God's Choices

BOOKS BY JAMES D. QUIGGLE

DOCTRINAL SERIES

Biblical Homosexuality
A Biblical Response to Same-gender Marriage
Marriage and Family: A Biblical Perspective

Adam and Eve, a Biography and Theology
Angelology, a True History of Angels
Biblical Essays
Biblical Essays II

First Steps, Becoming a Follower of Jesus Christ
Christian Living and Doctrine
Spiritual Gifts
Why Christians Should Not Tithe

Antichrist, His Genealogy, Kingdom, and Religion
Dispensational Eschatology, An Explanation and Defense of the Doctrine
Understanding Dispensational Theology
The Literal Hermeneutic, Explained and Illustrated

God's Choices, Doctrines of Foreordination, Election, and Predestination
God Became Incarnate
Life, Death, Eternity

COMMENTARY SERIES

The Old Testament:

A Private Commentary on the Bible: Judges
A Private Commentary on the Book of Ruth
A Private Commentary on the Bible: Esther
A Private Commentary on the Bible: Song of Solomon
A Private Commentary on the Bible: Daniel
A Private Commentary on the Bible: Jonah
A Private Commentary on the Bible: Haggai

The New Testament

The Gospels

A Private Commentary on the Bible: Matthew's Gospel
A Private Commentary on the Bible: Mark's Gospel
A Private Commentary on the Bible: John 1–12
A Private Commentary on the Bible: John 13–21

A Private Commentary on the Bible: John's Gospel
The Passion and Resurrection of Jesus the Christ
The Christmas Story, As Told By God

Pauline Letters

A Private Commentary on the Bible: Ephesians
A Private Commentary on the Bible: Colossians
A Private Commentary on the Bible: Philemon

General Letters

A Private Commentary on the Bible: Hebrews
A Private Commentary on the Bible: James
A Private Commentary on the Bible: 1 Peter
A Private Commentary on the Bible: 2 Peter
A Private Commentary on the Bible: John's Epistles
A Private Commentary on the Bible: Jude

Revelation

The Epistle of Jesus to the Church

REFERENCE SERIES

Old and New Testament Chronology

Also in individual volumes:

Old Testament Chronology
New Testament Chronology

Translation of Select Bible Books (Old And New Testament)
Dictionary of Doctrinal Words

Visit me at https://www.facebook.com/BooksOfQ

God's Choices

The Doctrines of Foreordination, Election, and Predestination

James D. Quiggle

God's Choices, The Doctrines of Foreordination, Election, and Predestination

Copyright © 2012, 2020 James D. Quiggle. All rights reserved. Except for brief quotations in critical publications or reviews, no part of this book may be reproduced in any manner without prior written permission from the Author. Email: booksofq@gmail.com. Subject: Permissions.

Revised March 2020, to include a brief discussion of Molinism.

Published by James D. Quiggle, 2020.

Scripture quotations are taken from the following translations.

The Authorized [King James] Version.

New King James Version®. Copyright © 1982, 1983 by Thomas Nelson Inc. Used by permission. All rights reserved.

The Holy Bible: New International Version (NIV), Copyright 1973, 1978, 1984 by International Bible Society. Used by permission of Zondervan Publishing House. All rights reserved.

Holman Christian Standard Bible (HCSB), Copyright 1999, 2000, 2002, 2003, by Holman Bible Publishers. Scripture quotations marked HCSB are from the Holman Christian Standard Bible®, Copyright © 1999, 2000, 2002, 2003 by Holman Bible Publishers. Used by permission. Holman Christian Standard Bible®, Holman CSB®, and HCSB® are federally registered trademarks of Holman Bible Publishers.

Parts of the present work appeared in a slightly different version in *Adam and Eve, A Biography and Theology*, James D. Quiggle, Author, Publisher, copyright 2011; *A Private commentary on the Epistle to the Ephesians*, James D. Quiggle, Author, Publisher, copyright 2012; *A Private Commentary on the Epistle to the Hebrews*, James D. Quiggle, Author, Publisher, copyright 2012.

This print edition contains the same material as in the digital editions.

Contents

Preface iii

Part One 1
1. Introduction 3
2. Preliminary Matters 5

Part Two 21
3. The Doctrine of Foreordination 23
4. The Doctrine of Election 55
5. The Doctrine of Predestination 107

Part Three 129
6. Divine Sovereignty and Human Freedom 131
7. Culpability and Inability 141
8. Saving Faith 159

Part Four 185
9. Persevering Faith 187
10. Good Works 205

Appendix: Molinism, Foreordination, And Election 221

Bibliography and Sources 227

PREFACE

If I were to title this work after the old Puritan method, it might be something like this: "An explanation of the doctrine of God's sovereignty as it is effected through God's choices in foreordination, election, and predestination; showing how God's sovereignty works through man's choices; with discussions of how sin creates culpability and inability in man, requiring God's electing choice to effect man's salvation; with concluding thoughts on how the doctrine of predestination affects man's choices in exercising persevering faith with good works."

As one might guess from the Puritan-style title, this work is about more than foreordination, election, and predestination. God's choices affect man's choices, a person's freely made choices are part of God's plan, and the sin attribute greatly affects a person's choice to do right or wrong. The doctrines explaining God's choices are inseparable from associated doctrines of sin (the sin attribute, culpability, inability) and faith (saving, persevering, working). These associated doctrines are required for a full understanding of the practical outworking of God's choices in the world, and are therefore included in the book.

The several doctrines concerning God's choices and man's choices interact at a minute level, and the details are of the utmost importance. For example, understanding the debilitating effects of sin in human nature is required to understand the necessity of election. An adequate understanding of God's sovereignty is necessary to a full understanding of God's choices as just, righteous, and holy.

I have struggled with a reasonable order in which to present these doctrines. Should God's choices in foreordination, election, and predestination be discussed before the doctrines of sin, faith, and good works? Or should man's sin attribute and his saving faith be presented first? The believer's choices as to persevering faith and good works must also be considered.

I have decided to follow the biblical order: God made his choices before man made his. The book is divided into four parts.

Part one presents a brief background, a discussion of what really matters, definitions of certain terms, the scriptures that define pertinent biblical words, and a brief analysis of those words in context. Part two is an explanation of God's choices in relation to the doctrines of foreordination, election, and predestination. Part three discusses man's choices in relation to the doctrines of God's sovereignty, man's sin, and saving faith. Part four examines God's and man's choices in regard to persevering faith and good works.

As we discuss these doctrines keep in mind the Christian religion is a super-natural religion: we believe in a God who is above and apart from the physical universe and the creatures he created. He acts according to his own will without consulting us. He made us in his image, and therefore we are required to conform to him, he does not conform to us. Additionally, let us remember there is always an element of faith in everything we understand about God. Faith is a reasoned and reasonable trust in the things God has taught us in the Scripture. But faith does not require complete understanding, or incontrovertible proof. God, nowhere in Scripture, presents an incontrovertible argument for his existence; yet the whole of Scripture presents reasonable evidence that God exists. So too with the doctrines we will examine. Let us also bear in mind that God adds conviction to faith. Conviction is God giving the believer assurance that the things he has revealed to us in Scripture are true. Let every reader seek understanding from God as to whether these things are so, and have faith in what he or she is convicted to believe.

Let me encourage you to become involved with these doctrines. This book is not designed for the learned but for those who want to learn. Diligent effort will be repaid with the precious coin of understanding and wisdom.

PART ONE

In which introductory and preliminary matters are discussed.

PART ONE

in which Freud Itzak and pre-Freddy me not tradition seed

1. INTRODUCTION

The Reformers of the sixteenth century revived the Augustinian (Augustine of Hippo, AD 354–430) understanding of certain biblical doctrines. Historians tend to focus on the Protestant Reformation's (AD 1517–1648[1]) revival of the doctrines of soteriology (saved by grace alone, through faith alone, in Jesus alone), and the work of reforming soteriology away from the salvation-by-works doctrines of Roman Catholicism. However, the reformation of soteriology would not have been possible without the revival of the doctrine of God's sovereignty. God's sovereignty was succinctly expressed in the Westminster Confession (AD 1647), chapter three, "Of God's Eternal Decree," of which the first article (of eight) states:

> God from all eternity did by the most wise and holy counsel of his own will, freely and unchangeably ordain whatsoever comes to pass; yet so as thereby neither is God the author of sin; nor is violence offered to the will of the creatures, nor is the liberty or contingency of second causes taken away, but rather established.[2]

Stated in less precise terms: before he created anything, God foreordained all that would come to pass; he elected some sinners to salvation; he predestined the saved to be conformed to be like Christ. In doing these things God did not cause his sentient creatures to sin. He did not limit the exercise of their sentience. In addition to himself as the active agent of events and outcomes, he ordained other things and beings to be agents of events and outcomes. The purpose of this book is to provide a reasonable explanation of these things within the biblical context.

In the view of the Reformers and their spiritual heirs, election and predestination were synonyms. In their preaching and writings the term predestination represented the entire system of salvation God created in his foreordaining and electing decrees. I have found that each of these doctrines is closely linked to the others, but

---

[1] The Protestant Reformation is usually dated from the publication of Martin Luther's *Ninety-five Theses* to the Treaty of Westphalia which ended Europe's religious wars.

[2] http://www.reformed.org/documents/westminster_conf_of_faith.html

Introduction

Scripture also makes each distinctive. The doctrine of foreordination addresses the entire created order, election addresses the salvation of sinners, and predestination addresses the spiritual growth and future of the saved. We will examine these doctrines in their proper order, and then discuss the doctrines affected by these three: sovereignty, sin, salvation, perseverance, and good works.

The theology the Reformers developed from the Augustinian system, and which was reflected in the Westminster Confession, has become known as Calvinism. Calvin (AD 1509–1564) "did not, of course, originate the system but only set forth what appeared to him to shine forth so clearly from the pages of Holy Scripture."[1] Nor, as so many wrongly believe, do the doctrines of sovereignty and election comprise the whole system of Calvinism. John Calvin was responsible for the development of many of the doctrines enshrined in the creeds and statements of faith in most Protestant and Dissenter denominations. These include such doctrines as: the verbal and plenary inspiration of the Bible; God is a Trinity, one essence in three persons, Father, Son, Spirit; the deity of Jesus, his consubstantiality and coequality with the Father and Spirit; the real humanity of Jesus, that he was and is the God-man; the deity and personality of the Holy Spirit, his consubstantiality and coequality with the Father and Son; the works of the Holy Spirit; the unsaved person is personally guilty for sin; redemption by Jesus alone, through grace alone, by faith alone; Jesus' ministry as prophet, priest, and king; the Person and work of the Holy Spirit in redemption and in the church; the final perseverance of the saved; eternal judgment for the lost; eternal heaven for the saved; the necessity of personal holiness of life; the saved required to maintain good works.

The explanation of biblical doctrine presented in this book is aligned with the Calvinistic view. However, this book is not a defense of Calvinism. That argument has been made by better theologians than me. This book is the result of my examination of the scriptures to determine what the Bible has to say about foreordination, election, predestination, sin, faith, and good works. The thoughts of other writers are included, but this book reflects my conclusions, neither more nor less, on the subjects it addresses.

---

[1] Boettner, *Predestination*, 4.

2. PRELIMINARY MATTERS

PRACTICAL MATTERS

In most cases it helps to know the destination before beginning the journey. This book is an explanation of three biblical doctrines: foreordination, election, and predestination. Foreordination is among the doctrines dealing with God's sovereignty. Election and predestination are part of the group of biblical doctrines known as soteriology. "Doctrine" is a word meaning "teaching." The doctrine of soteriology is what the Bible teaches about the salvation of sinners. Soteriology defines salvation, why salvation is possible, who can be saved, how they can be saved, and the result of salvation. The doctrine of election concerns the cause of salvation; the doctrine of predestination concerns the result of salvation. The doctrine of election answers the question, "Who can be saved?" The doctrine of predestination answers the question, "What happens after salvation?"

At the beginning of our study we want to take note of some things that really matter. The first is the transition of the soul from sinner to saved. What is salvation? Salvation is believing on Jesus Christ as the one who can save me, a sinner, from the guilt and penalty of sin. Why is salvation possible? God has made salvation possible through personal faith in Jesus. Who can be saved? Any person can be saved when he or she believes on Jesus as their Savior. How can I be saved? By God's gift of grace through my faith in Jesus as Savior. As Paul told the Philippian jailor, Acts 16:31, (translating according to Paul's use of grammar and syntax), "At once, and once for all, put your complete trust in the Lord Jesus Christ, and you will be saved!"

Another thing that matters is the result of salvation. Believing on Jesus as Savior results in forgiveness of the guilt of sin, release from the penalty of sin, deliverance from the power of sin, and in heaven to be forever free from the presence of sin. In the here-and-now of this mortal life salvation delivers the believer from the penalty, power, and pleasure of sin. The believer is given a new nature, holy and righteous. As a result he or she desires to do good works, and is able to say "No," to the temptations of sin, and mean it. What really matters? Decide right now and for all time to put your complete trust in Jesus to keep your soul safe in the here-and-now and for eternity.

Preliminary Matters

The doctrine of election—God choosing some to salvation, but leaving others just as they are—is troubling to some who may ask, "Am I among the elect?" If you believe in Jesus as your Savior then you are among the elect. What matters in election—in every practical sense—is that God never reveals (1) his reasons for choosing one but not another, and (2) just who he has chosen. In every practical sense what matters is to put your faith in Jesus as your Savior and be saved. The Gospel calls everyone to their moral responsibility to believe and be saved. God will respond with salvation to whosoever will choose to believe in Jesus as their Savior. With all your heart, mind, and soul seek salvation from God by believing on the Lord Jesus Christ as the One who can save you from sin's penalty. God will respond to your faith by giving you an eternal salvation.

The testimony of the gospel of salvation is another thing that matters. The end result of election, which is the salvation of souls, is accomplished through the gospel message. A believer's testimony of the gospel is one of the means foreordained by God in order that sinners may be saved. Every believer is responsible to speak the good news of salvation in Jesus Christ. Every sinner is responsible to believe and be saved.

Let us, then, as we study these doctrines, remember what really matters: the testimony of the gospel, the moral responsibility to believe, and the salvation of every person who does by faith believe. These are the ways in which foreordination, election, and predestination work out in the world to the salvation of sinful souls. Our study of these doctrines will confirm what really matters.

TERMS AND DEFINITIONS

Amos 3:3 asks, "Can two walk together, unless they are agreed?" The sense is to be in agreement at the beginning of their walk, else each may have a different path or a different destination in mind. In order for writer and reader to "walk together" we must at the beginning agree on the meaning of certain terms used in this Bible study.

Domain, God: because God is self-existent and increate, he is his own reality or domain. Any, all, and every other reality or domain that exists or may exist was created by God and exists within the reality that is God, without being made from his substance, or being part of his substance, or partaking of his nature. There are no realities or domains other than God himself and that which God created. God created other realities or domains from nothing (ex nihilo) through the sovereign exercise of his omnipotence and omniscience. All realities or domains created by God are limited and finite, have boundaries, a beginning, and an ending.

Domain, material: a reality created by God where all material created things and creatures live out their physical existence. Part of the universe God created. See Universe.

Domain, spirit: a reality created by God where all spirit created things and creatures dwell. Part of the universe God created. See Universe.

Effectuate: to effect; to bring about; to cause to come to pass; to cause a potential event to pass from possible to actual. In the decree of foreordination God effectuated certain events out of all possible events to become actual events.

Election: the choice of a sovereign God, 1) to give the gift of grace-faith-salvation to effect the salvation of some sinners, and 2) to take no action, positive or negative, to either effect or deny salvation to other sinners. The decree of election includes all means necessary to effectuate salvation in those elected.

Eternal, God: God is increate, self-existent, without beginning and without end. Only God is eternal. All which is not God was created by God and continues in existence because maintained by God. All created things have a beginning, some have an end (see Universe), and some are immortal (see Immortality).

Eternal life of the believer: the duration and quality of life experienced by the believer. The duration is everlasting. The quality of eternal life is God sharing his communicable attributes in the fullest measure possible for a saved finite soul to receive, thus effecting intimate fellowship and communion between God and the believer. The believer has eternal life as a present possession, and experiences it in part during his or her mortal life (as he or she is being made conformed by the Holy Spirit to the likeness of Christ), but the fullness of eternal life begins following physical death.

Eternity (1): a term used to identify the reality that is God himself, to identify the timeless and eternal existence of the increate God as separate from the time-bound existence of all things he has created, Genesis 1:1, or will create, Revelation 21:1.

Eternity (2): a term used to describe the duration of the life of the saved in heaven and of the unsaved in the lake of fire.

Eternity-past: the timeless state of reality when the increate God alone existed, before he created anything that was created. God himself is the one genuine, timeless, eternal reality within which the created time-bound reality that is our universe has its existence.

Eternity-future: the created reality that will exist when the present created reality, our universe, is destroyed and replaced, Revelation 21:1. In eternity-future the unsaved will experience everlasting woe in the lake of fire, Revelation 20:10–15; the saved will experience everlasting bliss by dwelling for eternity in the immediate presence of God, Revelation 21:22–27.

Foreknowledge: "When we attribute prescience [foreknowledge] to God, we mean that all things always were, and ever continue, under his eye; that to his knowledge there is no past or future, but all things are present, and indeed so present, that it is not merely the idea of them that is before him (as those objects are which we retain in our memory), but he truly sees and contemplates them as actually under his immediate inspection. This prescience extends to the whole circuit of the world [universe], and to all creatures."[1]

Foreordination: the decree of God occurring between his decision to create and his act of creation as to which agents, events, and outcomes, out of all possible agents, events, and outcomes potential in the decision to create, would pass from possible to actual, in which the liberty or contingency of secondary causes is established, in which God is not the author of sin, and in which no violence is done to the free will of his creatures.

Free will: the ability of sentient creatures to make decisions within the boundaries of their nature. The will is not neutrally suspended between good and evil, but is inclined toward one or the other by the several principles of life which compose the sentient nature. In the case of human beings, the will is inclined toward sin because of the principle of evil (the sin attribute) that became part of human nature following Adam's sin and propagation. When, in the ensuing

---

[1] Calvin, *Institutes*, 2:206 (3.21.5).

discussions, I speak of "free choice" or "freely made choices," it means choices made within the context of the will as circumscribed by the nature of the sentient being (human, angelic, demonic) making the choice. See also "will" and "volition."

Grace-faith-salvation: a term derived from Ephesians 2:8 indicating the complete salvation principle: saved by grace through faith. The gift of God in the salvation of sinners is grace-faith-salvation.

Heaven (1): there are three heavens. The first heaven is the material domain: earth's atmosphere and "outer space" extending to the boundary of the universe. The second heaven is the spirit domain: the habitation of all angels. The third heaven is a location within the second heaven where God has placed a permanent manifestation of his presence, Revelation 4.

Heaven (2): a location in the spirit domain where the souls of saved human beings go after physical death to await the resurrection. Whereas "to be absent from the body," physical death, "is to be present with the Lord," the location of heaven must be the third heaven where God maintains a permanent manifestation of his presence. See Heaven (1).

Hell (hades): a location in the spirit domain where the souls of unsaved human beings go after physical death to await resurrection and final judgment, Revelation 20:4–6, 11–15. There are no angels in hell, only unsaved human beings. Hell is a jail for unsaved souls awaiting eternal imprisonment in the lake of fire. See Lake of Fire.

Historical-present: a term to distinguish between the eternity of God's increate existence and the time-bound universe God created. The historical-present is the continuous succession of time from past to present to future. God made decisions in eternity-past (foreordination) and effects those decisions (providence) in the historical-present. In the context of human experience, the historical-present refers to the succession of circumstances, events, and outcomes a person has experienced, is experiencing, and will experience.

Immortality: created existence continuing without foreseeable end. All sentient beings were created to be immortal. In regard to human beings, every soul will live forever, united to the body with which it was propagated. God did not give the soul self-subsistence, but he created the soul without susceptibility to corruption, so that it has no process of natural decay and there is no natural power that can effect its dissolution; therefore it will naturally continue of itself. The soul does depend on God for its continuance, because he has the power to destroy or annihilate it should he think fit, but the testimony of Scripture is that God intends to sustain the soul in being forever. The resurrection of the saved and unsaved demonstrates human beings will continue forever alive in body and soul.[1]

Inspiration of Scripture: God's work of superintendence by which he presided over the human authors in their entire work of writing, with the design and effect of rendering that writing an errorless record of the matters he designed them to communicate.[2] Because the Bible is an inspired revelation from God it is an authentic, credible, and accurate account of the words and deeds of God, man, and angel.

Judgment, eternal: human beings are judged guilty of sin and deserving punishment if they die unsaved, i.e., if they physically die without having believed on Christ as their Savior. The punishment is eternal separation from God and eternal torment in the lake of fire. The judgment of the unsaved soul is executed in part at the moment of physical death. At physical death the unsaved soul is eternally separated from God, without hope of salvation, and is sent to hell (hades), to wait there, in torment (Luke 16:23), until resurrection and the Great White Throne (GWT) judgment, Revelation 20:11–15. In the book I sometimes refer to the GWT as final or eternal judgment. The GWT is the sentencing phase of judgment, after which the unsaved person is cast into the lake of fire. See Hell. See Lake of Fire.

Lake of Fire: a place, presumably located in the spirit domain, which was originally created for the devil and his angels, Matthew 25:41, and where they will be imprisoned for eternity, Revelation 20:10, at the end of the ages. The place where unsaved human beings will spend eternity, Revelation 20:14–15. The lake of fire is described as burning with fire and brimstone, Revelation 14:10; 19:20; 20:10; 21:8. See Hell.

---

[1] See Shedd, *Theology*, 1:257.
[2] Hodge and Warfield, *Inspiration*, 17.

Predestination: God's decree to conform the believer to be like Christ according to certain aspects of Christ's spiritual character and physical form, and to place the believer in the legal position of God's son and heir, so that the believer has an inheritance from God and is God's heritage.

Processes, plans, and purpose: This phrase, and these words, indicate the way in which God fulfills his purpose in creating the universe. A purpose assumes a plan by which the purpose can be fulfilled. A plan requires processes by which the plan is accomplished. For example, God's purpose to bring Israel into the Promised Land required a plan: free the Israelites from slavery in Egypt and bring them across the desert to Palestine. The plan required processes, e.g., the leadership of Moses, the contest with Pharaoh, the Passover, the passage through the Red Sea, etc., by which the plan could be accomplish and the purpose fulfilled.

Propitiation: The satisfaction Christ made to God for sin by dying on the cross as the sin-bearer, 2 Corinthians 5:21; Romans 3:25; Hebrews 2:17; 1 John 2:2; 4:10. Christ's propitiation fully satisfied God's holiness and justice for the crime of sin. Christ's propitiation was of infinite merit, because his Person is of infinite worth. The application of that merit is personally made by each sinner to his or her sin through faith in God's testimony of Christ as the only Savior.

Providence: That which God's foreordination effectuated in eternity-past, God's providence accomplishes in historical-present. Providence is a term used to describe God's unceasing works by which he maintains and preserves the universe and all his creatures, and governs its operations and their actions, so as to accomplish his plans and eternal purpose. See God, omnipotence; God, omniscient.

Reprobation: to be disqualified from heaven and subject to judgment and eternal punishment. Prior to the decree of election God viewed all human beings as sinners. God chose (elected) to save some of those sinners. In electing some God passed by the rest, taking no action to effect or deny their salvation. The doctrine of reprobation refers to the non-elect sinner as being disqualified from heaven and subject to judgment and eternal punishment. There is no divine decree of reprobation that would directly deny salvation to the non-elect. See election.

Salvation: The outworking of the doctrines of foreordination, election, and predestination encompasses the entire historical-present between eternity-past and eternity-future. Therefore, it is important salvation be defined not only for this New Testament age, but for all the ages between eternity-past and eternity-future. The ages (dispensations, economies) of the world in relation to salvation are Adam to Noah, Noah to Abraham, Abraham to Moses, Moses to Christ, Christ (first advent) to Christ (second advent/Millennial Kingdom), Christ (Millennial Kingdom) to eternity-future.

> Salvation is God by grace forgiving a sinner's sin-guilt and remitting sin's penalty through the application of Christ's infinite merit. Salvation is gained by receiving God's gift of grace-faith-salvation and applying that gift by means of personal faith in the content of faith God has revealed in any particular age or dispensation.
>
> The basis of salvation in every age is the propitiation made by Christ; the requirement for salvation in every age is faith; the object of faith in every age is God; the content of faith changes in the various dispensations.[1]
>
> Whether the content of faith is, e.g., believe in the judgment to come and get in the ark (Noah's dispensation), or bring the proper sacrifice in repentance and confession (Moses' dispensation) the salvific elements are: the believer's faith in the content of faith as the way of salvation; God's gift of grace-faith-salvation infallibly convicting the sinner to accept that content as the way of salvation; God by grace applying Christ's merit to save the believing sinner.
>
> Salvation is obtained only by grace through faith, not by works, and is maintained by grace through faith, not by works.
>
> Salvation in this New Testament age occurs when a sinner repents of his or her sins and believes on Christ as their Savior, Acts 2:38; 3:19–20; 11:18; Romans 3:22–26; 10:9–

---

[1] Ryrie, *Dispensationalism*, 115. Ryrie's opening phrase is, "the basis of salvation in every age is the death of Christ." I have changed "the death of Christ" to "the propitiation made by Christ."

10, 13; Galatians 3:22; 1 Peter 1:21; 1 John 3:23.

Scripture: God's words accurately delivered to mankind in writing through individuals chosen by God to communicate his revelation. The Bible is the only Scripture.

Sentience: a quality of self-awareness and self-actualization that only God, man, and angel have. All other creatures live according to instinct.

Sin: the legal violation of God's laws by disobedience and the moral violation of God's holiness by failure to conform to the image and likeness in which he created human nature.

Sin attribute: a life-principle of evil that became part of human nature when Adam sinned. Adam propagated the sin attribute to his children. The sin attribute resides in the soul with all the other life-principles of human nature. The sin attribute works constructively with all the other life-principles to continuously influence the will to choose to rebel against God and disobey his laws. See sin, volition, will.

Space-time: a mechanism God created to operate and regulate the functions of the universe he created. We experience space as the height, length, width, and depth of the material creation. We experience time as a continuous succession of events in the material creation that have occurred (the past), are presently occurring (the present), and will occur (the future).

Universe: Within the reality or domain that is God, God created what man and angel understand as the universe. The universe is not part of God's being nor was it created from his substance. God created the universe from nothing (ex nihilo) through his omnipotence and omniscience. After the universe was created God shaped and formed it by his omnipotence and omniscience as a suitable habitation for the things and creatures God would create. God created the universe with spirit and material domains and created all things and creatures in these domains. The universe depends upon God for its operation, maintenance, and continuance. The universe is finite in all aspects: limited dimensions of height, length, width, depth, and time; an all-encompassing boundary; limited to one place and excluded from all other places; a beginning, Genesis 1:1; an end, Revelation 21:1. See Domain.

Volition: the expressive faculty used by the will to carry out its choices through actions in thoughts and deeds. The will chooses the principles determining the how and why of action, volition carries out those choices through individual actions. The outward act, volition, is not the source of who we are, it is the result of who we are.

Will: "that voluntary power of human nature which determines the continuous movement of the soul toward its ultimate reason for living, according to those principles of life which together make up human nature."[1] Through the will the person chooses which principles of life (good, evil) will govern his or her behavior in general and in any particular circumstance. The choices made by the will are the expression of the whole person.

These terms reflect a conservative theology developed from a "literal" interpretation of the scriptures. A literal interpretation understands words in their normal sense and plain meaning. It does this by performing a lexical, syntactical, contextual, genre, theological, and doctrinal analysis of the scripture passage to be interpreted, and evaluating the result of that analysis in the context of the history and culture of the writer and his original readers. The goal of the literal method is to discover the meaning the writer intended (interpretation), and from the intended meaning to understand the significance (application) of the passage. This book uses the literal method.

PERTINENT BIBLICAL WORDS

One of the issues affecting an understanding of foreordination, election, and predestination is the meaning in context of the biblical words so translated.

Foreordination and Foreknowledge

God's foreknowledge is based on his foreordination and is associated with election and predestination. There are two words indicating "foreknowledge," one of which is also used to indicate foreordination. The first is *próginoskō*.[2] This word means to perceive or recognize beforehand; to know previously; to foreknow. This word is translated knew, foreknew, foreordained, beforehand.

---

[1] Shedd, *Essays*, 233–234.
[2] Zodhiates, *WSDNT*, s. v. "4267."

This word is used five times:

> Acts 26:5, "knew," indicating prior knowledge of Paul by his accusers.
>
> Romans 8:29, "foreknew," referencing those God has called, v. 28.
>
> Romans 11:2, "foreknew," referencing God's knowledge of Israel.
>
> 1 Peter 1:20, "foreordained," Christ's propitiation decreed in eternity-past.
>
> 2 Peter 3:17, "beforehand," Peter referencing his prophecy in vv. 10–13.

The second word is *prógnōsis*,[1] the feminine noun form of *próginoskō*. This word means to know beforehand; foreknowledge. This word is translated foreknowledge. This word is used twice:

> Acts 2:23, "foreknowledge," God's foreknowledge of Christ's crucifixion.
>
> 1 Peter 1:2, "foreknowledge," God's foreknowledge of his elect.

Election

There are three Greek words pertaining to election whose meaning is to choose or select. The first is *eklégō*.[2] This word means to select, choose, and is translated choose, chose, chosen, elect. It involves preference and selection from among many choices. A relationship is established between the one choosing and the object chosen. This word is used twenty-two times:

> Mark 13:20, "elect," those who will be saved during the Tribulation period.
>
> Luke 6:13, "chose," the selection of the twelve apostles.
>
> Luke 10:42, "chosen," Mary of Bethany made a choice.
>
> Luke 14:7, "chose," those invited chose the best seating.
>
> John 6:70, "choose," Jesus chose the twelve apostles.
>
> John 13:18, "chosen," Jesus knows who (of the 12 apostles) he had chosen.
>
> John 15:16, "choose; chose," Jesus chose the twelve apostles.
>
> John 15:19, "chose," Jesus chose the twelve out of the world.
>
> Acts 1:2, "chosen," Jesus chose the apostles.

---

[1] Ibid., s. v. "4268."
[2] Ibid., s. v. "1586."

Acts 1:24, "chosen," who did God choose to replace Judas?

Acts 6:5, "chose," the church chose seven men to serve.

Acts 13:17, "chose," God chose Israel.

Acts 15:7, "chose," God chose Peter as the first witness to the Gentiles.

Acts 15:22, "chosen," the church sent chosen men with Paul and Barnabas.

Acts 15:25, "chosen," the church sent chosen men with Paul and Barnabas.

1 Corinthians 1:27, "chosen," God has chosen the foolish, the weak, etc.

1 Corinthians 1:28, same as v. 27.

Ephesians 1:4; "chose," God chose us in Christ.

James 2:5, "chosen," God has chosen the poor to be rich in faith.

The second word is *eklektós*.[1] This word means to choose, to select, and is translated chosen, elect. Same meaning as *eklégō*, as influenced by context. This word is used twenty-two times:

Matthew 22:14, "chosen," for many are called, but few are chosen.

Matthew 24:22, "elect," those who will be saved during the Tribulation period.

Matthew 24:24, "elect," same as v. 22.

Matthew 24:31, "elect," same as v. 22.

Mark 13:20, "elect," those who will be saved during the Tribulation period.

Mark 13:22, "elect," same as v. 20.

Mark 13:27, "elect," same as v. 20.

Luke 18:7, "elect," those whom God has chosen.

Luke 23:35, "chosen," mocking Jesus as the chosen of God.

Romans 8:33, "elect," those whom God has chosen.

Romans 16:13, "chosen," Rufus was chosen in the Lord.

Colossians 3:12, "elect," those whom God has chosen.

1 Timothy 5:21, "elect," angels whom God has chosen.

2 Timothy 2:10, "elect," those who have been chosen.

Titus 1:1, "elect," those whom God has chosen.

---

[1] Ibid., s. v. "1588."

Preliminary Matters

1 Peter 1:2, "elect," those whom God has chosen.

1 Peter 2:4, "chosen," chosen by God.

1 Peter 2:6, "elect," referring to Christ.

1 Peter 2:9, "chosen," believers are a chosen generation.

2 John 1, "elect," John's correspondent, the elect lady.

2 John 13, "elect," John's reference to "your elect sister."

Revelation 17:14, "chosen," those with Christ are chosen.

The third word is *eklogé*.[1] This word means choice, selection, and is translated chosen, election, elect. Same meaning as *eklégō*, as influenced by context. This word is used seven times:

Acts 9:15, "chosen," Paul a chosen vessel of the Lord.

Romans 9:11, "election," God selected Isaac over Esau.

Romans 11:5, "election," election is of grace.

Romans 11:7, "elect," those chosen.

Romans 11:28; "election," reference to the act of selection.

1 Thessalonians 1:4; "election," Thessalonian believers chosen by God.

2 Peter 1:10, "election," the fact of having been elected.

These words, as used by the Greeks and Romans, and as used by the New Testament writers, do not necessarily imply an adverse or negative action toward those not chosen. Nor, as used by the New Testament writers in regard to election to salvation, do these words imply something meritorious in those chosen, or something undesirable in those not chosen. When used with regard to salvation, they simply mean God made a choice.

Predestination

There is one word translated "predestination." That word is *proorízō*.[2] This word means to determine or decree beforehand. The word is translated determined before, predestined, ordained. This word is used six times:

Acts 4:28, "determined before," referring to the decree that Christ would be crucified.

Romans 8:29, "predestinate," referring to the decree to conform

---

[1] Ibid., s. v. "1589."
[2] Ibid., s. v. "4309."

the believer to be like Christ.

Romans 8:30, "predestined," referring to v. 29.

1 Corinthians 2:7, "ordained," referring to God's decrees in eternity-past.

Ephesians 1:5, "predestined," the decree of adoption as a son of God.

Ephesians 1:11, "predestined," the decree of an inheritance.

BRIEF ANALYSIS

I strongly encourage the reader to read each verse listed above in their biblical contexts before continuing. A definition, no matter how well constructed, cannot substitute for reading a word as it is used in context by the New Testament writers. Following is a brief analysis of the words and Scripture passages relevant to foreordination, election, and predestination.

Foreordination and Foreknowledge

As used in Acts 26:5 and 2 Peter 3:17, the word *próginoskō* is not about God's choices, but reflect a present knowledge (Paul's enemies; Peter's readers) based on what had occurred in the past and was now remembered. God's foreknowledge is knowledge of the future based on his decrees which determined the shape of that future.

At Acts 2:23 God has *prógnōsis* of Christ's crucifixion just because he had decided to deliver Christ to wicked hands to be crucified. Christ was delivered according to God's *horízō boulé*. In this context *boulé* means the deliberation and reflection underlying God's decision,[1] and *horízō* means God's decree as a result of his *boulé*. God made a choice and decree. His foreknowledge of the event is based on that decree.

God foreknew, Romans 8:29, those whom he had called, 8:28, just because he had first called them: God's foreknowledge of his people is based on his prior act of calling them according to his purpose. At Romans 11:2 Paul said God had not cast away his people whom he foreknew. In these verses "foreknew" acts as the opposite of "cast away" (rejected), and therefore the meaning of "foreknew," *próginoskō*, is closer to "chose"; God has not rejected his people whom he chose.

---

[1] Ibid., s. v. "1012."

At 1 Peter 1:20, Christ was *próginoskō* before the foundation of the world. Was he known, foreknown, or foreordained? The context is redemption and the contrast is the relationship between the redemptive decree in eternity-past and the redemptive act in historical-present. The past decree effected the redemptive act, and therefore Christ was foreordained, i.e., appointed beforehand in eternity-past, to be the redeemer in historical-present. In other words, Peter is not saying God foresaw when Christ would come but that he foreordained when Christ would come.

At 1 Peter 1:1–2 Peter addresses believers as, NKJV, "to the Pilgrims of the dispersion. . . elect according to the foreknowledge of God the Father." The literal word order in the Greek text is "to elect pilgrims . . . according to foreknowledge of God Father." God knows his elect people as pilgrims traveling through this mortal life on the way to heaven. Peter is not saying God predicted their conversion, which is what a foreknowledge view of salvation would require. God knew and sustains his elect people in their pilgrimage because he chose (elected) and initiated a relationship (salvation) with them.

> For surely when Peter says that Christ was "delivered by the determinate counsel and foreknowledge of God," (Acts 2:23,) he does not represent God as contemplating merely, but as actually accomplishing our salvation. Thus also Peter, in saying that the believers to whom he writes are elect "according to the foreknowledge of God," (1 Peter 1:2,) properly expresses that secret predestination by which God has sealed those whom he has been pleased to adopt as sons.[1]

What Peter is saying is that God's foreknowing them during their pilgrimage is based on his choosing them. Peter meant this as an encouragement to a people wandering the earth waiting for their home-going.

Election

The word *eklégō* means the selection of some out of many. The word *eklektós* indicates those who have been selected. The word *eklogé* refers to the act of selection. The selection of some out of many never indicates malice or prejudice toward those not selected. For example, Jesus chose twelve disciples out of many disciples to

---

[1] Calvin, *Institutes*, 2:218 (3.22.6).

be his apostles. There is no indication of anything wrong with those not chosen, no indication of future prejudice or bias against those not chosen. Those not chosen continued to be disciples, even though they were not chosen to be apostles. Nor is there any indication of merit or special character in those chosen. In Acts 6:5 the Jerusalem church chose seven men to make the daily distribution to the needy. Obviously the many from whom the seven were selected was the male population of the church who met the qualifications set at 6:3. Many males met those qualifications; seven were chosen. Those not selected continued as they were.

In every use of these words, no reason is given as to why some were selected but not others. Acts 6:3–5 and 1:15–26 are not exceptions. The conditions set in these passages establishes who will be in the total number from which the selection is to be made. There is never any prejudice against those not chosen; they are left to continue as they were before the selection was made.

When we come to God's choices in salvation these same conditions apply. God chose to save some. The qualification required to be among the group from which the selection was to be made was to be a sinner: the entire population of human beings from Adam forward to eternity-future. The reason why some sinners were chosen to salvation and others were not is never stated. There is no action, negative or positive, taken toward those not chosen; they are left to continue in their original state.

Predestination

In four out of six uses the word *proorízō* refers to God's purposes regarding the believer. To wit, the believer is to be conformed to the likeness of Christ, be adopted as a Son of God, to be God's heritage, and to receive an inheritance from God. Although the Reformers, and their spiritual heirs today, use *proorízō* in the sense of election, the Scripture testimony is that *proorízō* expresses God's decrees affecting the believer after his or her salvation. The order in which predestination works out in the decrees of God is elected in eternity-past, saved in historical-present, and then the decree of predestination begins its sanctifying work.

PART TWO

In which the doctrines of foreordination, election, and predestination are stated, explained, and discussed.

3. THE DOCTRINE OF FOREORDINATION

STATEMENT OF THE DOCTRINE

Statement of the doctrine: foreordination is the decree of God occurring between his decision to create and his act of creation as to which agents, events, and outcomes, out of all possible agents, events, and outcomes potential in the decision to create, would pass from possible to actual, in which the liberty or contingency of secondary causes is established, in which God is not the author of sin, and in which no violence is done to the free will of his creatures.

How is it that God knows, *próginoskō*, an event, its outcome, and the agent by which it will be accomplished, before the occurrence? Because he has foreordained, *próginoskō*, the agent, event, and outcome. In eternity-past, out of all the possible agents, events, and outcomes in potential from his decision to create, God chose to effectuate certain agents, events, and outcomes from possible to actual by his decree of foreordination.

EXPLANATION

Before the beginning, there was only God. He only is increate and he alone created all things. God, then, is the cause of all things. Before the beginning the Godhead deliberated and determined a suitable purpose for their divine activity: the manifestation of God's glory and its appreciation by sentient creatures. Then God chose, and by his choice foreordained, the plans and processes that would fulfill the purpose. The omniscient and eternal God understood every possible agent, event, and outcome in regard to all circumstances, things, creatures, and sentient beings that could result from his decision to create. We might imagine these possible events and outcomes as many alternate realities that could result from the one decision to create. Out of many possible realities God chose to create the reality which is our universe. When a human being makes a decision he wonders what might happen. When God makes a decision, he understands all possible events and outcomes that could happen, and decrees which of these will actually occur. That decree is foreordination.

God decreed which particular events and outcomes, out of every possible event and outcome of the decision to create, he would effectuate from possible to actual, thereby establishing the actual events and outcomes that would take place in the universe he would create. An event must have a cause—an agent whose actions are the event or result in the event. God decreed himself to be the agent that would cause some events and outcomes. God intentionally and purposefully decreed to permit other events and outcomes to be caused by some agent he expressly purposed to bring into existence.[1] "Some agent" should be understood broadly of naturally occurring activity (such as heat, cold, rain, wind, flood, earthquake, feast, famine, disease, etc.), the recurring activities of non-sentient and sentient beings, and the consequences resulting from the events caused by these agents. Before he created, God decided which events would take place (out of every possible potential event), how each event would take place, through what agent, the outcome of each event, and the relationship between each agent, event, and outcome. He did this by knowing all potential agents, events, and outcomes and decreeing which would pass from possible to actual.

To effectuate (directly or permissively) some agents, events, and outcomes, out of every possible agent, event, and outcome, is to foreordain and decree those agents, events, and outcomes. The only way anything potential can pass from possibility to reality is by God's decree. Therefore, after the decision to create, but before the act of creation, God chose what would happen, and by whom and how and when it would happen, and by those choices foreordained everything that he created—all things, creatures, agents, events, and outcomes.

To understand what God has done, we might imagine a series of possible agents, events, and outcomes, and name them agents A-B-C, events 1-2-3, and outcomes X-Y-Z. To create the plans and processes that would fulfill his purpose God might have chosen agents A and B to cause events 2 and 3 to create outcomes X and Z. Our reality, then, our universe, would be composed of the agents, events, and outcomes A-B-2-3-X-Z. God could have chosen any agents, events, and outcomes, but he chose some out of the many possible to create a universe that would fulfill his purpose.

God's foreordination does not do violence to the free will of his sentient creatures (man, angel). In the context of eternity-past, their choices and actions are made certain by foreordination,

---

[1] Boettner, *Predestination*, 45.

because God chose to effectuate certain freely made choices and actions out of the whole range of all possible freely made choices and actions. From the historical-present perspective of his sentient creatures, their actions are a result of their freely made decisions: a natural response of their (human or angelic) nature to life's circumstances. Their choices are certain because foreordained, but not coerced or necessary, because their choices are the natural and freely made response of their nature.

Freely made choices include wrong choices (sinful choices). Foreordination does not make God the culpable author of sin. God permissively allows his sentient creatures to exercise their sentience, i.e., to make a choice, and sovereignly makes their choices—whether a right or wrong choice—to accomplish his plans and fulfill his purpose. Sinful persons, whether unsaved human or fallen angel, respond to life's circumstances as influenced by the principle of evil (sin) which is part of their nature, just as holy angels and saved persons respond to life's circumstances as influenced by the principle of holiness which is part of their nature. God's sovereignty causes all freely made choices to work out to accomplish his processes, plans, and purpose. Sinful choices are permitted (foreordination), known (foreknowledge), and sovereignly controlled and overruled (providence) to be part of the processes that accomplish God's plans and fulfill his purpose. Some may ask, how can a good God allow his creatures to make sinful choices? The brief answer is that freely made choices are a necessary part of sentience.

God's choice of particular agents, events, and outcomes made each certain. By determining which potentially possible events would become actual events, and by determining the agents (himself or others) by which these events would be effectuated, God decreed every actual agent, event, and outcome of his decision to create. This is foreordination: by his choice to effectuate particular agents, events, and outcomes (selecting some out of all possible) God predetermined every agent, event, and outcome that would happen in the creation he would create. Foreordination made these things certain, but did not make them necessary. For example, Adam was not compelled to sin. His act of sin was the result of his free will making a choice in response to circumstances. Instead of preventing the free choice of his sentient creature, God respected the sentience he had created. He permitted Adam's choice and effectuated the agents, events, and outcomes leading to and resulting from that choice. Thus, Adam's choice to sin was certain, because foreordained, but not necessary, because it was Adam's freely made choice.

If, as is the case, God saw all possible realities resulting from his decision to create, was there a reality in which Adam did not choose to sin? And, if such a reality was possible, why didn't God choose to effectuate that reality? Such hypothetical questions serve one purpose: to accuse and condemn God in the court of man's judgment. Who is man to judge his Creator, and to say that had he been in charge of creation he would have made a better, more perfect choice? How does God answer this charge? "O man, who are you to reply against God? Will the thing formed say to him who formed it, why have you made me like this" (Romans 9:20; Isaiah 29:16)? God chose to create man as a sentient being, to respect man's sentient faculty of choice, and to effectuate the choices made by man that would fulfill the purpose God had in creating man and the universe. What might have been is unknown and unknowable (perhaps in every possible reality Adam chose to sin?); only what God has created is real and knowable. A perfect, holy, righteous God has a perfect, holy, and righteous plan to fulfill his purpose; we, the creatures in that plan, must have faith in, submit to, and worship our Creator. Those choices will lead to salvation and eternal life.

God's foreknowledge is a result of his foreordination. The actions of agents other than God, including the freely willed acts of angels and men, are foreseen because they are certain to take place. God knows what will happen, because as the first cause he made choices as to what would take place and how those things would be accomplished. God knows the end from the beginning, Isaiah 46:9, 10, because he has foreordained the end, the beginning, and every agent, event, and outcome in between. God knows what will happen—his foreknowledge—because he chose what would happen—his foreordination.

UNDERSTANDING GOD'S CHOICES

Because we are finite creatures, as we consider God's choices in eternity-past and our choices in historical-present, we are incapable of holding in our mind every aspect, every event, every choice, and every outcome in our life that influences our choices.

Yet, no one can deny that his or her choices have been influenced by circumstances, whether past, present, or potential, and by the innumerable minutia of everyday life that affects our moods, choices, and actions. Perhaps one morning we didn't have time for our coffee or tea—having awoken later than usual, because the alarm was accidentally turned off, and it was cloudy, and therefore darker than usual in the bedroom—so we chose to give in to our anger by driving too fast and had a traffic accident; or perhaps all that frustration reminded us we tend to get angry when things do not go as planned, so we made an effort to be more careful and arrived at work late, but without incident. In both cases a choice was freely made out of one's nature in response to external influences. I have given a very simple example, but the reality is there are many events that influence our freely made choices, some observable, some unseen, including events influencing others, who in turn influence us.

God's choices are uninfluenced by any consideration other than his own sovereign will, Isaiah 14:24; 40:14; Romans 11:34. All the choices God made, which choices included man as a free agent, influence people to freely make certain choices, which God has foreordained to be the processes that accomplish the plans that fulfill his purpose. More simply, a person acts according to his or her own nature in response to events and circumstances, yet does exactly what God has planned for that person to do. That is because God's infinite omniscience allowed him to understand every possible freely made choice that might be made in response to every possible circumstance, and then God chose—foreordained—which circumstances and which choices would be the processes that would accomplish his plans and purpose. It may be that God effectuated one specific choice to accomplish his processes, plans, and purpose; it may be that God permissively effectuated more than one choice, because multiple choices (within specific circumstances) also accomplished his processes, plans, and purpose. Therefore, man freely decides to do that which God has sovereignly chosen.

Understanding the relationship between divine sovereignty and human freedom is important. Please allow me to restate the above in more detail. God knew every possible event and outcome in regard to all circumstances, things, creatures, and sentient beings that could result from his decision to create. In regard to his creature man—in regard to every person from Adam forward—God knew—not by foreknowledge but by an omniscient understanding or calculation of every consequence that might lead to any act and might arise from any act—God knew every possible freely made choice that might be made in response to every possible circumstance affecting every person throughout his or her lifetime. The eternity-past decree to effectuate some of those freely made choices from possible to actual—to foreordain them—does not make those choices less free when the person makes those choices during the course of their life as their natural response to life's circumstances. No one knows in advance what God has foreordained. Prophecy might be considered an exception to the rule. However, oft times those persons living out the prophecy are ignorant of the prophecy; therefore they make choices without knowing what God has foreordained.

A person, whether angel or man, freely decides to do that which God has sovereignly chosen. "The actions of free agents do not take place because they are foreseen, but they are foreseen because they are certain to take place."[1]

ILLUSTRATIONS

God's Omniscience

Let us reason on this doctrine through three analogies. The first analogy illustrates the minute detail of God's choices. Today we know that even a tiny change in the environment can have a great impact on the ecology of a region, or even the whole world. There is a chain of circumstances leading to a particular outcome that result from a change in the environment. Make a change, or several changes, in the chain of circumstances as it progresses, and a different outcome is obtained. Every possible change brings about a chain of circumstances leading to a particular outcome. The same observation applies to God's choices. Every human being's freely made choices are influenced by preceding events and influence succeeding events. Every circumstance, be it mundane or significant, effects the outcome. God's choices extend to the tiniest detail of circumstance, to the smallest act of free will. Before he performed the act of creation God's omniscience knew and understood every possible freely made choice that every person

---

[1] Ibid., 46.

might make. In choosing to effectuate particular agents, events, and outcomes, God foreordained a particular set of circumstances that would lead to certain freely made choices that would accomplish the purpose he had in mind when he created. In regard to sentient beings, those certain freely made choices God decreed to effectuate were selected out of all their possible freely made choices. So although the choices a person makes are certain, because foreordained, those choices are freely made as the person's natural response to the external influences of God's choice of agents, events, and outcomes. This includes a person's wrong choices, because God sovereignly permits his sentient creatures to make a wrong choice.

God's Choices

The second analogy illustrates the complexity of God's choices. Let us imagine that we want to drive from the east side to the west side of the city. There will be more than one path to travel to our destination, and at every intersection we can make more than one choice. If we consider all the main streets and all the side streets and all the streets running through neighborhoods and business areas, we realize there are many thousands of paths available to reach our destination, some simple and direct, others complex and circuitous. We might choose a simple path which knows no obstacles; or perhaps one more complicated to avoid traffic or go around accidents that slow or bar the way. So, too, God chose the paths he and his sentient creatures would travel from the moment of creation to the fulfillment of his purpose. The difference between our imagined city and God's choices is that God decided his and our path before he created the universe and pathways. In terms of the analogy, God could have created any one of many different cities with many different roads and streets, but he chose to create a certain city with certain roads and streets. To complete the analogy: God knew all the possible roads and streets men and angels might freely choose as they drove though his city; he chose which of their free choices he would effectuate from possible to actual; by his choice he made their free choices to be part of the processes and plans by which he would fulfill his purpose. A person freely decides to do what God has sovereignly chosen.

God's Sovereignty

Foreordination

The third analogy illustrates God's sovereignty. Let us consider a computer and its programmer. When I turn on my computer a certain chain of events leads to the display of my desktop. However, these are not the only possible events. The person who programmed the operating system (OS) had many choices of possible events resulting from the act of applying power. He chose some but not others. He chose the order in which the chosen events would occur. He chose the activities of the OS that would continue between turn-on and turn-off. He chose the order of events when the power was turned off. In biblical terms, the programmer foreordained what would happen at turn-on, operation, and turn-off. He has foreknowledge of those events because he foreordained them. His choice of events made those events the certain result of turning the power on. God's act of creation was the power-on of a certain chosen reality. The OS of the universe runs as God foreordained prior to power-on. God has foreknowledge of these necessary and certain events because he foreordained them. This analogy, of course, has certain limitations. Man is not a programmed machine. Man freely acts, is freely acted upon, and freely responds according to the attributes and characteristics of his human nature. He does so in accordance with God's foreordination of the agents, events, and outcomes acting in and upon his creation. A person freely acts according to his or her nature, yet does exactly what God has planned for that person to do.

SCRIPTURE SUPPORT

Scripture supports God's foreordaining decree of agents, events, and outcomes, and Scripture supports man as freely choosing a response to life's circumstances. Prophecy demonstrates both: God decrees the act that will take place and people make choices that cause the act to take place. That the choices a person makes are not fate or determinism is seen in that God holds a person accountable for their acts. For example, prophecy foretold that Babylon would take Israel captive (2 Kings 20:17–18), and prophecy foretold Babylon would be destroyed for their cruelty to Israel (Isaiah 13). Nebuchadnezzar and his father knew nothing of these prophecies. Their choice to expand their empire by conquering other peoples led to the captivity of Israel and razing of Jerusalem. Nearly a century later the Medo-Persians conquered Babylon without knowing the prophecy, Isaiah 45:1. Prophecy

Foreordination

foretold that Cyrus, king of the Medo-Persians, would allow the captive Jews to return to Jerusalem and rebuild the temple, Isaiah 44:28; 2 Chronicles 36:22–23; Ezra 1:1–4. We know Cyrus did not know this prophecy because history tells us his decree was issued to all the peoples made captive by Babylon, so that any might return to their homeland on the condition they build a temple and offer sacrifices for King Cyrus and his empire.

Scripture foretold that Jesus would be betrayed by his friend, Psalm 41:9, and Judas fulfilled that Scripture, Luke 22:22; Acts 1:16. Yet, Judas freely made choices that fulfilled the prophecy. He chose to be a thief, John 12:6. Jesus knew who would betray him, John 6:64, but Judas did not know until he had made that choice. Judas chose to betray Jesus for money, Luke 22:4–6. His immorality, his greed, his willingness to betray Jesus, led to such an evil disposition that Satan could enter his soul and influence his actions, Luke 22:3; John 13:27. Yet, Judas had choices. He experienced spiritual power, Mark 3:14–19, that should have influenced him to have faith in Jesus. Jesus gave him an opportunity for repentance in Gethsemane, Luke 22:48; John 18:5–6. In fact, Judas could have repented a year earlier at John 6:67–71. After his act of betrayal Judas experienced remorse, and could have chosen to repent and be saved. Instead he chose to give up hope and kill himself, Matthew 27:3–10.

Scripture says God "chose us in Christ," Ephesians 1:4, and Scripture calls on sinners to "believe on the Lord Jesus Christ and you shall be saved," Acts 16:31. Scripture says God chose Israel to be his covenant people, Deuteronomy 7:6, and Scripture calls upon Israel to "choose for yourselves this day whom you will serve," Joshua 24:15. God "saved us and called us . . . according to his own purpose and grace," yet we are saved "through faith," Ephesians 2:8, a freely made choice. Jesus was crucified according to the "determined counsel and foreknowledge of God," but "you have taken [Jesus] by lawless hands, have crucified [him], and put [him] to death," Acts 2:23, indicating the free choices sinners made to crucify Jesus. Scripture is replete with examples, but only one more must suffice. Joseph's brothers sold him into slavery out of envy. They "meant it for evil against me [Joseph], but God meant it for good," Genesis 50:20. God intended for Joseph to be in Egypt during the famine in order to save his family, and sovereignly permitted and used the freely made and evil choices of his brothers

Foreordination

as part of the processes that would accomplish that plan.

Boettner has categorized some of the scriptures supporting foreordination.[1]

> God's plan is eternal: Psalm 33:11; 139:16; Isaiah 37:26; 46:9–10; Jeremiah 31:3; Matthew 25:34; Acts 15:18; 2 Thessalonians 2:13; 2 Timothy 1:9; 1 Peter 1:20.
>
> God's plan is unchangeable: Numbers 23:19; Isaiah 14:24; 4610–11; Malachi 3:6; James 1:17.
>
> The divine plan includes the future acts of men: Daniel 2:28; Matthew 20:18–19; John 6:64 (Under this heading, prophecy, e.g., Micah 5:2; cf. with Matthew 2:5–6; Luke 2:1–7).
>
> The divine plan includes (what seem to be) fortuitous events or chance happenings: 1 Kings 22:28, 34; Job 5:6; 36:32; Proverbs 16:33; Jonah 1:7; Mark 14:30; Acts 1:24, 26. (Genesis 37:28; cf. with 45:5; 1 Samuel 9:15–16; cf. with 9:5–10.)
>
> Some events are recorded as fixed or inevitably certain: Genesis 41:32; Job 14:5; Jeremiah 15:2; 27:7; Habakkuk 2:3; Matthew 24:36; Luke 21:24; 22:22; John 8:20.
>
> Even sinful acts are included and overruled for good: Genesis 50:20; Isaiah 45:7; Amos 3:18; Matthew 21:42; Acts 3:18; Romans 8:28.
>
> God is sovereign in his choices: Genesis 18:14; Job 42:2; Psalm 115:3; 135:6; Isaiah 14:24, 27; 46:9, 10, 11; 55:11; Jeremiah 32:17; Daniel 4:35; Matthew 28:18; Romans 9:20–21; Ephesians 1:11, 22

GOD'S DECREES ARE CONSISTENT WITH HIS CHARACTER

"Though we often speak of the decrees of God in the plural, yet in its own nature the divine decree is but a single act of God . . . His knowledge is all immediate and simultaneous, rather than successive like ours, and his comprehension of it is always complete. And the decree that is founded on it is also a single, all-comprehensive, and simultaneous act. As an eternal and immutable decree it could not be otherwise. There is, therefore, no series of decrees in God, but simply one comprehensive plan, embracing all that comes to pass. Our finite comprehension, however, constrains us to make distinctions, and this accounts for the fact that we often

---

[1] Ibid., 26–29, 33–34.

speak of the decrees of God in the plural."[1] Therefore, as man views the act of God in eternity-past, there is a reasonable order to God's decrees that agrees with Scripture's portrait of God. In the case of foreordination God decided:

> The decision to manifest his glory to sentient creatures.
>
> The decision to create a universe in which his glory would be manifested
>
> The decree to foreordain the agents, events, and outcomes that would accomplish his purpose.
>
> The act of creating the universe.

Although God's acts in eternity past are surely timeless and simultaneous, arranging them in an orderly list helps us to understand God. He is worthy of worship, Revelation 4:11; 5:12, and thus the decision to create sentient creatures to appreciate his glory is consistent with his deity. The decision to create is consistent with his sovereignty, for God did not need to manifest his glory but chose to do so. His decision to foreordain certain agents, events, and outcomes to accomplish his purpose is consistent with his omniscience and wisdom. His decision to permit sinful choices is consistent with his decision to create sentient creatures. His foreordination to make even sinful choices accomplish his processes and plans is consistent with his providence by which he makes all things work together to fulfill his purpose in creating. The act of creation is consistent with his omnipotence and omniscience, for he brought the universe into existence from nothing, and shaped it to be a suitable habitation for his creatures.

The Godhead existed in perfect harmony and satisfaction in eternity past, neither wanting nor needing anything to fulfill or complete them. God's decision to create was a decision to share his glory, not in a participatory way, but to demonstrate his glory for the appreciation and praise of those whom he would create. A perfectly wise and powerful God would create all means to accomplish his goal, and therefore the choices God made—foreordination—are consistent with his sovereign purpose, his omniscient knowledge and wisdom, and his omnipotence to effect his choices.

---

[1] Berkhoff, *Theology*, 102.

Foreordination

This short list does not exhaust the subject of God's decrees. We might consider the doctrine of election, which is dependent on the decree of foreordination. In the decree of foreordination God chose the agents, events, and outcomes that would be the processes which would accomplish the plans that would fulfill the purpose to manifest his glory. The eternal salvation of some—their election—was part of that foreordaining decree, containing all means to accomplish the ends. Is the foreordaining decree of election consistent with what is known of God's character? That is, was election an arbitrary choice, or is it consistent with God's love, holiness, mercy, compassion, sovereignty, omniscience, and omnipotence?

To answer that question we will ask, "Were the objects [mankind] of the divine decree [of election] contemplated as fallen creatures? or were they contemplated merely as men whom God would create, all being equal?"[1] The respective views are known as supralapsarian, infralapsarianism, and sublapsarianism. The suffix -lapsarianism refers to the "lapse" in man's holiness, i.e., Adam's sin.

The supralapsarian view says God decided to elect some to salvation and others to reprobation.

> To elect to life some of the persons who were to be created, and to condemn to destruction the other persons who were to be created.
>
> To create.
>
> To permit the fall of mankind into sin.
>
> To send Christ to redeem the elect.
>
> To send the Holy Spirit to apply this redemption to the elect.

According to the supralapsarianism order, election precedes creation and the fall. The problem with this view is that men who are not contemplated as sinners are ordained to eternal punishment. Since, in this view, God decided the eternal fate of men before the decision to create, then he specifically created some men to eternal damnation. This view is opposed by Scriptural ideas of God as just, e.g., Genesis 18:25, "Shall not the Judge of all the earth do right?" The supralapsarianism view sees God as electing

---

[1] Harrison, *Dictionary*, s. v. "Predestination."

Foreordination

the righteous person to eternal condemnation—righteous because not yet fallen in the order of God's decrees according to the supralapsarianism view. This view also contradicts scriptural ideas concerning the treatment of the innocent (as a concordance search on the word "innocent" will clearly demonstrate).

The infralapsarian view understands the order of God's foreordaining decrees to be the following. God decided:

> To create.
>
> To permit the fall.
>
> To elect some out of this fallen mass to be saved, and to leave the others as they were.
>
> To provide a redeemer for the elect.
>
> To send the Holy Spirit to apply this redemption to the elect.

According to the infralapsarian view the decree of election followed the decree permitting the fall. Sin was the background in which God viewed all human beings, and from which he chose to save some. None were innocent because the fall was permitted before the election; in deciding who to elect God contemplated all as sinners. God chose to rescue some from sin. He chose to take no action, pro or con, toward those not chosen. In this view man is the author of his eternal punishment, God the author of eternal salvation. This view agrees with Scripture, e.g., those who are saved were chosen out of the world, i.e., chosen out of the world in which all are sinful. All men are made of the same lump of sinful clay, Romans 9:21, out of which God took some clay and fashioned it into vessels of honor.

The sublapsarian view is similar to the infralapsarian view. The difference is the order of "provide a redeemer" and "election" are reversed.

> To create.
>
> To permit the fall.
>
> To provide a redeemer
>
> To elect some out of this fallen mass to be saved, and to leave the others as they were.
>
> To send the Holy Spirit to apply this redemption to the elect.

Foreordination

My view is closest to the sublapsarian view.

> To create.
>
> To permit the fall.
>
> To satisfy God's justice through a propitiation for sin
>
> To elect some out of this fallen mass to be saved, and to leave the others as they were.
>
> To send the Holy Spirit to the propitiation to redeem the elect.

The reason my view is different is because the Scripture teaches atonement is not redemption. Atonement is the propitiation (the full satisfaction) of God's justice for the crime of sin through a suitable vicarious sacrifice suffering the judicial penalty against sin.

Every Old Testament sacrifice for sin teaches this basic redemptive truth, that propitiation and redemption are separate acts. The animal is sacrificed on behalf of the sinner, and then the blood of the sacrifice, which represents the merit that cancels the debt of sin, must be applied to the altar to effect forgiveness of sin.

God satisfied his justice against the crime of sin through the propitiation of Jesus Christ on the cross. The merit of that propitiation is limitless, sufficient to forgive all sin. Then, God's justice having been satisfied, God could act redemptively. God applies the limitless merit of the propitiation according to the decree of election (Ephesians 1:4) through the gift of grace-faith-salvation (Ephesians 2:8). Thus, Unlimited Propitiation, Limited (or Particular) Redemption. (Which is the teaching found in the Canons of the Synod of Dort.)

(Recognizing atonement-propitiation is not redemption has three benefits. One, the offer of the gospel to all persons is a legitimate offer. God does not prevent any sinner from coming and believing, their own desire for sin prevents them. Two, salvation is not universal but particular. Three, God would act savingly toward any non-elect who would come, if they could come.)

The decree of foreordination, then, includes both righteous and sinful choices persons will make, and sovereignly causes all choices, holy or sinful, to accomplish the purpose God had in mind when he created the universe. The order of God's foreordaining and electing decrees (including the subsequent decree of predestination) is proposed to be:

Foreordination

The decision to manifest his glory.

The decision to manifest his glory in a particular manner by creating a universe populated with sentient creatures.

The exercise of his omniscient knowledge and wisdom to understand all possible agents, events, and outcomes in the proposed universe that *could* fulfill his purpose.

The decree of foreordination: to create a particular universe by choosing to effectuate certain agents, events, and outcomes (out of all possible) that *would* fulfill his purpose.

The decision to permit the fall of mankind into sin.

The decree to satisfy God's justice through a propitiation for sin.

The decree to elect some sinful persons to be saved and to leave the others as they were.

The decree to send the Holy Spirit to apply the merit of Jesus Christ's propitiation to effect the redemption of the elect.

The decree of predestination to conform the saved person to the image of Christ, and to adopt him or her as a son of God and joint-heir with Christ.

The omnipotent act of creating the universe.

No list, of course, can fully capture, nor accurately define, exactly what God thought and did in eternity-past. However, based on what God has recorded in Scripture about his decisions and subsequent events, and applying reason and logic to what the Scripture says, this order seems a rational view of God's decisions, decrees, and actions concerning foreordination, election, and predestination.

OBJECTIONS TO THE DOCTRINE

There are several objections raised against foreordination. Each requires a limitation to God or a judgment of God by man. I will state and discuss the objections and give a biblical response.

Objection: God Doesn't Foreordain Events He Creates Events

This view says God makes choices without regard to the choices of free agents. There are two possible outcomes to this view. The first is that there is no free will because God has predetermined everything a person will do. The second is that free will is active but has no effect, i.e., whatever choices a person might make, those choices have no effect on God's predetermined processes and plans. The practical result of either outcome is that there is no free will but only determinism. The scriptures do not support this view. For example, God destroyed the earth with a flood, Genesis 6:7, 13, 17, just because the peoples of the earth had become so sinful they were useless to his processes and plans, Genesis 6:5–6, 11–13. The wickedness of all the people led to the decision to start over with one man and his family. In terms of the foreordination in eternity-past, God chose to allow the free choices that resulted in "every intent of the thoughts of his [mankind's] heart was only evil continually." God chose to destroy the earth with a flood, because his sentient creatures freely made wrong choices continually, which choices were permitted by God's foreordination.

The conditional nature of God's dealings with man reveal man has a free will. For example, at 1 Samuel 2:27–36, God repudiates what seemed to be, when first given, an unconditional promise. First Samuel 2:30 is the key verse, "Therefore the Lord God of Israel says, 'I said indeed that your house and the house of your father would walk before Me forever.' But now the LORD says: 'Far be it from me; for those who honor me I will honor, and those who despise me shall be lightly esteemed.' " In this passage God states that Eli and his descendants shall no longer be priests to God, even though God had called Aaron and his sons to serve God as priests, Exodus 29:9, "The priesthood shall be theirs for a perpetual statute." The implication is that the descendants of Aaron and his sons, Nadab, Abihu, Eleazar, and Ithamar, Exodus 28:1, would serve God as priests on behalf of the nation of Israel. Yet this is a conditional statement. Nadab and Abihu were killed for offering strange fire before the Lord, Leviticus 10:1–2. First Chronicles 24:2 tells us that "Nadab and Abihu died before their father, and had no children; therefore Eleazar and Ithamar ministered as priests." The condition of priestly service was, "By those who come near me [YHWH] I must be regarded as holy; and before all the people I must be glorified," Leviticus 10:3. Because Nadab and Abihu did not "regard the Lord as holy" and did not glorify the Lord "before all the people," their priestly line was cut short. The same condition affected Eli and his sons some 400–500 years later: "those who despise me shall be lightly esteemed," 1 Samuel 2:30. Eli was a descendant of Ithamar, whose line slowly died out. When King

Foreordination

David set up the courses of priestly service for the Temple, it was found, 1 Chronicles 24:4, "There were more leaders found of the sons of Eleazar than of the sons of Ithamar." The promise of Exodus 29:9 was fulfilled through Eleazar, because he and his descendants honored and glorified the Lord before the people.

God's choices incorporate man's choices. The God who knows the end from the beginning knew Nadab and Abihu wouldn't serve long, because they would choose not to fulfill their moral obligations. Yet, the promise of a "perpetual statute" was given to them as well as to Ithamar and Eleazar because it established their moral responsibility and treated them as free agents who could choose to meet their obligations. God knew they would not, but their point of view was that they should and were free to choose whether or not they would. Eleazar and his descendants made right choices, until Eli and his sons chose to make wrong choices. Each person in the priestly line made a free choice to honor and glorify the Lord, or not, a free choice God incorporated into the processes that accomplish his plans and purpose. As to the Lord's promise to Eli, at 1 Kings 2:27, "Solomon removed Abiathar from being priest to the LORD, that he might fulfill the word of the LORD which He spoke concerning the house of Eli at Shiloh."

What the above scriptures show is that actions have consequences. Events happen because the choices of sentient creatures are the agents that cause events to happen. For example, to live one's life as an alcoholic or drug addict is to cause events resulting in an early (and probably painful) death. In a more positive view of life, prayer causes events. God has decreed that prayer is one of the agents that causes events and outcomes.[1] God has foreordained that the choices and actions of sentient beings have consequences moral, physical, and spiritual. He has foreordained that events will occur by our causing them. He has effectuated the choices and actions that are the agents causing the events.

> A man's heart devises his way, but the Lord directs his steps, Proverbs 16:9, intimating that the eternal decrees of God by no means prevent us from proceeding, under his will, to provide for ourselves, and arrange all our affairs. And the reason for this is

---

[1] God is sovereign in his answers. He may answer no, not yet, yes, or here is more than you asked for.

Foreordination

clear. For he who has fixed the boundaries of our life, has at the same time intrusted [sic] us with the care of it, provided us with the means of preserving it, forewarned us of the dangers to which we are exposed, and supplied cautions and remedies, that we may not be overwhelmed unawares. Now, our duty is clear, namely, since the Lord has committed to us the defence of our life,—to defend it; since he offers assistance,—to use it; since he forewarns us of danger,—not to rush on heedless; since he supplies remedies,—not to neglect them.[1]

[T]he Lord has furnished men with the arts of deliberation and caution, that they may employ them in subservience to his providence, in the preservation of their life; while, on the contrary, by neglect and sloth, they bring upon themselves the evils which he has annexed to them. How comes it that a provident man, which he consults for his safety, disentangles himself from impending evils; while a foolish man, through unadvised temerity, perishes, unless it be that prudence and folly are, in either case, instruments of divine dispensation? God has been pleased to conceal from us all future events that we may prepare for them as doubtful, and cease not to apply the provided remedies until they have either been overcome, or have proved too much for all our care. Hence, as I formerly observed, that the Providence of God does not interpose simply; but, by employing means, assumes, as it were, a visible form.[2]

Each person is responsible for the choices he or she makes. I do not know in advance which of my choices God has foreordained; but I do know the choices God wants me to make. He wants me to believe on Jesus as my Savior; he wants me to lead a godly life, making wise choices that lead to righteous actions. He wants me to worship him, depend on him, and make choices that glorify him, i.e., choices that demonstrate his holy and righteous power at work in me. God's choices work with a person's responsibility to accomplish God's will. God has made us morally responsible to have faith in him as the Savior and to exercise faith to live our life according to his values, through obedient response to his commandments. Our choices determine what kind of person we will be today, tomorrow, and for eternity. We are responsible to make right choices, culpable for wrong choices. God works with our choices to accomplish his plans and purpose.

---

[1] Calvin, *Institutes*, 1:187 (1.17.4).
[2] Ibid.

Foreordination

God is the agent for certain events and outcomes, but not all. God did not create the choices his sentient creatures will make, nor did he create the events that are the outcome of their choices. Rather, he foreordained events with regard to the choices of sentient beings exercising their free will. Knowing all the possible free choices that might be made by his sentient creatures, God sovereignly foreordained those choices that would accomplish his processes, plans, and purpose. It may be that more than one choice would lead to the same outcome, and God's sovereignty is such that any one of multiple possible choices would accomplish his processes, plans, and purpose, and thus multiple possible choices were effectuated as liable to being chosen by his sentient creatures in their historical-present.

This is, perhaps, too complicated for our finite mind; but it is clear from Scripture that, whether God effectuates one specific choice, or permissively effectuates more than one choice, our freely made choices cause events and outcomes. If there were no choices then there would be no moral responsibility to be righteous, no accountability for sin, and no liability to punishment for the sinful. If there were no choices then Scripture would not exhort believers to live a righteous life, and there would be no reward for the righteous. However, Scripture does exhort the righteous to look toward an eternal reward, and does warn the sinful of eternal punishment. God does not create our choices, or the events resulting from our choices. He sovereignly causes our choices and the events and outcomes resulting from those choices to fulfill his purpose. That is foreordination.

Objection: God Can Only Know Actual Events

I have described God's foreordination as creating a plan and the processes to accomplish that plan by choosing to effectuate certain agents, events, and outcomes out of all those that were possible. The objection is that God cannot know the choices made by free agents because the choice of which action to take under a particular circumstance is variable (contingent) and therefore cannot be known with certainty. By their very nature free choices are uncertain, at least from our point of view. For example, if the circumstance is, "I am thirsty," will my choice be water, juice, or soda? If water will it be from the tap, or bottled; or perhaps tap water I have previously bottled and put in the refrigerator with the

Foreordination

juice and soda? At different times I might respond with a different solution to the exact same circumstance. Therefore, in this view, a person's free choices cannot be foreknown.

The answer to this objection is in three parts. First, God's omniscience is not only knowledge but also understanding. Knowledge and understanding add to form wisdom, which is the skill to put knowledge to right uses. God is able to understand—we might say calculate—every possible circumstance and freely made choice, and he is able to choose wisely the circumstances and choices that will infallibly accomplish his purpose. (Moreover, as previously suggested, God may have chosen to effectuate multiple choices as responses to particular circumstances.) Second, God is infinite: he is beyond any limitation of essence. As to his omnipresence, he is not infinite in the sense of the space-time in which we live, but is immeasurable because he has no material dimension, incomprehensible because he has no all-encompassing boundary, and everywhere because there is no place from which he is excluded and no place to which he is limited.[1] As to his omniscience, there are no exceptions to his knowledge and no exclusions to his understanding. As to his omnipotence there are no limits or boundaries to his authority and power. A God without limits is fully capable of understanding every possible circumstance and every possible free choice. This leads to the third part: a God without limits is omnipotently sovereign to choose the circumstances and freely made choices that fulfill his purpose.

There are two possibilities resulting from a consideration of God's infinite omniscience and omnipotence. One, God's wisdom understood that from circumstance A the free decisions B, C, or D might result. He then foreordained the free decision C to be the outcome of circumstance A. The second possibility is that God foreordained to allow any of the possible decisions, B, C, or D to be the outcome of circumstance A, and through his sovereignty caused that free decision to result in a process that accomplished his plan. Regardless of the way God's foreordination did its work, the decree of foreordination does not destroy the freedom of agents to choose, because God's choice was to effectuate a person's freely made choice or choices.

The point of these arguments is, it is impossible a perfect, all-

---

[1] Ames, *Marrow*, 86.

knowing, all-wise, all-powerful, omnipresent being cannot take infallible action to accomplish his purpose. The infinitely omniscient and omnipotent God must know all possibilities springing from his own actions and the actions of others in order effect the plans and processes that will fulfill his purpose. Man's choices in response to circumstances may be variable, but God knows the actual choice because he selected that choice (or those choices) to become actuality out of all possibilities. God *knew* all possible free choices because of his omniscience, and he *knows* all actual free choices because of his omnipotence.

Objection: God's Decrees are based on His Foreknowledge

In essence, this view states God knows what will happen because he has seen it happen. This wrong view limits God's knowledge to his omnipresence only (eliminating acts of omnipotence and omniscience). The basis for this view is God's relation to the universe. God, being increate, is his own reality, his own domain. He is the only genuine and permanent reality (the present universe is temporary and will be replaced, 2 Peter 3:10–13; Revelation 20:11; 21:1). The universe exists within the reality that is God himself, not as part of his substance, nor as being made from his substance, but existing within him and dependent on him for its maintenance and continuance. God interpenetrates the universe, and therefore is present everywhere at once in the universe. Since he is an eternal being, God interpenetrates the universe in time as well as space (space-time being God's creation). Therefore, everything we understand as past, present, and future is to God ever-present. Moreover, as an omniscient God, from the moment of his decision to create, the universe that would be created existed in potential in his "mind's eye" (so-to-speak), and God saw what would happen throughout time in the universe he was about to create. Therefore, says this view, God knows not because he has foreordained, but because he foresaw.

The essential problem with this view is that it makes God's plan dependent on man's choices. In the foreknowledge view God becomes the reactor not the initiator and actor. God ceases to be sovereign, since he must accommodate man's choices. However, Scripture teaches that God omnipotently initiates and effects, he does not wait and respond. God says, "I am God and there is none like me; declaring the end from the beginning . . . my counsel shall stand, and I will do all my pleasure," Isaiah 46:9, 10. The saints in heaven testify, "You [God] created all things and by your will they exist and were created," Revelation 4:11. God says, "Surely, as I have thought, so shall it come to pass; and as I have purposed, so shall it stand," Isaiah 14:24. And again, "My counsel shall stand and I will do all my pleasure . . . yea, I have spoken, and I will also bring it to pass; I have purposed, I will also do it," Isaiah 46:10. Paul is quite clear that it is God who decides and acts, and his creatures who respond, for believers are "called according to his purpose," Romans 8:28. If believers were called according to foreseen faith, then God would call them according to their purpose, not his. But since faith is God's gift which men must receive, then it is God who calls by initiating faith in the object of his purpose.

We should note that objections made to foreordination equally apply to foreknowledge. In order to foreknow a future event that event must be certain, but the foreknowledge view makes God react to the uncertain choices of his sentient creatures. The true doctrine is that "God foreknows only because he has pre-determined, and it is therefore also that he brings it to pass; his foreknowledge, in other words, is at bottom a knowledge of his own will, and his works of providence are merely the execution of his all-embracing plan."[1] The defense made for foreordination applies with equal force to a proper understanding of foreknowledge.

Objection: Foreordination Makes God the Author of Sin

Some may ask, since God chose everything that would happen, could he not have chosen to prevent sinful choices? The answer is that God chose to create sentient creatures. A necessary property of sentience is the capacity for freely made choices.

Sentience is a quality of self-awareness and self-actualization that only God, man, and angel have. All other creatures live according to instinct. One of the key differences between sentient and non-sentient creatures is the power and authority to choose. For example, sentient creatures can choose to worship God, but non-sentient creatures—every living thing other than God, man, and angel—worship by instinct: "let everything that has breath praise the Lord," Psalm 150:6. Revelation 5:13, "And every creature which is in heaven and on the earth and under the earth and such as are

---

[1] Warfield, *Works*, 2:18.

in the sea, and all that are in them, I heard saying: 'Blessing and honor and glory and power be to Him who sits on the throne, and to the Lamb, forever and ever!' " God created some creatures with sentience because he wanted those creatures to make a voluntary choice to worship him, serve him, obey him, and have intimate fellowship with him. The choice to permit sin began with the choice to create sentient creatures. Sentient creatures make rational (and irrational) choices—freely made choices—that are the result of their individuality responding to life's circumstances. If their choices are truly free, then a wrong choice must be possible. This does not mean a wrong choice is inevitable, or even necessary, to the exercise of free will, as exampled by the holy angels who did not sin and have never sinned. All angels had the power and authority to continue in holiness or choose sin. Some chose to sin, some did not. The ones who chose to remain holy exercised their power of free choice just as surely as the ones who freely chose to sin.

A practical example from biblical history will illustrate the issues of sentience and free choice. Adam and Eve were the first human beings who sinned, a choice that affected all their posterity. They exercised their sentience by choosing between God and self. Every aspect of their complex humanity was oriented toward choosing obedience to the command that restricted their authority (Genesis 2:17). They were created sinless; they were created holy and righteous. They were created with every ability, authority, and moral disposition to maintain their original state, and created without sin or any inclination or disposition to commit an act of sin. They had been given the grace (holiness) necessary to maintain their sinless state. God gave them a test which would let them choose to remain dependent on him or become morally autonomous. Implicit in the test was God's desire they choose to remain holy and in fellowship with him, and his permission to choose to disobey the command and lose their holiness and fellowship. The foreordaining event, which was the decision in eternity-past to create beings with a sentient nature, came with the power and authority to choose righteous obedience or sinful disobedience. To foreordain one outcome only, that of righteous obedience, would be to injure the sentient nature by limiting its full exercise; it would be to create sentient beings who could only act in non-sentient ways.

Adam and Eve were dependent on God, for they exercised a

delegated authority over the earth—authority God had given them, Genesis 1:26, and to which he had commanded the submission of every creature, Genesis 1:28–30. God placed a limit on their authority, Genesis 2:17, one which had little impact on their life. The point of the limitation was a test of submission or autonomy. To continue in their holy and righteous state they must submit to God and depend on him to guide their life and sustain their relationship with him. Through their act of disobedience they become morally autonomous in defiance of God and his commandments.

Though Adam and Eve were created sinless, and righteous, and given the grace of holiness to maintain their sinless state, God also made them mutable—able to change—and did not give them the one grace—indefectibility—that would have led them to reject the temptation. Mutability was necessary if they were to grow emotionally, mentally, spiritually, and physically. However, mutability also meant their human nature could be changed through an act of disobedience. Mutability was necessary to the test of their sentient capacity to choose voluntary submission to God or rebellious autonomy. Withholding the grace of indefectibility meant they must use the righteousness and holiness present within their sinless human nature to decide for God. The righteous and holy human nature God had given them was sufficient to the task. Had they chosen for God they would have merited and immediately received the grace of indefectibility as the reward for their obedience. But they disobeyed the commandment, and their mutable human nature was changed by their disobedience from sinless to sinful.

So God made them sentient; and thereby made them creatures with the power and authority of choice; and he gave them every ability necessary to make the right choice. But they decided to make the wrong choice—a choice they knew was wrong—and turn away from God in sin. They self-originated sin in their perfect human nature; they voluntarily chose to disobey God. Every human being faces that same choice throughout their life.

To act on the basis of instinct is to be non-sentient. To be able to choose between alternatives is a necessary component of sentience. The sentient capacity for choice is why God permitted, and continues to permit, individuals to sin. To prevent sin through the decree of foreordination in eternity-past would be to not create sentient beings. To prevent sin in historical-present would be to deny sentient beings the capacity to exercise their sentience. To prevent the choice of sin God would have had to make human beings non-sentient. But, he made us sentient and permitted the choice of worship or sin. Because he chose to make us sentient, he chose to permit our freely made sinful choices.

As to the problem of sin in the world, the doctrine of foreordination means God sovereignly uses man's choices as parts of the processes that accomplish his plans and purpose. God makes all things work to manifest his glory. For example, the wrong acts of some turn others to God, and God is glorified in their salvation. Sin presents God and his saved people manifold opportunities to act in mercy, compassion, and love. When unsaved sinners face their eternal judgment, God will be glorified in the exercise of his holiness and righteousness in his judgment against sinners. I am not saying that sin is necessary to the exercise of godliness and righteousness—it is not—but that God has decreed to allow his sentient creatures to choose how they shall live in this world, and therefore sinful choices are permitted.

God does warn his creatures not to make wrong choices, and he punishes the unsaved (and chastises the saved) when wrong choices are made. God does give grace and does exercise his omnipotence to prevent some sinful acts. That there is some measure of love, kindness, compassion, mercy, and justice in the world indicates individuals are not always allowed to act on every sinful impulse. God gives grace to influence their decisions to not sin. Moreover, God acts in providence to prevent some from suffering who might otherwise have suffered, and in mercy to alleviate the suffering of those who are suffering.

God's foreordination of all events includes two events that will be the end of sin. One, every unsaved sinner (man, angel) will be imprisoned for eternity in the lake of fire, Revelation 20:11–15. Two, just as he did for the holy angels, God will give his saved people the grace of indefectibility when they enter heaven. The holy angels freely made a choice to remain in the holy state in which God had created them. God rewarded that choice with the grace of indefectibility, so that they will not turn from God and commit sin. This grace, like every other grace, does not prevent the free exercise of their will, but so works with their free will as to positively and inevitably and eternally influence them to choose to turn away

Foreordination

from sin. So too with those saved by faith in Christ. In eternity they will have this grace to preserve them from sin; and even now God gives grace so that they persevere in their faith.

The grace God gives his people influences them to choose him; it does not control their choices. Grace influences the saved person's will as one principle of life among the many that compose human nature. The grace of holiness is a life-principle that continually influences the person to choose to worship, obey, serve, and fellowship with God. The influence of grace does not mean the saved person does not possess any freedom of will, but because grace is an innate principle of holiness in man's nature, his will is of itself inclined to choose holiness and, as being in an intimate relationship with God, never desires to change its inclination to choose holiness. The grace of holiness works constructively with all the other life-principles in human nature to influence the will to choose to live in holiness and maintain one's relationship with God in Christ. In the redeemed in heaven the influence of the grace of indefectibility is so pervasive and so powerful they will by choice never turn from God to sin.

God, then, is not the author of sin, but the creator of sentience. Man decides what he will do with his sentience: worship his Creator and God, or worship himself. God permits sin as a possible outcome of sentience.

THE FAITH OF THE CHURCH

The terms election and predestination were very often used by the theologians and preachers of the church to communicate the idea of foreordination. On occasion foreordination and foreknowledge were used as synonyms. Some identified foreordination with providence. However, there are passages in their writings where what is in view is God determining the agents, events, and outcomes of the world he is about to create. Not in those terms, of course, but the idea is present. The following testimonies were gleaned from the Church Fathers.

> Clement of Alexandria, AD 153–217, ". . . whom God hath foreordained before the foundation of the world (Ephesians 1:4, 5) to be enrolled in the highest 'adoption.'"[1]
>
> Minucius Felix, AD 210, "For what else is fate than what God has

---

[1] Roberts and Donaldson, *Ante-Nicene Fathers.* 2:492.

Foreordination

spoken of each one of us? who, since he can foresee our constitution, determines also the fates for us, according to the deserts and the qualities of individuals."[1]

Lactantius, AD 260–330, "First a question arises: whether there is any providence which made or governs the world? [Almost all philosophers, except the Epicureans agree that there is such providence.] For who can doubt respecting a providence, when he sees that the heavens and earth have been so arranged, and that all things have been so regulated . . . that, therefore, which exists in accordance with a plan, cannot have had its beginning without a plan."[2]

Augustine, AD 354–430, "Thou existest, and art the God and Lord of thy creatures; and with thee fixedly abide the causes of all unstable things, the unchanging sources of all things changeable, and the eternal reasons for all things unreasoning and temporal."[3]

Augustine, "For what else is to be understood by that invariable refrain, 'And God saw that it was good,' than the approval of the work in its design, which is the wisdom of God? For certainly God did not in the actual achievement of the work first learn that it was good, but, on the contrary, nothing would have been made had it not been first known by him."[4]

Augustine, "So great is his [God's] wisdom and power, that all things which seem adverse to his purpose do still tend towards those just and good ends and issues which he himself has foreknown . . . [those events] which from eternity ha[ve] been prepared in his unchangeable will, shall, then come to pass."[5]

Chrysostom, AD 400, Homily III on Acts 1:12, "So confident were they, that assuredly one of them must be appointed. They said not, Choose, but 'Show the chosen one'; knowing that all things were foreordained by God."[6]

Gregory Nazianzen, AD 329–389, "Or are the disturbances and changes of the universe (which was originally constituted, blended, bound together, and set in motion in a harmony known only to him who gave it motion,) directed by reason and order

---

[1] Ibid., 4:195.
[2] Ibid., 7:224.
[3] Schaff, *Nicene and Post-Nicene Fathers*, First Series. 1:47.
[4] Ibid., 2:216.
[5] Ibid., 2:480.
[6] Ibid, 11:21.

Foreordination

under the guidance of the reins of providence?"[1] [He affirms this statement.]

Beginning with the Reformation, theologians began to develop the modern understanding of the term.

> Calvin, AD 1504–1564, "God is the disposer and ruler of all things,—that from the remotest eternity, according to his own wisdom, he decreed what he was to do, and now, by his power executes what he decreed. Hence we maintain that, by his providence, not heaven and earth and inanimate creatures only, but also the counsels and wills of man are so governed as to move exactly in the course which he has destined."[2]

> William Ames, AD 1576–1633, "God's will determines all things without exception: the greatest, the least, the contingent, the necessary, the free." . . . "By his will, however, he does not will all things which he can, but all things he judges should be willed, or all things that actually happen." . . . "The will of God does not imply a necessity in all future things, but only a certainty in regard to the event. Thus the event was certain that Christ's bones should not be broken, because God willed that they should not be. But there was no necessity imposed upon the soldiers, their spears, and other secondary causes then present." . . . "The will of God . . . effectively foreordains certain effects to follow certain causes." . . . "In the things which God wills . . . he wills the end before the means . . . he wills first those [means] which come nearest the end; that which is first in order of execution is last in order of intention and vice versa."[3]

> Westminster Confession, 1647, chapter three, paragraphs 1, 2, "God from all eternity, did, by the most wise and holy counsel of His own will, freely, and unchangeably ordain whatsoever comes to pass; yet so, as thereby neither is God the author of sin, nor is violence offered to the will of the creatures; nor is the liberty or contingency of second causes taken away, but rather established. Although God knows whatsoever may or can come to pass upon all supposed conditions; yet has He not decreed anything because He foresaw it as future, or as that which would come to pass upon

---

[1] Schaff and Wace, *Nicene and Post-Nicene Fathers*, Second Series. 7:248.
[2] Calvin, *Institutes*, 1:179 (1.16.8).
[3] Ames, *Marrow*, 99–101.

Foreordination

such conditions."[1]

Westminster Confession, chapter five, paragraphs 1–3, "God the great Creator of all things does uphold, direct, dispose, and govern all creatures, actions, and things, from the greatest even to the least, by His most wise and holy providence, according to His infallible foreknowledge, and the free and immutable counsel of His own will, to the praise of the glory of His wisdom, power, justice, goodness, and mercy. Although, in relation to the foreknowledge and decree of God, the first Cause, all things come to pass immutably, and infallibly; yet, by the same providence, He orders them to fall out, according to the nature of second causes, either necessarily, freely, or contingently. God, in His ordinary providence, makes use of means, yet is free to work without, above, and against them, at His pleasure."[2]

John Owen, AD 1616–1683, "Divines, for distinction's sake, ascribe unto God a twofold knowledge; one, intuitive or intellective, whereby he foreknows and sees all things that are possible,—that is, all things that can be done by his almighty power,—without any respect to their future existence, whether they shall come to pass or no. Yea, infinite things, whose actual being eternity shall never behold, are thus open and naked unto him; for was there not strength and power in his hand to have created another world? was there not counsel in the storehouse of his wisdom to have created this otherwise, or not to have created it at all? Shall we say that his providence extends itself every way to the utmost of its activity? or can he not produce innumerable things in the world which now he doth not. Now, all these, and every thing else that is feasible to his infinite power, he foresees and knows, "scientia," as they speak, "simplicis intelligentiae," by his essential knowledge. Out of this large and boundless territory of things possible, God by his decrees freely determines what shall come to pass, and makes them future which before were but possible. After this decree, as they commonly speak, follows, or together with it, as others more exactly, taketh place, that prescience of God which they call "visionis" [sic], "of vision," whereby he infallibly sees all things in their proper causes, and how and when they shall come to pass. Now, these two sorts of knowledge differ, inasmuch as by the one God knows what it is possible may come to pass; by the other, only what it is impossible should not come to pass. Things are possible in regard of God's power, future in regard of his decree.

---

[1] http://www.reformed.org/documents/wcf_with_proofs/index.html
[2] Ibid.

Foreordination

So that (if I may so say) the measure of the first kind of science is God's omnipotency, what he can do; of the other his purpose, what certainly he will do, or permit to be done. With this prescience, then, God foresees all, and nothing but what he hath decreed shall come to pass."[1]

Moving into the modern era, we discover the same faith.

Charles Hodge, AD 1797–1878, "The decrees of God are his eternal purpose, according to the counsel of his will, whereby for his own glory he hath foreordained whatsoever comes to pass." . . . "[f]rom the indefinite number of systems, or series of possible events, present to the divine mind, God determined on the futurition or actual occurrence of the existing order of things, with all its changes, minute as well as great, from the beginning of time to all eternity." . . . "All events embraced in the purpose of God are certain, whether he has determined to bring them to pass by his own power, or simply to permit their occurrence through the agency of his creatures."[2]

Louis Berkhoff, AD 1874–1957, "God has decreed all things, and has decreed them with their causes and conditions in the exact order in which they come to pass."[3] . . . "The decree itself provides in every case that the event shall be affected by causes acting in a manner perfectly consistent with the nature of the event in question. Thus in the case of every free act of a moral agent the decree provides at the same time — (a) That the agent shall be a free agent. (b) That his antecedents and all the antecedents of the act in question shall be what they are. (c) That all the present conditions [emphasis original] of the act shall be what they are. (d) That the act shall be perfectly spontaneous and free on the part of the agent. (e) That it shall be certainly future. Psalm 33:11; Proverbs 19:21; Isaiah 46:10."[4]

Lewis Sperry Chafer, AD 1871–1952, "The whole order of events from the least detail unto the greatest operates under the determining decree of God so as to take place according to his sovereign purpose."[5] . . . "According to the Scriptural conception, God foreknows because he has foreordained all things, and because in his providence he will certainly bring all to pass. His

---

[1] Owen, *Works*, 10:23–24.
[2] Hodge, *Theology*, 1:534, 537.
[3] Berkhoff, *Theology*, 67.
[4] Ibid., 104 (quoting A. A. Hodge, *Outlines of Theology*, 203).
[5] Chafer, *Theology*, 7:158.

Foreordination

foreknowledge is not a dependent one which must wait upon events, but is simply the knowledge which God has of his own eternal purpose."[1]

Emery Bancroft, died AD 1944, "The counsel of God [Ephesians 1:11] is that eternal scheme of all things adopted by the divine mind which embraces all his original designs, including everything in the creative and redemptive program of God, and involving or embracing the free actions of man . . . the counsel covers a multitude of things which are in reality but infinitesimal parts of an infinite whole, and embraces, not only effects, but also causes; not only the ends to be secured, but also the means needful to secure them."[2]

J. Oliver Buswell, AD 1895–1977. "[w]ith infinite power and infinite wisdom God has, from all eternity past, decided and chosen and determined the course of all events without exception for all eternity to come."[3]

Wayne Grudem, AD 1948–Present, "The decrees of God are the eternal plans of God whereby, before the creation of the world, he determined to bring about everything that happens."[4]

I have provided these quotations from various centuries of church history so the reader may understand that mine is no novel doctrine of foreordination and foreknowledge.

---

[1] Ibid., 7:159, (quoting Dr. Caspar Wistar Hodge from the 1915 edition of the *International Standard Bible Encyclopedia*, 2:1129–30).
[2] Bancroft, *Theology*, 106–7.
[3] Buswell, *Theology*, 1:163.
[4] Grudem, *Theology*, 332.

4. THE DOCTRINE OF ELECTION

STATEMENT AND ILLUSTRATION OF THE DOCTRINE

Statement of the doctrine: election is the choice of a sovereign God, 1) to give the gift of grace-faith-salvation to some sinners to effect their salvation, and 2) to take no action, positive or negative, to either effect or deny the salvation of other sinners. The decree of election includes all means necessary to effect salvation.

An illustration of the doctrine:

> The river of sinful humanity is justly racing toward the waterfall of death emptying into the lake of eternal fire; God reaches into the river and saves many; he prevents no one from swimming to the safety of the heavenly shore; he will receive any person who comes to him by way of Christ. The saved are standing on the shore urging everyone in the river to come to Christ.

The illustration communicates the important aspects of the doctrine of election: 1) every human being is a sinner and thus is justly due eternal judgment in the lake of fire; 2) God takes direct action to save some sinners from eternal punishment; 3) God does not take any action which would prevent any sinner from coming to him to receive salvation; 4) God sends his saved people to evangelize the unsaved.

ELECTION IN ETERNITY-PAST

In the previous chapter we discussed the choices God made in eternity-past. Of interest to the present chapter was God's decision to permit the fall of mankind into sin, and his decree to elect some sinful persons to be saved and to leave the others as they were. The Epistle to the Ephesians deals directly with God's choices in election. Paul's letter to the Ephesians might be called advanced instruction for advanced Christians.[1] The doctrines of election and predestination in the first chapter certainly meet that definition.

The theme of Ephesians 1:3–14 is announced in v. 3: God has blessed the believer with every spiritual blessing in Christ. What those spiritual blessings are is stated in vv. 4–14. Ephesians 1:4 clearly states God chose some human beings to salvation: "just as

---

[1] Eadie, *Ephesians*, xxxii. "The letter was intended for advanced Christians."

Election

God chose us in Christ before the foundation of the world, that we should be holy and without blame before Him in love." Paul is addressing a certain group of people, those who had previously believed on Jesus as their Savior, and therefore what he has said explains how they came to believe: God chose them.[1] To choose "us" implies a "them" who were not so chosen.

The Greek adverbial conjunction opening v. 4, *kathós*, can have a comparative meaning, hence the NKJV translation "just as." The conjunction can also have a causal sense, with the rendering "because", "since", or "for." Both meanings are in view. The work of the Trinity in blessing a believer, v. 3, is both the manner and basis for blessings. "The election of the Father, the redemption of the Son, and the seal of the Holy Spirit are themselves spiritual benefits as well as being the basis for every spiritual benefit."[2] Election is one of the acts of God by which he blesses his people with every spiritual blessing.

The phrase "before the foundation of the world," v. 4, means eternity-past, before the universe was created. The Greek word, *eklégō*, "he chose," is in the middle voice and means to choose or select for one's self. In both biblical and secular use the word indicated "a careful selection out of known options where the subject can freely make a choice according to his or her known preference with no idea of dislike toward the options not selected."[3] Jesus, for example, chose twelve disciples to be his apostles out of the multitude of disciples; the church chose seven disciples to be deacons out of the multitude of believers. When Jesus chose twelve to be his apostles it did not mean he had a personal dislike for the ones not chosen, nor that he prevented them from continuing to be his disciples. When the church chose seven deacons those not chosen were not disliked or sent away. The act of choosing says nothing about the ones not chosen. Equally as important, the ones chosen did not have some claim on the one choosing; there was nothing about them that obligated the one choosing to choose them over others. Finally, the use of *eklégō* never indicates the reprobation of those not chosen. God chooses to save, but that choice does not directly deny salvation to the ones not chosen. The

---

[1] Paul presents the man-ward side of salvation in Ephesians 2. I will discuss man's choice in a later chapter.
[2] Hoehner, *Ephesians*, 175.
[3] Ibid., 186.

biblical doctrine is that sinners are reprobate because of their freely made choices throughout their lifetime to reject Jesus as their Savior and continue in sin.

In regard to election, "God is the one who chooses the believer. His choice of the believer is in the light of all known options, namely the entire human race. There is no reference in this context [Ephesians 1:4], as in any other context, to those not chosen, and hence there is no indication of dislike toward other human beings. The [grammatical construction] aorist middle voice expresses personal interest in God's choice. The believer is chosen for God's own benefit. The whole action shows God's grace in taking the initiative. It shows that he freely chose the believer due to his grace and not because the believer had some legal claim on God. The past action is denoted by the phrase 'before the foundation of the world.' Knowing all options, God chose with personal interest the believer (who had no legal claim on God) in eternity-past."[1]

The choice of God to save some sinners out of the entire group of sinners (the human race) is the doctrine of election. Though this might be a difficult doctrine to some, we should remember that God is always just and holy. Is God just and holy and righteous only when I understand; or only when I approve his actions? Who is man to judge God? Whatever God's choices, and whatever God's reasons for his choices (reasons he never states or explains), God cannot sin; he cannot make an error in judgment. God is holy, God is righteous, God's choices are just. Understanding the doctrines of foreordination and election begins with the scriptural knowledge that God made choices. Those choices were not made capriciously, in ignorance, malevolently, nor isolated from the whole of God's character and attributes. Every aspect of God's being, from his love to his holiness, worked in harmony to make the perfect choices that would perfectly fulfill his purpose. God decided toward whom he would act in unmerited blessing (grace) by electing them to salvation, and toward whom he would not so act. Those choices were made in a manner that was consistent with God's sovereignty, knowledge, wisdom, holiness, righteousness, and love.

A Discussion of God's love

I want to digress for a moment to discuss God's love in

---

[1] Ibid.

election. Given what most people understand as love, a "God of love" seems inconsistent in not saving every sinner. God's electing choice affected the eternal destiny of all. How could a God of love choose to act in grace to save some, but not all? The answer is that grace is unmerited by any. God acts sovereignly to give grace to whom he chooses. However, the question remains. Wouldn't a God of love choose to extend his grace to all? The short answer is that God's sovereignty, grace, and love work together without conflict.

God's electing choice is consistent with all of God's attributes working together in harmony. Election required the exercise of God's love as well as his grace, holiness, righteousness, justice, mercy—indeed, all his attributes were exercised in harmony in the decree of election. All God's attributes work together without conflict because God is a unity of essence and attributes, not a union. A union is a joining together of dissimilar components. For example, man is a union of material body and immaterial soul. That the "spirit is willing but the flesh is weak" efficiently describes the conflict many experience between body and soul. Man's human nature is composed of many life-principles (or attributes) which do not always agree, hence the confusion and frustration—even insanity—that afflicts human beings.

God is a unity, an undivided state of oneness. Each Person in the Trinity possesses the same one essence in whole. The whole essence is in each divine attribute. There is no separation, division, or conflict between or among the Persons or their attributes. Each divine Person participates in the work of any one of the Persons, because God is one essence. No one attribute operates apart from all other attributes, because the whole essence is in each attribute.

Therefore, as an example of the unity of God's attributes: his holiness was violated by the crime of sin; his righteousness demanded he take action to punish sin; his justice applied the penalty of sin to the sinner; his mercy delayed justice to give the sinner time to find saving faith, and his mercy relieved the suffering caused by sin; his love led him to become incarnate and suffer sin's penalty on behalf of the sinner, thus satisfying his holiness, righteousness, and justice; his grace applied the satisfaction (propitiation) he made for sin to the sinner's need, by giving the gift of grace-faith-salvation. All God's attributes worked in harmony to accomplish the redemption of sinners. In another example, God's holiness, righteousness, and justice punishes sinners who will not believe; those same attributes act to chastise believers who commit sin, and act to restore believers to fellowship upon their repentance. In every act God commits, without exception, all of God's attributes act in harmony because they are in a state of oneness: "the whole essence is in each attribute and the attribute is the essence."[1] Therefore, God's love is consistent with his electing choice, because the exercise of his sovereignty, knowledge, wisdom, holiness, righteousness, and justice in election was in union and harmony with his mercy and love, in extending saving grace to some but not all.

The problem we sinners have with accepting God's love in election is that we understand love as emotion. However, love is not merely emotion. Love has two aspects. One aspect is emotional. The emotional aspect of love is based in having something in common with another person. God has nothing in common with sinners that could be the basis for an emotional relationship, such as fellowship. Furthermore, God doesn't punish sinners out of malice or anger, but from his holiness, righteousness, and justice: their crime of sin violated God's law, engaging the penalty required by that law. God actions toward all sinners is not grounded in emotion, but in a decision of his will formed by all his attributes acting in harmony.

A decision of the will is the other aspect of love. Love is a decision of the will to seek the best good for another person, without expectation of recompense, reciprocity, or recognition, and without consideration of merit or demerit. This is the love God exercised in election. This is love believers are to exercise toward one another, and toward the world. This love is not dependent on affection, fondness, or friendship. Although emotion may develop during its exercise, this love begins as a decision, not an emotion, and does not require emotion for its exercise. I need not have the emotion love in order to decide to help (to love) the homeless stranger in need of food, clothing, shelter, or medical treatment; I may in fact feel decidedly unfriendly or disgusted. The decision to help—the decision of the will to seek the best good for another person, without expectation of recompense, reciprocity, or recognition, and without consideration of merit or demerit—is love.

Of course, as a human being, various emotions, such as

---

[1] Shedd, *Theology*, 1:334.

compassion, or friendship, or malice, or disgust, contribute to the decision-making function of the will. However, a decision to seek the best good for another—the decision to act toward another in love—can be, and should be, independent of positive or negative emotions. Otherwise our love is a respecter of persons, helping those we like and ignoring those we have no reason to like. Christians are to exercise their love as God exercises his love, by decision apart from sentiment (emotions). Because human attributes are not always in harmony, and are subject to conflicting emotions, this kind of love—the decision to exercise godly, self-sacrificial love for the best good of another—can be exercised only through the spiritual power provided by the Holy Spirit.

God, of course, also has emotions. Man, who was created in God's image, has emotions, and therefore the Person in whose image man was created must have emotions. God loves, is angry, is joyful and at peace, offers friendship and fellowship, etc. However, God is a union of essence and attributes: his emotions do not conflict with his will. Put another way, God's emotional state always agrees with his decisions.

The love God exercised in choosing some to salvation was a decision of his will. This is clear from the order of God's decrees. At the moment when the electing choice was made, God contemplated all human beings as sinners, because he had previously decreed to permit the fall into sin. Therefore, no person was lovable; no person had anything in common with God from which to form a basis for friendship, fellowship, or the emotion of love. Every person was obnoxious to God's holiness, disgusting (an abomination) to his righteousness, and an offense to his justice. Every person was in spiritual darkness unable to comprehend God, John 1:5; every person was in spiritual darkness and had no place in the presence of God, 1 John 1:5. An emotional decision would have rejected every person and allowed every person to continue on to eternal punishment in the lake of fire.

God's decision to save some was not an emotional decision, but was an act of his will—a choice formed by all his attributes acting in harmony—to exercise his love in such a way as to fulfill his purpose. God's decision to love was and is expressed through covenant and salvific relationships. For example, God told Israel he chose them out of all other peoples because he loved them. His love toward Israel was expressed through the covenant he made with Abraham,

Deuteronomy 7:7–9. Taking another example, God loved Jacob and hated Esau, Malachi 1:2–3. Paul used this verse to explain election, Romans 9:6–11. How did God express his love for Jacob? He chose Jacob to be a member of the covenant he had made with Abraham; a covenant God faithfully kept with the nation Israel, on whom he set his love, expressed by the making and maintaining of that covenant.

The choice of Jacob but not Esau was not based on any good or evil Jacob might have done—in other words not an emotional response to Jacob—"for the children not yet being born, nor having done any good or evil, that the purpose of God according to election might stand, not of works but of Him who calls," Romans 9:11. The same applies to Esau. His non-election was not some emotional response on the part of God, because he too was "not yet born." God made a decision to choose Jacob not Esau, a decision of his will made for reasons not stated, except to say they were not emotional reasons, and the choice was part of the plan to fulfill God's purpose. Why then is it said, "Jacob I have loved, but Esau I have hated." Not out of emotional love for Jacob or emotional malice for Esau. God's electing love is his decision to bring a person into a covenant and salvific relationship with himself. He did not elect Esau. Therefore, it is said that he "loved" the one and "hated" the other, because he elected one to salvation and did not elect the other. An emotional bias toward the one and emotional prejudice toward the other was not at all part of God's electing decision. His love for Jacob was bringing him into the covenant; his hatred of Esau was not bringing him into the covenant.

If, then, we would understand God's electing love, we must set aside, as best we can, the emotional content we assign to the words "love" and "hate." God's love was his decision to establish a relationship with Jacob. God's hate was his decision not to establish a relationship with Esau. God, through the decree of election in eternity-past, ordained certain sinners to a relationship with himself; he loved them.

God, with all his attributes acting in union and harmony, chose to establish a covenant relationship with some sinners, and bring them into that covenant through salvation. God made a decision of his will, not an emotional decision. His decision toward the non-elect, which was to leave them as he found them (in sin), was also not an emotional decision, but a decision of his will that, like the decision to elect some, would fulfill his purpose. God's love in election was his decision to seek the best good for some sinners, without expectation of recompense or reciprocity, and without consideration of their merit (they had none) or demerit. He made this decision without favoritism toward the elect and without malice—without any negative emotion—toward those not chosen. Those God elected were chosen in love and mercy (Ephesians 1:4; 2:4) to be saved, sanctified, and adopted, to the praise of his glory.

VIEWS OF ELECTION

The Foreknowledge View

God never says why he made an electing choice, nor the reasons for the choice, nor the reasons for his particular choices (which individuals he would elect). There are man-made explanations of election that try to explain why God in eternity-past chose certain (as-yet-uncreated) sinners for salvation in Christ. The basis for these man-made explanations is foreknowledge: that God chose certain persons just because he knew they would believe when hearing the gospel; that certain persons were elected because God had foreseen their faith. This view eliminates the sovereignty of God and makes man his own savior: God reacts to man's choices; a person becomes elect because he is foreknown to believe.

I have explained in the chapter on foreordination that all events and outcomes are certain because God chose which potential events and outcomes would pass from possible to actual. God knows what circumstances, agents, events, and outcomes will happen because he chose what would happen. God chose who he would elect. He chose those particular persons to salvation for his own benefit: to fulfill the purpose for which he created the universe and all things and creatures in it, including all human beings, saved and unsaved. Election means God chose the circumstances, agents, and events that would lead the elected persons to freely make a decision to believe the gospel of salvation. Election means God will extend to those he has chosen the efficient agent of salvation, which is God's gift of grace-faith-salvation, and not extend the same to those not chosen. Those who are elected will freely respond to God's gift by means of faith, which is the instrumental agent of their salvation: faith is the hand of the soul receiving God's gift. God gives the gift of grace-faith-salvation to the elect; by means of their faith the elect freely choose to receive the gift and appropriate the truth of the gospel to their specific circumstances.

Acts 2:23 demonstrates that God's foreknowledge is subordinate to (depends upon, comes after) God's "determined purpose" i.e., his foreordination. The applicable portion of the verse states, "Him [Christ], being delivered by the determined purpose and foreknowledge of God." God's "determined purpose" caused Christ to be delivered to sinners to be crucified. God's foreknowledge was based on the foreordination which made this event certain. I will discuss in a moment the part God's foreknowledge played in Christ's crucifixion.

God is a sovereign God. Before he contemplated what he would create, he decided why he would create: his purpose. Then he decided how he would accomplish his purpose: his plans. Then he contemplated what he would create as the processes to accomplish the plans and fulfill the purpose. After he had decided his purpose and plans, then he decided all things that would occur in his creation from its beginning to its end. God selected those freely made choices which would accomplish his predetermined purpose and plans. Therefore, what his creatures might or might not do did not influence God's decisions which were made before he contemplated their choices.

God alone decided the purpose for which he would create. God alone decided what to create. God alone decided the agents, events, and outcomes that would take place in the creation he would create. God alone decided the processes in the creation that would accomplish the plans by which he would fulfill his purpose. What his sentient creatures would freely choose to do was part of the agents, events, and outcomes God chose to effectuate to fulfill his purpose.

God, therefore, decides what he will do uninfluenced by what others will do. Scripture clearly teaches God decides apart from any external influence, e.g., Isaiah 41:28; Romans 11:34, "For who has known the mind of the LORD? Or who has become his counselor?" Therefore, God's foreknowledge of an event is not the reason God made a choice or decision; if foreknowledge was the reason for a decision, then God was deciding what to do based on what others had decided to do. If such was the case, then God would not be a sovereign God but a God who reacts rather than initiates action.

God's foreknowledge of any event is based on his decision to effectuate that event. Because he has decreed it, he knows it. Because he has decreed it, it is certain, Isaiah 46:10. Because he knows the event, his sovereignty uses the event to accomplish his purpose. God's use of his foreknowledge is to integrate the freely made choices of his sentient creatures into the processes that accomplish his plans and purposes. First, God made a decision independent of the decisions and actions of others: God decided to create a universe that would display his glory. Then his foreordination effectuated all things—including the decisions and activities of sentient beings—that would fulfill his purpose in creating. Then his foreknowledge integrated the decisions and acts of others to accomplish what he foreordained. In chapter 2 we noted that God's foreordination and his foreknowledge are, respectively, his *próginoskō*, and *prógnōsis*. The latter is the feminine noun form of the former. In essence, God's foreknowledge is the same as his foreordination: he foreknows because he foreordained.

Returning to Acts 2:23, the means by which sinners would be saved illustrates the relationship between foreordination and foreknowledge. God's plan is that sinners will be saved through the death of Jesus on the cross. Jesus was killed by lawless hands, Acts 2:24, meaning that certain men made a conscious and free decision to crucify Jesus. Those men were able to crucify Jesus because God's plan of salvation decreed his Son would redeem sinners through his death by crucifixion, Acts 2:23. God then effected his decree (in the fullness of time) through the conscious and free decision of certain sinners to kill Jesus. Those certain sinners and their choice to sin was foreknown, because God had foreordained all events, including the freely made choice of certain sinners to crucify Jesus. God's foreknowledge was not the origin of the decree to crucify the Redeemer, nor the origin of the sinner's choice to crucify Jesus, but was part of the process by which God effectuated the decree. The death of Jesus to redeem sinners, and all events and circumstances leading up to that act, was foreordained, including the freely made wrong choices of the sinners who caused the crucifixion and the sinners who performed the crucifixion. God's foreknowledge of the sinners' choices—foreknowledge based on the foreordination that selected those particular choices to accomplish God's plans and purpose—caused those choices to be incorporated as part of the processes by which the crucifixion was to be accomplished.

For argument's sake, let us rewrite Acts 2:23 and interpret the crucifixion using the foreknowledge view: "Him [Christ], being delivered by the foreknowledge and determined purpose of God." If foreknowledge of their actions was the reason certain sinners were chosen to crucify Jesus in order to fulfill God's purpose to redeem sinners, then the origin and cause of redemption from sin is a sinful act by sinful men. That, of course, is not what happened. God's decree to redeem sinners through Jesus' crucifixion caused the wrong decision of those certain men to become an integral part of the processes by which the decree to crucify Jesus was effected. The decree came first, and then foreknowledge became an integral part of putting the decision into effect. So too with the decree to save. God chose to save certain sinners, and then his foreknowledge put the decision into effect by incorporating foreordained circumstances, events, and agents into the processes necessary to achieve the outcome.

Let us look at this view of foreknowledge as the basis of saving faith from a temporal point of view. God decreed to permit the fall into sin. Sinful persons cannot initiate saving faith (discussed in a later chapter), because the sin attribute strongly influences a person to reject God, disobey his commandments, and seek salvation by his own hand. The sinner does not desire to seek God, Romans 3:11, and has no desire to change his inclination to turn away from God, Romans 3:12. The decree of election followed the decree to permit sin. God, by the decree of election, decided to act as the effectuating agent of saving faith. Therefore, foreknowledge of faith cannot be the ground of election because faith is the very blessing to which sinners are elected.[1] (Molinism proposes a foreknowledge view. See Appendix, Molinism and Election.)

Sinful human beings will choose to reject God, no matter what circumstances, events, and outcomes—other than divine intervention—might be brought to bear in that person's life. God is the agent that effectuates faith, by giving the gift of grace-faith-salvation. He gives the gift according to his decree of election in eternity-past. Therefore God's decree of election, not foreseen faith, is the reason sinners are saved.

In the logical order in which God's decision making process

---

[1] Hodge, *Ephesians*, 30.

must occur, God decides what to do, and then decrees agents, events, and outcomes as the processes by which his decision is effected in the world. God has decided to redeem certain sinners; his decree of election is the origin of all the processes required to effect his decision. His foreknowledge flows from his decrees, integrating the acts of his agents (himself and others) to effect his decision.

Pelagian, Semi-Pelagian, and Armenian Views

In the Pelagian, Semi-Pelagian, and Armenian views, God passively reacts to man's choices, i.e., election is based on foreseen faith. Pelagianism is the origin of the foreknowledge view. Pelagianism was named after the monk Pelagius (AD 354–420), who first proposed the foreknowledge view of election in opposition to the Augustinian view of biblical doctrine. Pelagianism taught:

> The will was always as free to choose good as evil. There was no inherited inclination to evil in human nature . . . .. denied original sin . . . .. denied the need of internal grace to keep God's commandments. Human nature was created good; and was endowed by its Creator with power to live an upright life easily if a man will to . . . .. [it is] rationalized moralism. Man created with free will has no longer to do with God but with himself alone. God only re-enters at the last judgment.[1]

Under these conditions God, at the last judgment, would choose to save the person who had chosen to follow God during his or her lifetime.

The Pelagian view was declared heretical at the Council of Carthage in AD 418 and at the Council of Ephesus in AD 431. The Pelagian view survived here and there in Italy, Sicily, Africa, and Britain through the fifth century, but was modified into what was later called Semi-Pelagianism, which rejected aspects of Pelagianism and Augustinianism. Semi-Pelagianism was maintained in Africa and Gaul (France) until AD 531 when Boniface II approved the decision of the Synod of Orange (AD 529) to reject the doctrine. Semi-Pelagianism subsequently declined, but "the pivotal issue . . . the priority of the human will over the grace of God in the initial work of salvation—did not die out."[2]

---

[1] Harrison, *Dictionary*, s. v. "Pelagianism."
[2] Elwell, *Dictionary*, s. v. "Semi-Pelagianism."

Semi-Pelagianism opposed the Augustinian doctrines of unconditional election, irresistible grace, and infallible perseverance. It taught that "although grace is essential to salvation, it is added when the first steps are taken by the will of man."[1] The practical effect of Semi-Pelagianism is that a person must first chose God, and then God will respond by giving grace leading to salvation. In other terms, God is not the actor effecting his choices, but the reactor to man's choices. A God who reacts to the choices made by others is a God who is neither omniscient or omnipotent; he is not a sovereign God. The Semi-Pelagian view was also rejected as heretical.

The Semi-Pelagian view underwent further development and became Arminianism, which was a reaction to Augustinian theology as developed by John Calvin.[2] Jacob Arminius (AD 1560–1609) was among the next generation of theologians after John Calvin (AD 1509–1564). He developed doctrines concerning the sovereignty of God in salvation (and related themes) that opposed those same doctrines as explained by Calvin. After the death of Arminius his followers, who became known as Armenians or Remonstrants, developed five articles or statements of doctrine to oppose the tenets of Calvin. Article one speaks to the subject of election, stating that God elects on the basis of foreseen faith or reproves on the basis of foreseen unbelief.

Arminian soteriology has been adopted by many in evangelical Christianity, in greater or lesser degree, regardless of denominational affiliation. John Wesley (1703–1791) in England, and Charles Finney (1792–1875) in America, popularized Arminian soteriology. Today, denominations as diverse as Methodists and Baptists (most of the thirty-one Baptist denominations) embrace some form of Wesleyan-Finney Arminianism.

A Discussion of Arminian Theology

To understand Arminianism, one must understand how Arminianism understands prevenient grace. Prevenient Grace is the biblical teaching that God gives grace to enable the sinner's faith. But differences in how and when that prevenient grace is given defines Calvinistic and Arminian soteriologies. Prevenient grace is

---

[1] Harrison, *Dictionary*, s. v. "Semi-Pelagianism."
[2] Ibid., s. v. "Arminianism."

Election

viewed differently by Arminian and Calvinistic soteriology.

Calvinistic soteriology views prevenient grace as that grace given by God through his gift of grace-faith-salvation (the salvation principle in Ephesians 2:8, saved by grace through faith) that infallibly and irresistible results in the salvation of the sinner receiving God's gift. God' gift of grace-faith-salvation is given only to those whom he, "elected before the foundation of the world."

Arminian soteriology views prevenient grace as God giving every sinner the grace needed to freely decide for him or herself whether or not to believe the gospel and be saved. In the Arminian view, God gives this prevenient grace to all because of Christ's work on the cross, so that all people are capable of hearing and responding gospel as they may choose. Arminian soteriology views the application of prevenient grace in three distinct ways, depending on who in the Arminian camp you are speaking with.

> In the first Arminian view, the sinner is in bondage to sin until he/she hears the gospel, and the hearing of the gospel is itself the application of prevenient grace, by which the sinner is enabled to exercise saving faith, or not, as he/she may choose.
>
> In the second Arminian view, the sinner is in partial bondage to sin, but God is always indiscriminately drawing sinners to Christ, and this act of drawing is the prevenient grace which, as the gospel is heard, makes the sinner capable of hearing and responding gospel as he or she may choose to believe and be saved, or not.
>
> The third, and modern, Arminian view (developed by Charles Wesley) is that because of the first coming and atoning work of Christ, God has dispensed a universal prevenient grace that fully negates the depravity of every person. This prevenient grace places sinners in a neutral spiritual state, so when the gospel is presented they may freely choose to believe unto salvation, or not. Wesleyan prevenient grace is universal in its scope (every human being) and effect (completely freed from the effects of sin).

The Armenian position teaches an election that is conditional, a redemption that is universal, and a grace that is resistible. The Bible presents election as God's choice of particular undeserving persons. Arminian theology says, "I owe my election to my faith," whereas the Bible teaches, "I owe my faith to my election." Arminian theology teaches, "I could not have gained my salvation without Calvary," whereas the Bible teaches, "Christ gained my salvation for me at Calvary." The end result of the evolution of Pelagianism to Arminianism is that many believers reject the doctrine of election, in their practice if not in their creeds or statements of faith.

In Arminian theology God's gift of grace in salvation is defined as "moral suasion," the bare bestowal of an understanding of God's truth. The Bible defines God's gift of grace in salvation as the regenerating work of God in sinners, his almighty power effectually drawing them to Jesus Christ, yet so as they come willingly, being made willing by his grace. Arminian theology says, "I decided for Christ, I made up my mind to be a Christian, whereas the Bible teaches salvation is gained by God's gift of grace-faith-salvation which regenerates the soul and brings the sinners to freely confess his sins and believe on Christ as Savior. The Christian will say, "I did not save myself, God saved me."[1] The biblical way of salvation is that God chose particular sinners to salvation, to be accomplished by the regenerating act of the Holy Spirit, and the sinner's belief of the truth, 2 Thessalonians 2:13. Salvation is of the Lord.

What, then, are the real differences between these two theologies of salvation? Let us note first that the differences are not simply an issue of soteriology (salvation) but a biblical view of God, man, sin, and the Savior. The Arminian theology originates in two philosophical principles. One, divine sovereignty is not compatible with human freedom, nor therefore with human responsibility. Two, ability limits obligation. Therefore, faith cannot originate in God, but is a free and responsible human act exercised independent of God, and since the Bible regards faith as obligatory, then the ability to believe must be universal.[2]

The Arminian view is the foreknowledge view expanded into a consistent but unbiblical theology. For example, article four indirectly addresses the issue of election: "this grace [of God for salvation and good works] may be resisted." However, if, as is the case, God has elected some sinners to salvation, then his perfections and sovereignty must accomplish what his will has foreordained. When God gives the gift of grace-faith-salvation it is always freely received (I will explain why in chapter 8).

One logical result of the Arminian view is that because the individual is the one deciding whether or not to be saved, that

---

[1] Preceding paragraph drawn from Packer, *Quest*, 130–132.
[2] Paragraph drawn from Packer, *Quest*, 127–128.

person can make a decision to become unsaved, either by some sin, or by deciding to reject what he (or she) once believed. Most denominations who follow the Arminian view of salvation believe a person can lose their salvation (by sin or by choice) and regain it by works or by renewed faith. However, the Armenian position is wrong. Hebrews 6:4–6 teaches that if a believer could lose their salvation, that person could not be saved again. Believers cannot lose their salvation. Since salvation is determined by the decree of God, and obtained on the merits of Christ, then God himself stands as surety for the eternal salvation of his elect people.

The biblical view is that salvation is of the Lord, divine sovereignty works with human ability to accomplish God's purpose, man is responsible for his choices, and ability does not limit obligation. As to this last, all human law recognizes the obligation to obey is not dependent on the ability to obey. For example, the driver under the influence of drugs and alcohol may not have the ability to obey traffic laws, but he is obligated to obey, and subject to penalties should he not obey. This is a universally accepted truth resting firmly on biblical truth.

The differences between the Arminian philosophy and biblical truth may be summed in a series of contrasting statements drawn from the Arminian Remonstrants and the response of the Synod of Dort.[1]

> *Arminian:* Man is never so completely corrupted by sin that he cannot savingly believe the gospel when he hears it.
> *Bible:* Sinful man in his natural state lacks all power to believe the gospel, just as he lacks all power to believe the law, despite all external incentives that may be extended to him.
>
> *Arminian:* Man is never so completely controlled by God that he cannot reject the gospel.
> *Bible:* God's election is a free, sovereign, unconditional choice of sinners, as sinners, to be redeemed by Christ, given faith, and brought to glory.
>
> *Arminian:* God's election of those who can be saved is prompted by his foreseeing that they will of their own accord believe.
> *Bible:* The redeeming work of Christ has as its end and goal the salvation of the elect.
>
> *Arminian:* Christ's death did not ensure the salvation of anyone,

---

[1] Ibid., 128.

> for it did not secure the gift of faith to anyone (there is no such gift); what it did was rather to create a possibility of salvation for everyone if they believe.
> *Bible:* The work of the Holy Spirit in bringing a person to faith never fails to achieve its object.
>
> *Arminian:* It rests with believers to keep themselves in a state of grace by keeping up their faith; those who fail here fall away and are lost.
> *Bible:* Believers are kept in faith and grace by the unconquerable power of God till they come to glory.

Arminian theology makes man, not God, the sovereign decider. In the Arminian view man's salvation depends on man himself, because saving faith is man's work, not God's work in man. The Bible teaches salvation is of the Lord from beginning to end. The weakness in the churches today stems from combining these two incompatible views of God's saving work. "A half-truth masquerading as the whole truth becomes a complete untruth. Thus, we appeal to men as if they all had the ability to receive Christ at any time; we speak of his redeeming work as if he had done no more by dying that make it possible for us to save ourselves by believing; we speak of God's love as if it were no more than a general willingness to receive any who will turn and trust; and we depict the Father and the Son, not as sovereignly active in drawing sinners to themselves, but as waiting in quiet impotence 'at the door of our hearts' for us to let them in."[1]

The biblical truth is that God's free election is the ultimate cause of salvation, because of man's inability to believe, and that Christ died to create salvation for those whom God elected to be his people: "here am I and the children whom God has given me," Hebrews 2:13b; "All that the Father gives me will come to me," John 6:37; "No one can come to me unless the Father who sent me draws him," John 6:44. All men are sinners who cannot save themselves. Jesus Christ is the Savior of sinners, even the worst. God acts (through the gift of grace-faith-salvation, Ephesians 2:8–9) to create faith in those whom he has elected. God will save and keep all who come to him through faith in Christ.

I know that many ideas, perhaps ideas new, strange, or foreign to the reader's understanding of the Bible, have been introduced in

---

[1] Ibid., 126–127.

this discussion of Armenian theology. The doctrines—the theology—underlying the biblical view cannot be presented "all at once." I ask for patience and diligence. All will be explained as the reader perseveres through the book all the way to the end.

Return to the Discussion of Foreknowledge.

The foreknowledge view, in any of its various forms, makes man, not God, the sovereign decider. In this view salvation is not an effectual act by God to save, but merely an offer of salvation contingent on man's decision. However, sin is awesomely terrible: it leads sinners to reject God. If salvation were merely an impotent offer contingent for acceptance on man's decision alone, then the decision would always be to reject the offer and continue in sin. The biblical testimony is clear that sinners love the darkness of their sinful lives and do not desire the light of a salvific relationship with God.

A sovereign God must infallibly accomplish his purposes: if he offers salvation, then his purpose in so offering must be to save sinners; therefore he must act to accomplish their salvation. A sovereign God does not offer a potential salvation; he is the active agent of salvation. As to sin, since the fall of Adam sin has been part of human nature. Sin is transgression against God, both his character and his laws. Sin is a crime whose penalty is death and eternal punishment. Sin—as a principle of evil, as the guilt of a crime against God, and as the cause of the penalty of death—is such a powerful force in man's nature that no one can overcome it without sovereign grace from God. The cause of that sovereign grace extended to save the sinner is election, not foreknowledge.

The Biblical View

A perfect God decrees the means (the processes) to accomplish his plans and purpose. The election of a person to salvation is one of the decrees God made before he created. God's choice to see certain sinners as being in Christ was part of the decree to redemption as means are to end. A sinner's choice to act in faith is part of the events, agents, and outcomes foreordained by God, as the sure and certain act of the will in the human nature after receiving God's gift of grace-faith-salvation. Man's will is the expression of his nature. Since sin is an innate part of that nature, man is always inclined to sin and not inclined to God. How then can saving faith be exercised as an act of the will in the human nature? Because men are chosen to salvation. The means to salvation, 2 Thessalonians 2:13, are twofold: the sinner is first set apart to salvation by the Holy Spirit; then the sinner makes a choice to believe in the truth (cf. 1 Peter 1:2, elected; set apart; saved). The order of salvation is God electing, God seeking and drawing the elect sinner through the gospel call to salvation, God regenerating the soul of the sinner who responds to his drawing, and the conversion from sinner to saved through the sinner's conviction of sin, repentance from sin, and faith in Jesus as their Savior. Although the individual processes of regeneration and conversion are virtually simultaneous, regeneration must precede conversion because one must have the spiritual perception to be convicted of sin, salvation, and the Savior before he or she can understand the need for conversion, and then exercise saving faith and be saved.

Colossians 2:13 states the sinner was dead in his trespasses and sins, but God "has made [the sinner] alive together with him," having forgiven all trespasses. Second Thessalonians 2:13 is even clearer as to the order (election, regeneration, conversion): "Because God from the beginning chose you to salvation [election] through sanctification[1] by the Spirit [regeneration] and belief in the truth [conversion through conviction, repentance, and faith]." Ephesians 2:8–9 is equally as clear. One is saved through receiving God's gift of grace-faith-salvation. God's gift is not only grace, not only faith, not only salvation; it is grace-faith-salvation. Grammatically these cannot be separated so that one, but not another, is the gift. The gift of grace-faith-salvation regenerates the soul, giving the sinner perception of spiritual truth, leading to conviction and the freely made choice to exercise saving faith.

By a definite act God extends his gift of grace-faith-salvation to a sinner so that sinner can personally appropriate the truth of his sin and of Christ as Savior to his or her specific spiritual need. Faith in Christ as Savior is the unmerited gift of God, Ephesians 2:8, not a work of man arising out of his unsaved human nature. God's gift of grace infallibly inclines the sinner's will to receive God's gift of faith, so that he might receive God's gift of salvation. God's sovereignty in

---

[1] Sanctification in relation to salvation has two necessary aspects: the Spirit cleanses and separates the person from sin's defilement; the Spirit dedicates the person to God. In illustration, my toothbrush is sanctified: it is separated from all other uses (clean and separated from defilement) and dedicated to one use.

election incorporates the means—the Spirit's work, the sinner's act of faith—which accomplishes the end, salvation. God chooses, draws, and makes the sinner willing. The same decree that elects to salvation requires the sinner to make the choice to receive the faith that accomplishes the decree, i.e., the sinner's free exercise of faith is as much a part of the decree to redeem as is God's electing choice. God commands, "Seek salvation in Christ;" he offers the sinner the map, faith, that will infallibly lead him or her to Christ; he gives the sinner grace that will infallibly bring him to receive the gift of salvation. Such is the doctrine of election: not that we loved God, but that he loved us, chose us in Christ in eternity-past, and therefore we love him because he first loved us.

REACTION TO THE DOCTRINE

The electing choice of God angers sinners, who want to believe they, not God, are the sovereign rulers of their universe. Self-determination is the essential attribute of the sin attribute, so sinners must believe that they and they alone can decide to take or leave God. God, as they believe, must abide by their choices, because their self-determination is the most important doctrine in their universe. Common sense and universal experience deny that belief, but it is the belief of sinners everywhere. What person truly decides his path in life? Every person experiences the capricious circumstances and the actions, willful or accidental, caused by others. Every person affects the choices made by others. But, sin is a deceiver, and every person believes he or she made and owns the ship of their life, and infallibly commands its course to the destination they alone can choose.

The electing choice of God discourages some sinners. Why should I seek after God, if I may not be one of the elect? If I am elect, I shall be saved; if not, I am damned. In answer, first know that God has ordained means as well as ends. He who elected sinners to salvation also decreed the means by which they would be called to saving faith in Christ. The elect are sinners before they are saved, and therefore must come to Christ through the means God has ordained for their salvation. The elect will receive and use these means and be saved. If you want to know if you are among the elect, get up and seek God!

Second, there is one infallible means by which you may know you are among the elect: believe on Jesus Christ as your Savior.

Election

> How do we know that God has elected us before the foundation of the world? By believing in Jesus Christ. I said before that faith proceeds from election and is the fruit of it, which shows that the root is hidden within. Whosoever then believes is thereby assured that God has worked in him, and faith is, as it were, the duplicate copy that God gives us of the original of our adoption.[1]

Do not be discouraged. Call upon Christ: seek Christ, speak to Christ, cry out to Christ. Call upon Christ directly, confess your sin, confess your unbelief, and ask for Christ's forgiveness and mercy. Repent of your sins and ask him to take away your unbelief. Believe on Christ as your Savior by trusting him as best you can, asking him to give you grace to believe and be saved. Seek Christ, pray to Christ, read and hear his word, worship with his people. Continue with these things until you know in yourself that you have believed; that you have been changed from an unrepentant sinner to a believing person with new life through faith in Christ as your Savior.

The doctrine of election angers many believers. Some want to believe they chose God, not that God first chose them, but, 1 John 4:19, "we love him because he first loved us." Some might say that as Creator God owes man salvation for permitting him to fall. Scripture states God is debtor to no man, he owes us nothing (e.g., Job 41:11). A sovereign God decreed to allow man to choose whether he would be a sinner, or not. Man wrongfully used his power of choice to decide to sin, Genesis 2:17; 3:6.

Others want to believe a God of love rejects no man, but must sit and wait for man to accept or reject him. Yet, if man judges whether or not God is acceptable for his allegiance, then who has become sovereign? A God of love, holiness, righteousness, and justice seeks and saves, Luke 19:10; Matthew 18:11.

A God made up of love alone is a one-dimensional God incapable of judging good from evil. Is he not holy? Yes, Leviticus 11:44. Is he not a consuming fire? Yes, Deuteronomy 4:24. Is he not the judge of all the earth? Yes, Genesis 18:25; Psalm 75:5. Is he not sovereign in every decision, in every choice? Yes, Isaiah 45:22; 46:9; Daniel 4:35. He is holy, and righteously discerning, and does judge. He is sovereign, and although none seek after the one true God (Romans 3:10), he himself seeks after men according to his sovereign will (Romans 8:30). Some, with an uninformed

---

[1] Calvin, *Sermons*, 47.

religious conscience, want to believe the only difference God puts between men is whether or not each man is worthy and deserving of heaven. The yardstick these persons use to measure worthiness may be summed under two heads: either a man is religiously worthy, in that he has believed and accomplished all his religion requires of him; or he is morally worthy, in that God must love those who are virtuous. But, what religion or work of man is worthy of eternal life? What can a person do to glorify God, except to work the works of God? The works of God rest in the Savior sent by God, John 6:29. No self-determined religion or virtue is as worthy as Jesus dying on the cross for sin. The death of Jesus was foreordained, Acts 2:23, for the salvation of a chosen people, Hebrews 2:12, 13. Neither works nor religion will make a person worthy of salvation, Acts 4:12.

THE NECESSITY OF ELECTION

The necessity of election is seen two things. In relation to God's choices, we have seen salvation is initiated by God seeking the sinner. In relation to man's choices sin creates the inability to seek God. For example, Adam and Eve turned away from God, but God sought them. Their reluctance to confess their sin shows the same thought pattern. If God had not sought them, drawn out their confession, and forgiven their sin, they would have continued to hide from God. The inability caused by sin is the reason Jesus said, "No one can come to me except the Father who sent me draws him," John 6:44. The subjects of sin, culpability, and inability are discussed in chapters 6, 7. Anticipating the result of those discussions, election is necessary to overcome sin and save the sinner's soul.

THE PURPOSE OF ELECTION

A foundational issue regarding election and salvation is this: what is the purpose of God in the world? If God's purpose is man's salvation, then election is contrary to that purpose, for the election of some, but not all, would contradict the purpose to save all. If God's purpose is man's salvation, then the rejection of salvation by some would frustrate God's sovereignty. If God's purpose can be denied by man, then God is not sovereign, for a sovereign God is a God whose omnipotence, omniscience, omnipresence, holiness, and love work together to infallibly accomplish his purpose, plans, and processes.

The purpose of God in the world is his glory, e.g., Isaiah 6:3; 43:7; Luke 2:14; Ephesians 1:6, 12, 14. The larger purpose of God in creating the heavens and the earth with all its things and creatures was the manifestation of his own glory, Psalm 19:1–4. God did not initiate life in some simple organism and then step back to see what random chance and limitless time (evolution) would create. God created on purpose, with a purpose, and therefore everything in his creation was made for a purpose. A purpose requires plans to bring it to fulfillment, and processes that accomplish the plans. God created a being in his own image to display more clearly who he was as a person; a being who was to be a part of the processes that furthered God's plans to fulfill his purpose.

The election of the saved displays God's glory. Their selection reveals God's sovereignty: a decision of his will uninfluenced by external forces, designed to accomplish his plan to redeem a people for his glory throughout eternity-future. Their election reveals a God who is no respecter of persons but is sovereign and just, wise and holy. The certainty of their salvation reveals God's omnipotence and integrity: his purposes will come to pass and none can prevent him. A righteous and holy God is glorified when he saves sinners, for God is the One who draws and inclines men to salvation, therefore all the glory belongs to him. The eternal felicity of the saved glorifies God, for he keeps his promises.

The punishment of those who reject salvation also fulfills the purpose to display his glory, Proverbs 16:4, "The LORD has made all for Himself, yes, even the wicked for the day of doom." A righteous and holy God is glorified when he executes justice on those who reject him and his Christ. Election does not hinder a person's choices, and therefore God righteously holds a person accountable for the choices he or she makes.

Election to salvation is a decree of God that is consistent with God's nature, plans, purposes, and sovereignty. The electing act of God involves the outworking of God's sovereignty with man's responsibility to exercise saving faith. This is the interaction between God and man by which men choose and God infallibly fulfills his purpose.

THINGS TO KEEP IN MIND ABOUT ELECTION

Election

There are seven important things to remember.

> God never tells us the basis on which one was elected and another was not, other than God acts according to his sovereign will. A person's choices are not the reason for election. If a person's choices were the reason, then man, not God, would be sovereign, God would be reacting to man, and thus God would be arranging his plan of redemption to suit man's response.

> God's foreknowledge of faith cannot be the ground of election because faith is the very blessing to which sinners are elected. God's pre-knowing a believer as saved is not based on what they will do or believe, but is based on his decree concerning their redemption.

> The number of the elect is not revealed, although personally I believe a great number of redeemed gives God a great measure of glory.

> Election is not fate; the decree of election requires the exercise of individual faith, without which none can be saved. The decree does not substitute divine fiat for the means necessary to bring sinners to salvation: evangelism, personal testimony, a godly witness in the believer's manner of living, the promulgation of God's word in written and oral form; these are all decreed as the means whereby sinners are brought to salvation. The evangelizing work of the saved is decreed as a necessary means to bring the elect to salvation.

> Election does not substitute for grace: unmerited blessing is required as one of the means God uses to effect salvation.

> Election is not predestination. As will be discussed in chapter 5, the predestination Paul speaks of (Romans; Ephesians) is a decree affecting believers, not sinners. Predestination is a decree to adopt the believer as a son of God and conform believers to be like Christ.

> The election of some to salvation does not mean a corresponding election of others to reprobation; election speaks only of those chosen and says nothing of those not chosen. Every person is a sinner on his or her way to an eternal destiny in the lake of fire, and can be saved from it only by that faith in Jesus which results in personal salvation.

A SOVEREIGN CHOICE

The perfect decrees of a sovereign perfect God must include all the means to infallibly accomplish the ends established by his perfect purpose. Paul, Ephesians 1:4, is quite specific: God chose Paul and the Ephesian Christians in Christ before he created the universe. Paul uses the singular "us," to include himself with the Ephesian church, not the plural "you" which would mean the Ephesian church only. The singular "us" indicates chosen individuals making up a body of believers. The Scriptures were not intended for one body of believers only, but for all believers in the body of Christ; therefore Paul and the Spirit are saying that God chose each individual believer in Christ. Before he created anything God decreed to permit the fall, and he decreed to save some sinners out of sin. All human beings (Jesus excepted) are guilty of sin, and therefore all human beings justly deserve an eternity separated from God. God was not under obligation to save any. The marvelous wonder of election is that God chose any, because all human beings are sinners and deserve eternal punishment for their sin.

God "chose us in him," Ephesians 1:4, meaning God chose some sinners to be "in Christ." Several thoughts follow from this phrase. First, there was nothing in any sinner that caused God's choice to save. In sinners God saw sin and corruption and defilement. Second, God looked on Christ before he "chose us." Sinners are made acceptable to God because God has made them acceptable in Christ, Ephesians 1:6. Because God loves Christ, John 17:24, he loves all those in Christ, John 14:21; Romans 8:39. Therefore the election was made in Christ. This does not mean Christ is the elect one and all those in Christ are corporately elect with him. That view sidesteps the question as to how any person can come to be in Christ. One commentator has written, "Individuals are not elected and then put in Christ. They are in Christ and therefore elect."[1] Election does mean being in Christ, but this view confuses the natural force and order of God's decrees, by making the believer's faith the efficient cause of his being in Christ. Sinners do not become elect because they are in Christ; sinners are in Christ because God elected them to salvation. The sinner's faith is the instrumental cause of salvation, but God's election is the efficient cause. Election is the eternal act of God that establishes the sinner as saved in Christ; grace is the historical act of God that

---

[1] Snodgrass, *Ephesians*, 49.

inclines the sinner to receive faith in Christ; faith is the historical act of the sinner choosing salvation in Christ. All three—election, grace, faith—are required to place the believer in Christ in the fullness of time.

God elected individuals. The word "us" in Ephesians 1:4 ("he chose us") is a singular verb in the Greek text. The electing choice was a series of individual choices: he chose you; he chose me; he chose others. Every choice was a particular and purposeful choice: each choice was purposefully designed to be part of the processes to accomplish the plans to fulfill the purpose.

God chose us "in Christ." The merit of Christ is the sole ground for salvation. Election is God seeing the sinner in Christ, an act that occurred in eternity-past. In the timelessness of God's existence before he created, he elected those whom he would later in time create. God decreed to create man in holiness and blessedness; he decreed to permit man to fall by the self-determination of his own will; he decreed to elect a definite number of sinners to redemption in the Redeemer. God's act of election was the decision to see a sinner in Christ the Redeemer. Jesus is, as it were, the book of life, in whom the believer is written down and acknowledged by God as his child. Paul is much more explicit in Romans 9:10–13 about the act of election. God chose Jacob and not Esau before either man had been born, and therefore no act by them was the cause of Jacob's election, that it might be seen that election is according to God's will alone. God—not the sinner, not the believer—God only is the One who causes an individual to be in the number of his elect.

A final thought concerning the phrase "in Christ." In us there is no good thing, but "in Christ" is the cause of every good thing. Whatever praise, glory, holiness, righteousness, and future there is for a saved sinner, it all comes from Christ. The believer receives these things as spiritual blessings, in the heavenlies, in Christ, Ephesians 1:3.

INCENTIVE TO EVANGELISM

The doctrine of election is the greatest incentive to evangelism. The evangelist goes forth in the certain knowledge that the gospel is being used to accomplish God's decreed purpose, and that he is a servant fulfilling God's plan. An evangelistic witness of salvation is a decreed means in the decreed processes leading to the salvation of those sinners whom God has chosen to salvation. I can say this no plainer than to say that those who are elected to be saved must and will be saved through the means to their salvation that God has decreed. Therefore, the believer has a God-given responsibility to "preach the Word," and to "go . . . and make disciples." When he obeys, then he will see others saved.

What, then, is the gospel message that honors God, depends on God's truth, and calls sinners to believe and be saved? A biblical gospel has four components.[1]

> That all men are sinners, and cannot do anything to save themselves.

> That Jesus Christ, God's son, is a perfect Savior for sinners, even the worst.

> That the Father and the Son have promised that all who know themselves to be sinners and put faith in Christ as Saviour shall be received into favor [saved], and none cast out—which promise is a "certain infallible truth, grounded upon the superabundant sufficiency of the oblation [propitiation] of Christ in itself, for whomsoever (fewer or more) it be intended."[2]

> That God has made repentance and faith a duty, requiring of every person who hears the gospel "a serious full recumbency [rest] and rolling of the soul [dependence] upon Christ in the promise of the gospel, as an all-sufficient Savior, able to deliver and save to the utmost them that come to God by him; ready, able and willing, through the preciousness of his blood and sufficiency of his ransom, to save every soul that shall freely give up themselves unto him for that end."[3]

"The preacher's task, in other words, is to *display Christ*, to explain man's need of him, his sufficiency to save, and his offer of himself in the promises as Saviour to all who truly turn to him; and to show as fully and plainly as he can how these truths apply to the congregation before him."[4] Who has been elected and why they were elected is not the issue; the gospel never once calls upon us to ask the who or why of God's purpose in election. The gospel calls the sinner to simply exercise faith, which he is both authorized and required to do by God's command and promise.

---

[1] Packer, *Quest*, 139.
[2] Owen, *Works*, 10:315.
[3] Ibid., 10:407.
[4] Packer, *Quest*, 139 (emphasis original).

ASSURANCE OF SALVATION

The doctrine of election is also the greatest assurance of salvation, and the greatest incentive to perseverance. God has chosen; because he has chosen he draws, he saves, and he keeps by faith those to whom he has given faith, John 10:28–29. "No one seeks God and yet in his sovereign grace he chooses some for everlasting life in his presence. His selection was made with full knowledge of all the options and with intense personal interest, not in a random impersonal manner. Believers may take comfort in the fact that what God has begun in eternity-past will be completed in eternity-future."[1]

In the Armenian view of salvation (versus the biblical view), the sinner chooses to be saved; therefore he can chose to be unsaved. The Armenian view understands foreseen faith (the foreknowledge view) as the basis for election. Election, therefore, is not God's choice but contingent on the sinner's choice. Arminianism teaches that a person cannot be saved by God unless it is that person's will to be saved; therefore, a person cannot continue in salvation unless he (or she) continues to will to be saved. "As long as a man lives he may fall away from grace and lose his salvation."[2] A few examples from selected church doctrinal statements demonstrate the Armenian doctrine.

> [The] future obedience and final salvation [of the truly regenerate] are neither determined nor certain.[3]

> It is possible for a man to sin and lose his status with God in any phase of his experience.[4]

> It is possible for [those who have been saved] to fall from their steadfastness in Christ . . . therefore, the believer is secure from the judgments of God only as he maintains his fellowship with Christ.[5]

> The eternal security of the believer depends on his obedience to God's word . . . when a Christian sins or fails God . . . if he fails to repent and persists in willful disobedience, the ultimate result will

---

[1] Hoehner, *Ephesians*, 192.
[2] Harrison, *Dictionary*, s. v. "Arminianism."
[3] Melton, *Creeds*, 2:17 (Freewill Baptist Church of the Pentecostal Faith).
[4] Ibid., 2:47 (Pentecostal Church of Zion).
[5] Ibid., 2:58 (Associated Brotherhood of Christians).

Election

be spiritual death and eventually the lake of fire.[1]

The view that understands an unconditional election as the cause of salvation comprehends the believer's eternal security in that salvation. If, as is the case, Ephesians 1:4, election is God seeing the sinner "in Christ," then it is the infinite merit of Christ that secures the believer's faith and salvation. "Christ died to save a certain company of helpless sinners upon whom God had set his free saving love. Christ's death ensured the calling and keeping—the present and final salvation—of all whose sins he bore."[2]

Since the cause of salvation is the electing decree of God, then it is reasonable the cause of perseverance in that salvation is the work of God. And so say the scriptures.

> Philippians 1:6, He who has begun a good work in you will complete it until the day of Jesus Christ;
>
> John 6:39–40, This is the will of the Father who sent Me, that of all He has given Me I should lose nothing, but should raise it up at the last day. And this is the will of Him who sent Me, that everyone who sees the Son and believes in Him may have everlasting life; and I will raise him up at the last day."
>
> John 10:27–28, My sheep hear My voice, and I know them, and they follow Me. And I give them eternal life, and they shall never perish; neither shall anyone snatch them out of My hand.
>
> Jude 24–25, Now to Him who is able to keep you from stumbling, And to present you faultless before the presence of His glory with exceeding joy, to God our Savior, who alone is wise, be glory and majesty, dominion and power, both now and forever. Amen.

Assurance of salvation is also found in the decree of predestination. Each believer is predestined to be adopted as a son of God, to be conformed to be like Christ, to be God's heritage in the world, and to receive an inheritance, "incorruptible and undefiled and that does not fade away, reserved in heaven for you, who are kept by the power of God through faith for salvation," (1 Peter 1:4, 5). I will speak of these things in a later chapter, but here let us take note that the gifts and calling of God are irrevocable. Those whom God has called, he has predestined; therefore their salvation is assured by both election and

---

[1] Ibid., 2:59 (Bethel Ministerial Association).
[2] Packer, *Quest*, 138.

predestination.

This is not to say the believer need not persevere in the faith; he (or she) does need to persevere. But, there is always a God-ward side to faith as well as a man-ward side. God gives grace for the believer to persevere, Philippians 1:6, and the believer uses the grace God gives in order to persevere, Hebrews 10:35. I will discuss these things in a later chapter. Here it is sufficient to note the decrees of election and predestination secure the believing sinner's salvation for eternity.

THE OUTCOME OF ELECTION

In Ephesians 1:4 Paul states the result of God's choosing: that we should be holy and without blame before him; in a word, "sanctification." The sinner's sanctification is the immediate object of God's election in grace. How are these things to be accomplished?

Let us first define sanctification. The word translated "sanctification" is a form of the word meaning "holy." Sanctification means to be set apart from sin and dedicated to God. There are three aspects of sanctification. The first is positional sanctification. God declares the believer to be holy and righteous in Christ. This is one's "standing" before God: the state of the soul wherein the believer stands before God the Judge and is seen as guiltless and forgiven because God views the believer as in Christ. Since the righteousness of Christ has been imputed to the believer (e.g., Romans 4:11; 2 Corinthians 5:21), he or she is set apart from sin and dedicated to God. The positional aspect of sanctification accounts for the Scripture's declarations that the believer is holy and righteous apart from works.

The second aspect is experiential sanctification. This is one's state in the world, i.e., how a person habitually acts in the world. The believer has had holiness added to his human nature to oppose sin, and therefore is able to overcome temptation. Sin never stops tempting, and a believer may succumb to temptation and commit an occasional act of sin, but sin is not habitual in the believer. In the process of practicing the values of the Christian life, and through the guidance and power given by the Holy Spirit, the believer becomes more like Christ as his or her Christian life plays out over years and decades, so that his or her state of experiential sanctification looks more and more like their positional sanctification. The experiential aspect of sanctification accounts for the Scripture's exhortations to work hard to live a righteous and godly life.

The third aspect is eternal sanctification (sometimes called final sanctification). This is the believer's state and standing following physical death. The act of physical death removes the sin attribute from body and soul. Sanctification is complete, standing and state are the same, the believer is eternally sanctified. The eternal aspect of sanctification accounts for the Scripture's declarations of a transformed and redeemed body and soul in the resurrection and into eternity.

In Ephesians 1:4, one must decide if Paul means positional or experiential sanctification, when he says that the end of election is "that we should be holy and without blame before him." This is not a trivial question. One commentator (Lehman Strauss) states, "Chose us for what? Not to everlasting life, but that we should be spotless for himself! The election in the divine Mind was that all those in Christ should be 'holy ones,' free from every defilement of sin."[1] This is simply a clever way of saying that the decision to be saved resides in man alone, and then once he is saved he finds that God has chosen to make him holy. To Strauss, then, election is to sanctification, not salvation. A review of Strauss's statement in context reveals he is speaking of experiential sanctification. He knows that believers are not always holy in the ways they live out their mortal life. Therefore, in order to maintain his view of election, yet not accuse God of failure, he must displace the fulfillment of God's election to holiness to the time when Christ returns. Until that time, believers are to try and be perfect, even though no person can reach that goal in this life. In this view, the purpose of election is to enable the Christian to try and live a holy life.

Is sanctification (whether positional or experiential) or salvation the goal of election? Scripture teaches that sanctification is the result of salvation: the believer's soul spiritually stands before God as "holy and without blame" as a result of salvation, 1 Corinthians 1:2; 6:11; Jude 1. God's decree is election to salvation, and sanctification is one of the spiritual blessings God has given to the saved person. The subject of Ephesians 1:3–14 is stated in 1:3, the spiritual blessings with which God has blessed the believer in Christ.

---

[1] Strauss, *Ephesians*, 119.

Those blessings flow from election, 1:4. The first blessing Paul mentions is sanctification. Therefore, sanctification is a result of election.

The Writer of Hebrews, after stating the propitiation made by Christ takes away sins forever, 10:11, 12, plainly states the result: Christ has "perfected forever those who are sanctified" (HCSB). Those who are saved are positionally sanctified as a result of their salvation. The Writer follows those statements with the Old Testament witness of sins forgiven in the covenant made by Christ, vv. 15–18, and then the exhortation to live a holy life: experiential sanctification.

Paul, writing to the carnal church of the Corinthians, stated the believer is in this mortal life holy before God, "for the temple of God is holy, which temple you are" (1 Corinthians 3:17). Paul as plainly stated he had betrothed these believers to Christ with the intent of presenting him or her as a chaste virgin to Christ, 2 Corinthians 11:2. The betrothal in biblical times was as binding as the actual marriage, but there was no consummation until marriage: in spiritual terms marriage represents eternal sanctification, the betrothal experiential sanctification. Thus, in two letters to these saved people, Paul states they were holy—positional sanctification, and his intent was to guide them into a holy life— experiential sanctification, so he might present them as a chaste virgin to Christ—eternal sanctification.

In Colossians 1:21–22 Paul said Christ reconciled the believer to God through his crucifixion—in other words, salvation and positional sanctification—in order "to present you holy, and blameless, and above reproach in his [God's] sight," which is eternal sanctification. The present state of the believer in the world is found in the exhortation, v. 23, to live a life of experiential sanctification: "to continue in the faith, grounded and steadfast . . . not moved away from the hope." More to the point, in Colossians 3:12, Paul describes the believer as "the elect of God, holy and beloved," which is his or her present standing before God, and then describes, vv. 12–17, how the believer should live his or her life in the world, because of that present, positional standing of holiness.

Whether one views the believer's positional, experiential, or eternal sanctification before God, the work of sanctification is intrinsic to and inseparable from the act of God saving the sinning soul. God elects to salvation with the result the sinner is saved and sanctified: made holy and without blame before God. Speaking more precisely, to be without blame is justification and to be holy is sanctification. Justification is deliverance from the judicial guilt of and just penalty due the crime of sin. Sanctification makes the believer holy, which is to be eternally set apart from the defilement of sin and dedicated to God in fellowship and service. Both are the result of salvation, which is the result of election. Therefore, in viewing the purpose of election as to make the believer "holy and without blame," Paul is viewing the end result of the decree of election to redemption as incorporating the means, which is salvation.

The subject of Ephesians 1:3–14, is the spiritual blessing the believer has because he is in Christ in the heavenlies, a position indicating the spiritual standing of the believer's soul as redeemed and sanctified, therefore without blame. The purpose of election in bringing the believer into a standing of "holy and without blame before God" was accomplished at the moment of saving faith. It is not a matter of one's actions, nor a matter reserved for the future. The spiritual standing of the believer before God is always "in Christ" because chosen in Christ. Paul is speaking of real and present spiritual blessings the believer has in his incorporated relationship with Christ in the heavenlies. Is the believer presently before God "without blame" in Christ? Yes, as Paul said in Romans 8:1, "there is therefore now no condemnation to those who are in Christ Jesus."[1] Therefore, Paul teaches that the immediate purpose of election is salvation from sin, with the result the believer receives blessings from God, the first of which is sanctification. Christ fully propitiated God for the crime of sin. His payment for that crime is applied to those who believe on him as the One who made the full payment for their sin. The full payment made for the believer's sins means the believer stands before God without guilt, and therefore he stands before God blameless. The state of salvation means a believer is set apart from sin and dedicated unto God, therefore he stands holy in Christ before God. Christ's righteousness is imputed to the believer and he (or she) is declared without blame for the crime of sin: justification. The justified believer is declared holy: positional sanctification. The believer's human nature is regenerated

---

[1] The second part of Romans 8:1 is not a condition of having "no condemnation" but is the result of it, as v. 2ff indicates.

to spiritual life and the life-principle of holiness is added to it: experiential sanctification. In every way the believer presently stands before God in Christ holy and without blame. There is a future time when the believer will physically, as he now does spiritually, stand before God holy and without blame; then the "yet-future" state of the believer will equal his "now" standing—experiential and positional sanctification will become the same, resulting in eternal sanctification. The end result of election is sanctification, which is accomplished through salvation. One's election, therefore, is to salvation.

ELECTED IN LOVE

There are three major views as to how *en agápē*, "in love," in Ephesians 1:4 connects to the other words in the sentence. (Translations break up the sentence, but in the Greek text Ephesians 1:3–14 is one sentence.)

In the first view, "in love" is grammatically connected to "he chose." This view represents the interest God took in choosing, which was his love for the one's chosen. Hoehner gives three reasons why he believes this grammatical view is wrong. (Hoehner does not mean that God's love in election is a wrong view, but that the view which grammatically connects the words "in love" to the words "he chose" is wrong.[1]) First, the words "in love" are grammatically very far away from "he chose," being separated by twelve words. Although sentence construction in Greek is not as dependent on word order as it is English, the separation of the modifier (love) from the verb (chose) is a reasonable objection to the view connecting these words. Second, the act of election is itself an evidence of God's love, so no additional words are needed to express his love in election. Third, the predominant use of *agape* in Ephesians is to express the believer's love.

As to the first objection, I do not disagree with Hoehner that "love" is too far from "chose" to be grammatically connected. However, there are other points of view to be considered. To place the modifier at a far distance from the verb would be unusual, but not impossible. In looking at the order of the words, one sees that, in accordance with Greek sentence construction, the more important information is at the front. Believers were chosen in

---

[1] Hoehner, *Ephesians*, 182.

Christ, before the act of creation, with the intent they would be made fit for God's presence, and therefore chosen because of God's love. I am not saying connecting "in love" to "he chose" was Paul's grammatical intent, but simply that the distance of "in love" from "he chose" does not rule out the interpretation.

The second objection was that God's love needs no additional phrase to express the concept of his love in election. In answer to this objection, Deuteronomy 7:6–8 does connect God's election with his love:

> Deuteronomy 7:6–8, the Lord your God has chosen you [Israel] to be a people for Himself, a special treasure above all the peoples on the face of the earth. The Lord did not set His love on you nor choose you because you were more in number than any other people, for you were the least of all peoples; but because the Lord loves you, and because He would keep the oath which He swore to your fathers.

One should remember that God's love is not based in sentiment but in the choice of his will. God self-determined to act toward Israel in a manner other than how he would act toward other peoples. That manner involved a covenant with them. His love was his decision to establish that special relationship with that particular people. Sentiment was not excluded, but the choice of Israel over others was not an emotionally-based decision. Moses and the Spirit, however, thought it agreeable to the meaning of the text to add words concerning God's love as part of God's choice. God had determined to seek the best and highest spiritual good for Israel (love) by bringing them into a covenant relationship with himself, that they might be saved from sin and enjoy his presence as their God and his people. The phrase "because the Lord loves you," expresses the interest God had in making his choice. So too might Paul have thought it appropriate to indicate the same in Ephesians: "He chose us . . . in love."

Hoehner's third objection was the predominant use of *agape* in Ephesians to express the believer's love. There are fifteen[1] uses of *agape* in Ephesians, although the specific form used in 1:4 is found only ten times.[2] However, one does not decide a grammatical connection by averaging out how a word is generally used, but by

---

[1] 1:4, 15; 2:4; 3:17, 19; 4:2, 15, 16; 5:1, 2, 25, 28, 33; 6:26, 24.
[2] 1:4, 15; 2:4; 3:17, 19; 4:15, 16; 5:2; 6:23.

considering the individual context of each use, especially where the connection or use is uncertain. To argue that "in love" cannot be speaking of God's love in 1:4 because it is predominantly used of the believer's love in other parts of Ephesians is to assume, not prove, the point in contention. There are several verses where *agape* distinctly refers to God's love, and others where God's love is in view as the ground of the believer's love. We see, then, that these objections do not necessarily prevent a grammatical connection between the phrases "in love" and "he chose."

However, Hoehner is correct. The distance between "he chose" and "in love" is great enough that it is unlikely this proposed grammatical connection was intended. Eadie agrees, "The construction is highly improbable . . . would be so awkward . . . the entire verse intervenes between a reference to the act of election and the motive which is supposed to prompt to it."[1]

The second view is that "in love" connects with v. 5, "predestined." The proponents of this view do not connect "in love" with "holy and without blame" (still less with "he chose") because the words "before him" intervene. As noted above, the word order argument is not persuasive by itself, because in Greek grammar order is found in word endings not word order. In English it makes a great deal of difference whether the "cat ate the rat," or the "rat ate the cat." In English, the meaning is to be found in the order in which the words occur in the sentence. In other languages, the meaning is found according to the grammatical endings attached to the root word. A very clear example is in Ephesians 5:33. The word order in the Greek text is, "However also you everyone each his own wife so let love as himself," but the meaning, based on the grammatical word endings, is "However, also you—everyone—let each so love his own wife as himself." Therefore, the separation between "in love" and "holy and without blame" in 1:4 does not necessarily connect "in love" with "predestined." That there could be a connection is possible, in that it would be appropriate God's love is the reason for the believer's predestination. However, the addition of "in love" to predestination would, in this instance, be unnecessary, as vv. 5b–6 clearly state the reasons for the believer's predestination.

There is no need to separate love from election, sanctification,

---

[1] Eadie, *Ephesians*, 28–29.

or predestination. Every act of God is conditioned by his holiness and his love working together in perfect harmony. These cannot be separated, whether one considers election of sinners to salvation, sanctification as a result of salvation, or the predestinating of believers to be like Christ. Love and holiness together must be present, active, and working at all times in perfect harmony to accomplish God's purposes. However, to answer this view, Ephesians 2:4 indicates God's love was the impelling reason for election, and the nature of predestination (explained in chapter 5 of this book) indicates it follows election and salvation. The view that connects "in love" with "predestined" is not the best view.

The third view connects "in love" to the preceding "holy and without blame." This is the view taken by most present day commentators. The major reason is that the descriptions of God's actions always precede the qualifying phrases (all verses Ephesians 1):

> v. 3, he blessed us . . . with every spiritual blessing
>
> v. 4, he chose us . . . in Christ before the foundation of the world
>
> v. 5, he predestined us . . . to adoption
>
> v. 7, he redeemed us . . . through his blood according to his grace
>
> v. 8, he made abound to us . . . all wisdom and grace
>
> v. 9, he made known to us the mystery . . . according to his good pleasure
>
> v. 11, predestined . . . according to his will

Based upon this analysis, "in love" does not connect with either "he chose" or "predestined." Therefore, in this view, it must connect with "holy and without blame." This view states God elected sinners to salvation for the purpose of making them holy and without blame before him in love. Most who take this view understand it to indicate the moral actions of the believer as a result of election; more simply, the believer's present day-to-day state of experiential sanctification. Representatives of this view believe:

> Election is intended to achieve a life before God which is holy and blameless and lived in love.[1]

---

[1] O'Brien, *Ephesians*, 101.

> A person is to manifest love with holiness as a result of being elected.[1]
>
> God's choice of a people in Christ has a goal—that they should exhibit a particular quality of life, described here in terms of holiness and love.[2]
>
> Holiness before God is that of a pure conscience . . . the perfection of the believer consists in love . . . [as] an evidence of the fear of God and of obedience to the whole law.[3]

However, the subject of Ephesians 1:3–14 is, "blessed with every spiritual blessing in the heavenly places in Christ," v. 3, and as I proved before the sanctification in view is positional, not experiential. I do not deny that a life of holiness effected by love is required of the believer, for one's experiential state must always strive to serve one's positional standing before God. Paul's subject, however, is not practical Christian living, but the spiritual benefits of salvation as decreed by God. The epistle divides at chapter four between doctrine and practice. Chapters 1–3 concern doctrine. Chapters 4–6 concern putting doctrine into practice. Simply from a literary standpoint 1:4 cannot be about how one lives a holy life, but why one can live a holy life. One can live a holy life because of the spiritual benefits, 1:3, attained through election, 1:4. One's experiential sanctification (moral living) is the result of that positional sanctification (holy and without blame) which is a result of salvation. The believer is standing before God as the object of his love in the condition of being holy and without blame, because elected to be saved and through salvation made holy and without blame.

The "in love" in Ephesians 1:4 is God's love for man *not* man's love for God as expressed in holy living. The spiritual blessing of being holy and without blame in love originated with God in Christ, and therefore it is God's superlative blessing that is in view, not the believer's effort in day-to-day living. Paul's intent was to show that God's purpose in election was to bring a sinner into a relationship with himself; the words "in love" are the indicators of that relationship (just as at Deuteronomy 7:6–8). Election was God's decision to redeem sinners through a covenant between himself and

---

[1] Hoehner, *Ephesians*, 184.
[2] Lincoln, *Ephesians*, 24.
[3] Calvin, *Ephesians*, 200.

Election

the Son; that is love. Part of the terms and conditions of that covenant was to bring sinners immediately into a positional standing of holy and without blame before God; that is love. Their positional sanctification would inform and aid their experiential sanctification, with the end result being eternal sanctification. The phrase "in love" indicates the salvific relationship and positional sanctification resulting from the electing choice.

In other words, God's love is his bringing sinners into a relationship with himself by saving them and making them holy and without blame. The relationship was initiated by God's electing choice and effected in the believer's historical-present by salvation. God's electing decree brought salvation, which caused sanctification, creating a positional and eternal standing before God as holy and without blame. This standing is present in the here-and-now, and includes future eternal sanctification at death (or rapture), which removes the sin attribute, and results in the completed act of God's sovereign electing grace: to physically stand in his presence, in heaven, holy and blameless, having been brought into his presence and into that state of holiness by his love. God elects, calls, and inclines the sinner's heart to receive faith; God redeems, regenerates (which includes sanctification), preserves, and presents the saved sinner faultless before himself as a child of his love, through his sovereign electing grace and gift of saving faith.

Because of this relationship (in love), which has resulted in their standing (holy and without blame), God's grace produces holiness in believers and love toward one another in this present world. God intends a believer's moral actions (their experiential state in the world) to manifest love with holiness. Love without holiness is life without a standard of right and wrong; holiness without love is life without compassion, mercy, and kindness. Thus, in application, holiness effected with love is an outward evidence of election. Anyone who claims to be saved, but lives in sin and without love for the brethren, is not saved.

Thus, election is the efficient cause of salvation and sanctification. The believer's faith is the instrumental cause, and will be discussed in chapter 8.

OBJECTIONS TO THE DOCTRINE

Some objections to the doctrine of election were discussed in the sections concerning the foreknowledge view. There are other objections of a different order.

Election is said to be unjust. Since God is just, then he does not elect individuals, says this objection, because the condemnation of one guilty of sin, but not another just as guilty, would be unjust. The claim election is unjust misunderstands the doctrine of grace. Grace is God's favor and blessing given to those who are undeserving—positively undeserving, if we may use that terminology. Grace is unmerited favor: we cannot lay a claim upon God for grace. However, "grace is something more than 'unmerited favor.' To feed a tramp who calls on me is 'unmerited favor,' but it is scarcely *grace*. But suppose that after *robbing* me I should feed this starving tramp—that would be 'grace.' Grace, then, is favor shown where there is positive de-merit in the one receiving it."[1]

"All are under sin," says Paul, Romans 3:9, 23, drawing his doctrine from the Old Testament descriptions of man the sinner. It would be just for God to leave every person in their sins to suffer for eternity in the lake of fire. But grace is the sovereign exercise of God's blessings; he bestows his grace upon whom he will. Election is not a matter of justice, for all deserve eternal punishment. God draws some out of a deserved punishment as an eternal testimony to his grace, love, and mercy. God justly leaves others to the punishment of their sin, as a testimony to his holiness and justice. To deny God the right to exercise his grace as he sees fit is to deny God his sovereignty. It is to subject the Creator to the judgment of his creature.

Paul anticipated the "unjust" argument. At Romans 9:11 Paul says God chose Jacob, not Esau, before the children were born, "that the purpose of God according to election might stand." "Is there unrighteousness with God" in making such a choice? "Certainly Not!" says Paul. He presents two arguments to prove his case. One, God is sovereign. He has mercy and compassion on who he will. Second, the creature has no right to blame his Creator, for the sovereign God has the authority to choose one but not another. Both Esau and Jacob were sinners. Both were justly subject to God's wrath. God chose to justly leave one in his sin and in sovereign mercy extend grace to the other.

Moreover, Paul anticipated the foreknowledge view of election when he said that God chose Jacob (and not Esau) "not of works

---

[1] Pink, *Sovereignty*, 31, unnumbered note (emphasis original).

but of him [God] who calls." Since neither had performed any works, being in the womb, then the works Paul refers to—in saying that God's choice was apart from their works—must have been foreseen works. In other words, God's choice was "not of foreseen works, but of God who calls." Election is sovereign in its choices, made apart from any foreseen works or faith. All human beings are sinners justly deserving eternal punishment, so it is grace alone that separates the redeemed from the lost.

Scripture presents an argument for what might be called "common grace," as opposed to the special or electing grace that infallibly leads to salvation. In the view of some, common grace is defined as grace given to all to overcome the sin attribute and seek God, if they so choose.

That view is not the biblical view of common grace. Common grace regulates the working of the sin attribute so that there is a measure of justice, mercy, kindness and compassion in the world. Few persons are as bad as they might be, because sin is restrained by common grace.

Some identify the soul's built-in witness of God's existence as common grace,[1] but that is not common grace. The witness in the soul of the existence of God was designed by God into human nature in the first man, and propagated by him to all human beings. Every person knows God exists and that he (or she) must discover a relationship with God. The truth of that assertion is seen in its opposite: persons rejecting the one true God devise false gods to worship. They reject a relationship with the one true God and devise a substitute suitable to their sins. Even the atheist knows God exists, for his declaration, "There is no God," is in reality a cry of "No God for me!"[2]

Sinners can resist common grace, and Scripture is replete with examples. But God is just, and no respecter of persons, because he extends common grace to all. However, special grace, which is the grace of God that is the result of the decree of election, must be extended to a sinner if he is to receive and act upon God's gift of

---

[1] Elwell, *Dictionary*, s. v. "Grace."
[2] The correct translation of Psalm 14:1; 53:1, is "No God for me." See Perowne, *Psalms*, 1:183–84, "a practical rather than a theoretical atheism; not so much a denial of the *being* of a God as a denial of his *moral government* of the world." Also see Craigie, *Psalms*, 147, "The fool is one whose life is lived without the direction or acknowledgment of God."

grace-faith-salvation, and develop a relationship with him through faith in Christ.

A second objection is similar to the "election is unjust" view: that election makes God a respecter of persons. Not in the least. Let us think biblically: the Bible defines "a respecter of persons" as one who acts favorably toward another because of that person's power, position, privilege, or wealth. At James 2:1–9 the rich and powerful were wrongly given the best seats, because the church leaders preferred the rich over the poor. The judge who deals out one form of "justice" to the poor and another to the rich is condemned. On the other hand, in Ephesians 6:5–9 slaves and masters are to treat each other equitably, i.e., without regard for their respective position and power. God saves persons out of every nation, tribe, people, and tongue, Revelation 7:9, because he saves without regard to worldly circumstances. God blesses his people when they behave righteously and chastises them when they behave wrongly, because he is no respecter of persons. At the sinner's final judgment, Revelation 20:11–15, the book of life is searched to see if any standing before Christ the Judge should not be there. Then other books are opened, books detailing the works of the sinners standing for judgment, and each was "judged according to their works." In other words, everyone who is there is supposed to be there, having rejected Christ as Savior. And everyone there is individually judged and sentenced according to the works they did as sinners.

God is no respecter of persons. Every sinner is subject to the sentence of eternal punishment. In election God chose some sinners to salvation through the punishment of a substitute, Jesus the Christ. Divine holiness and justice are not waived for the elected sinner. On their behalf Jesus suffered God's wrath against sin; he endured God's penalty—spiritual and physical death—for sin. Jesus fully paid the debt the sinner owed for his or her sin. That judicial payment—the propitiation of God for the crime of sin—is applied to the sinner's spiritual need through personal faith. Those who have no-faith pay the penalty in their own persons. For those with faith, Jesus paid the penalty. Thus, God is no respecter of persons, having required the sin-debt be paid by all. Rather, God in sovereign grace, working to effect his decree of election, acted in person to pay the penalty for his elect, and justly left others to pay the penalty due from them. This is not to say Christ's propitiation wasn't sufficient for all, because it was. However, Christ's propitiation is efficient to salvation only for those who apply it by faith as payment for their sins. Since God does not prevent any sinner from seeking salvation, Christ's propitiation, as being all-sufficient, is available to any who will apply it by faith.

One objects that "God desires all men to be saved and to come to the knowledge of the truth," 1 Timothy 2:4. Yet, it is obvious that every person without exception is not saved. Either God is not sovereign, nor omnipotent, or there is an explanation that agrees with his sovereignty and omnipotence, as well as his decrees of foreordination and election. The answer that agrees with what Scripture teaches elsewhere about God's will in salvation is that the word "all" indicates all without distinction, not all without exception. God saves out of "all nations, tribes, peoples, and tongues," Revelation 7:9. The 1 Timothy verse means, "not that there is no man whose salvation he does not will, but that no man is saved apart from his will."[1]

Another objection is that the offer of salvation toward the non-elect is not genuine. As far as God is concerned the offer is genuine, for he elects to save sinners, not to exclude sinners from salvation. If the non-elect person would seek salvation in Christ apart from self-made or man-made means, then God would act savingly; after all, that is exactly how the elect are saved. As far as the person hearing the offer is concerned the offer is genuine: God will act savingly if that person responds to the offer by seeking salvation through faith alone in Christ alone. As far as the believer giving testimony of salvation is concerned, the offer is genuine. Neither believer nor unbeliever knows who is or is not elect. From the evangelizing believer's point of view every person he speaks to about Christ is salvable. He himself was a sinner, rejecting God, not seeking God, when some believer called him to Christ through a gospel witness.

From God's point of view whosoever shall call on the name of the Lord shall be saved (Acts 2:21; Romans 10:13); whosoever will, let him take of the water of life freely (Revelation 22:17); whosoever believes in Christ shall receive remission of sins (Acts 10:43). God chooses and calls according to the good pleasure of his will, yet he hinders no person from coming or willing (Horatio

---

[1] Schaff, *Nicene and Post-Nicene Fathers*, First Series, 3:270.

Bonar). The reason some are not saved is not their lack of election but their lack of desire to seek and find salvation only in Christ. The gospel call goes out; the sinner rejects it because he loves his sin more than God. The offer of salvation is as genuine as the sinner's rejection and the believer's saving faith.

It is objected that election is to a sanctified life. But as I proved before there is no sanctification without salvation. It is objected that Christ is the elected one, and therefore those who believe become elect in him. But this is a variation of the foreknowledge view, to wit, that God doesn't know who is elect until they respond to the gospel call and believe; then they become one of the elect. But salvation comes through the gift of grace-faith-salvation, Ephesians 2:8–9, which is efficaciously applied to those whom God has elected. We see this is so, because each believer is "God's workmanship, created in Christ Jesus," and God has prepared works for the saved person to accomplish after his or her salvation. That answers yet another objection, that believers are elected to service, not salvation. But service follows after salvation: "created in Christ Jesus for good works." Service is the very thing believers are supposed to do, not the thing which makes them believers; therefore their election is to salvation that they might afterwards serve as God has appointed for them.

The truth is that God chose us in Christ . . . according to the good pleasure of his will . . . to the praise of the glory of his grace . . . according to the riches of his grace. Salvation is all of grace; grace is sovereign; therefore God was and is not unjust, nor a respecter of persons, but acts as he will to accomplish his will and display his grace for the admiration and praise of his saved people.

It is objected that the church as a body was elected; whoever is saved becomes part of the elect church. But the church is the *ecclesia*, a Greek word meaning "called out." The church is composed of individuals who have been called out from the world to be joined to Christ by faith. Therefore, it is individuals who are elected to be saved: the Lord added to the church daily those who were being saved, Acts 2:47. First salvation, then incorporation into the body of Christ. If further proof be needed, then John 20:22 shows the disciples were saved before the Holy Spirit descended fifty days later and formed them into the church.

Some object that if there are elected persons, then why did Christ say more laborers are needed in the fields of the lost? The answer is that evangelism is ordained as a means to call the lost to salvation. Evangelism establishes the moral responsibility of all to believe, and effectually calls those who are elected to be saved. Christ stated, "No one can come to me unless the Father who sent me draws him," John 6:44. Laborers are needed to proclaim the gospel call; through their labor God calls his people to salvation, Romans 10:14.

One objects that, "Every man who by faith accepts the call is *eklektós*."[1] This is the foreknowledge view: one is elected because he or she has faith. We have examined this word before, verse by verse. To be *eklektós* is to be chosen, to be selected. The elect are those whom God has chosen: Luke 18:7; Romans 8:33; Colossians 3:12; 2 Timothy 2:10, etc. Remember, saving faith is the very thing to which one is elected. One cannot believe and then retroactively be selected to have saving faith.

Objections similar to these might be multiplied indefinitely. Ultimately it is a matter of God's sovereignty. Did God create a universe that fulfills his purpose? Did God act sovereignly in grace to elect some to salvation, and act in holiness and justice to leave others in their sin, taking no action for or against the salvation of their soul, but proclaiming the gospel to all, and his willingness to receive "whosoever will"? Yes, to all these. Every person, from Adam forward (after his sin) is in the river of life racing for the waterfall of death that empties into the lake of fire. God has chosen to reach into the river and save some from an eternal death by giving them a relationship with himself. He has left others in the river, taking no action for or against their souls. On the contrary, God uses his saved people to proclaim salvation to everyone, urging all to come to Jesus by faith and be saved. He will act savingly toward *anyone* who responds.

A WORD ABOUT REPROBATION

The Reformers (Calvin, his peers, their spiritual descendants in history and modern times) believed the predestination of the elect made certain the eternal damnation, or reprobation, of the non-elect.

> The doctrine of absolute predestination [unconditional election] of course logically holds that some are foreordained to death as truly

---

[1] Fisk, *Divine*, 49.

Election

> as others are foreordained to life. The very terms "elect" and "election" imply the terms "non-elect" and "reprobation."[1]
>
> By predestination we mean the eternal decree of God, by which he determined with himself whatever he wished to happen with regard to every man. All are not created on equal terms, but some are preordained to eternal life, others to eternal damnation; and, accordingly, as each has been created for one or other of these ends, we say that he has been predestinated to life or to death.[2]
>
> The secret counsel of God, by which he chooses some to salvation and appoints others to eternal destruction.[3]
>
> Again, in another place he [Augustine] says, "Who created the reprobate but God? And Why? Because he willed it. Why did he will it?—'Who art thou, O Man, that repliest against God?'"[4]
>
> Because he [God] predestines some to destruction from their very creation.[5]

On the other hand, Calvin also placed the reprobation of the non-elect in the context of their sinfulness. Commenting on Romans 9:21 he wrote, "The mind and intent of the apostle, therefore, in the use of this similitude, are to be carefully observed and held fast—that God, the Maker of men, forms out of the same lump in his hands one vessel, or man, to honour, and another to dishonour, according to his sovereign and absolute will. For he freely chooses some to life who are not yet born, leaving all others to their own destruction, which destruction all men by nature deserve.[6]

Again, Calvin wrote, "Now, if we are not really ashamed of the Gospel, we must of necessity acknowledge what is therein openly declared: that God by his eternal goodwill (for which there was no other cause than his own purpose), appointed those whom he pleased unto salvation, rejecting all the rest; and that those whom he blessed with this free adoption to be his sons he illumines by his Holy Spirit, that they may receive the life which is offered to them in Christ; while others, continuing of their own will in unbelief, are left

---

[1] Boettner, *Predestination*, 104.
[2] Calvin, *Institutes*, 2:206 (3.21.5).
[3] Calvin, *Calvin's Calvinism*, 25.
[4] Ibid., 40.
[5] Ibid., 58.
[6] Ibid., 75.

destitute of the light of faith, in total darkness."[1]

There is, then, in Reformed theology what Reformed theologians call a "double predestination" to eternal life and eternal death. Some interpret double predestination to mean that God made two decrees: the salvation of the elect and the reprobation of the non-elect. This view looks to the use of phrases such as "foreordained to death," "preordained (predestined) to . . . death," "appoints others to eternal destruction," "predestined some to destruction," and, "who created the reprobate but God?".

Others interpret double predestination to mean that God did not decree the reprobation of the non-elect, but rather by not electing them he passed by them to leave them in their sins. This is what a modern interpreter of Reformed theology teaches. "The positive side [of double predestination] refers to God's active intervention in the lives of the elect to work faith in their hearts. The negative refers, not to God's working unbelief in the hearts of the reprobate, but simply to his passing them by and withholding his regenerating grace from them."[2] This is the true Reformed view, which looks to all of Augustine's and Calvin's statements on election.

My objection is to the interpretation of double predestination which asserts that just as God decreed the salvation of the elect he also decreed the reprobation of the non-elect. I hold to the biblical view: that God foreordained to create man without sin, to permit the fall which made all mankind to be reprobate, to elect some to salvation out of the mass of the reprobate, and to leave the rest of the reprobate as they were, in their sins. Let us reason together.

There was a decree to permit the fall of Adam, and by reason of that decree all men equally became sinners doomed to reprobation. All mankind were in Adam seminally (by propagation) as well as federally (Adam was the legal representative of all his race in the covenant God made with him, Genesis 1:26–29; 2:17). The decision in eternity-past to permit Adam's sin would result in all persons propagated from Adam being born as sinners. God made a decree of election to save some out of this mass of sinners. He made no decree respecting the non-elect, quite simply because they were already in a state of reprobation, by reason of the decree to

---

[1] Ibid., 31.
[2] Sproul, *Grace*, 158.

Election

permit the fall of Adam. To leave the non-elect in their spiritual state, while choosing to elect others to an opposite state, is not the same as decreeing the reprobation of the non-elect. All persons yet-to-be-born were equally reprobate before the decree of election. The non-elect continued in that state after the decree of election. No decree of reprobation was required, or given.

The problem with a decree of reprobation is that it would prevent any non-elect person from the possibility of salvation. A decree of reprobation would loudly declare, "This person *cannot* be saved!" A decree of reprobation, if it existed, would make God unjust and dishonest in offering salvation to "whosoever will."

I freely admit that non-elect sinners will not, even cannot, initiate a saving relationship with God. However, that is a result of their sin, not God's decree. The negative force of sin in human nature strongly influences them against God—so much so that believers are said to have been freed from the dominion of sin, Romans 6:14. Also, the sinner's spiritual perception is so grossly dulled by sin that they "do not receive the things of the Spirit of God, for they are foolishness to him; nor can he know them, because they are spiritually discerned," 1 Corinthians 2:14. However, the inability caused by sin is not the same as a divine decree denying the possibility of salvation. The former makes man culpable for his sin and damnation; the latter makes God unjust.

Man the sinner believes that on his own, without God's help, he can choose to be saved, because in man's view sin is not so debilitating as to prevent him from securing his own salvation (the heart of the Arminian doctrines of sin and salvation).

However, God is a just God, and therefore he makes a genuine offer of salvation to all, including the non-elect, so that, if they will, they can choose to turn from their sin and seek God. It matters not that they will choose sin, not God; what matters is that they have a genuine opportunity to turn from their sin. God has met them in their spiritual state, and given them the opportunity to turn away from sin and receive Christ as savior, and he has provided himself a witness that he is just in his offer of the gospel, and righteous in punishing those who try to create their salvation apart from him. They are reprobate because they choose to continue in their sin.

When Jesus said "No person comes to me unless the Father draws him [to me]," he was not declaring a Divine obstruction to their salvation, but the sinner's inability to come unless drawn.

When Jesus said, "Every plant which my heavenly Father has not planted will be uprooted," Matthew 15:13 (one of Calvin's arguments in support of the reprobation of the non-elect), he was not saying "they are doomed and devoted to destruction"[1] in the sense of a specific decree of reprobation, he was saying that those persons who do not have a salvific relationship with God do not stand with him and cannot stand against him. Jesus was not speaking of reprobation via divine decree, but of the sinner's inability. And Calvin, in saying the non-elect are "doomed and devoted to destruction" was speaking of the reprobation of the non-elect stemming from the decree to permit the fall of man, which occurred prior to the decree of election, which decree left the non-elect in their existing state of reprobation.

God did make a choice to save some, a choice which by its very nature excluded others; but, it was not a choice to willfully obstruct or willfully deny salvation to those not chosen. The non-elect are without excuse; the Word of salvation comes to them equally as to the elect. They have the opportunity to respond to the Gospel call: whosoever shall call on the name of the Lord shall be saved (Acts 2:21; Romans 10:13); whosoever will, let him take of the water of life freely (Revelation 22:17); whosoever believes in Christ shall receive remission of sins (Acts 10:43).

God has decreed the salvation of some. He has not decreed the opposite, that all others cannot be saved. Rather, he has respect for the sentience he has created, and gives the non-elect a genuine opportunity to turn from their sin and choose to be saved. If such a thing could happen, God would act savingly toward "whosoever will." There is no decree of reprobation that prevents a person from being saved.

THE FAITH OF THE CHURCH

From the apostolic era forward, election to salvation was the common faith of the church. As with all doctrinal statements and church creeds there was a period of development before the full expression.

Clement, who lived circa AD 30–100, in his first epistle to the Corinthians (chapter 32), spoke of believers as "being called by his

---

[1] Calvin, *Institutes*, 2:226 (3.23.1).

will in Christ Jesus."[1] The author of the *Epistle of Mathetes to Diognetus*, circa AD 130, wrote,

> God formed in his own mind a great and unspeakable conception, which he communicated to his Son alone . . . but after he revealed and laid open, through his beloved Son, the things which had been prepared from the beginning, he conferred every blessing all at once upon us . . . and having made it manifest that in ourselves we were unable to enter into the kingdom of God, we might through the power of God be made able.[2]

Chrysostom, circa AD 395, had this to say on Ephesians 1:4, in his series of homilies on Ephesians (Homily 1). "What is meant by 'He chose us in him?' By means of the faith which is in him, Christ, he means, happily ordered this for us before we were born, nay more, before the foundation of the world."[3] In speaking of the blessings believers have in Christ because of their election before the foundation of the world, Chrysostom notes, "that ours is no novel system, but that it had thus been figured from the very first . . . had been in fact a divine dispensation and fore-ordained."[4]

Athanasius, AD 298–373, wrote in Discourse II of his *Four Discourses Against the Arians*, "that before the world there had been prepared for us in Christ the hope of life and salvation . . . having the spiritual life and blessing which before these things [the created world] have been prepared for us in the Word himself according to election."[5]

The works of Augustine against the Pelagians have already been mentioned. He taught that election is unconditional, that grace is the gift of God which brings salvation and is irresistible, and that man is required to exercise saving faith.

> For he worketh all these things in them who made them vessels of mercy, who also elected them in his Son before the foundation of the world by the election of grace . . . and they are elected because they are called according to the purpose—the purpose, however, not their own, but God's.[6]

---

[1] Roberts and Donaldson, *Ante-Nicene Fathers*, 1:13.
[2] Ibid., 1:28.
[3] Schaff, *Nicene and Post-Nicene Fathers*, First Series, 13:51.
[4] Ibid.
[5] Schaff and Wace, *Nicene and Post-Nicene Fathers*, Second Series, 4:390.
[6] Schaff, *Nicene and Post-Nicene Fathers*, First Series, 5:477.

Let us, then, understand the calling whereby they become elected,—not those who are elected because they have believed, but who are elected that they may believe. For the Lord himself also sufficiently explains this calling when he says, "Ye have not chosen me, but I have chosen you," (John 15:16). For if they had been elected because they had believed, then they themselves would certainly have first chosen him by believing in him, so that they should deserve to be elected. But he takes away this supposition altogether, when he says, "Ye have not chosen me, but I have chosen you." And yet they themselves, beyond a doubt, chose him when they believed on him. Whence it is not for any other reason that he says, "Ye have not chosen me, but I have chosen you," than because they did not choose him that he should choose them, but he chose them that they might choose him, because his mercy preceded them according to grace, not according to debt.[1]

Spurgeon quotes approvingly from the Waldensians (late 12th, early 13th century). "That God saves from corruption and damnation those whom he has chosen from the foundations of the world, not from any disposition, faith, or holiness that he foresaw in them, but of his mere mercy in Christ Jesus his son, passing by all the rest, according to the irreprehensible reason of his own free-will and justice."[2]

The thirty-nine articles of the faith of the Church of England were drawn up in AD 1563 and are still officially accepted as that church's expression of faith. Article seventeen states (in part), "Predestination to life is the everlasting purpose of God, whereby, (before the foundations of the world were laid) He hath constantly decreed by His counsel secret to us, to deliver from curse and damnation those whom He hath chosen in Christ out of mankind, and to bring them by Christ to everlasting salvation as vessels made to honour."[3]

In AD 1576 the Lutherans in Germany issued a statement of faith known as the "*Formula of* Concord." Article XI, paragraph 4 states, "But the predestination or eternal election of God extends only to the good and beloved children of God, and this is the cause of their salvation. For it procures their salvation, and appoints those

---

[1] Ibid., 5:514, 515.
[2] Spurgeon, *Collection*, Metropolitan Tabernacle, Vol. 1. Sermon No. 41–42.
[3] Thomas, *Principles*, 236.

things which pertain to it. Upon this predestination of God our salvation is so founded that the gates of hell can not prevail against it."[1]

The Baptist London Confession of AD 1677, which here closely follows the Westminster Confession of AD 1647, states, "by the decree of God for the manifestation of his glory some men and Angels, are predestinated, or fore-ordained to Eternal Life, through Jesus Christ to the praise of his glorious grace; others being left to act in their sin to their just condemnation, to the praise of his glorious justice."[2]

By the 1800s the Arminianism of Wesley and Finney had made inroads into the historic faith of the church. However, the AD 1833 New Hampshire Baptist Confession still confessed election, "We believe that Election is the eternal purpose of God, according to which he graciously regenerates, sanctifies, and saves sinners."[3]

In modern times some churches openly confess a belief in election, and others do not. Yet Scripture stands fast: God chose us in Christ before the foundation of the world.

---

[1] Schaff, *Creeds*, 2:166.
[2] http://www.ccel.org/creeds/bcf/bcf.htm
[3] Schaff, *Creeds*, 2:745.

5. THE DOCTRINE OF PREDESTINATION

STATEMENT OF THE DOCTRINE

Predestination is God's decree to (1) to adopt the believer as his son and heir, (2) to conform the believer to be like Christ according to certain aspects of Christ's spiritual character and physical form, (3) to give the believer an inheritance, and (4) to make the believer God's heritage. This is the order in which we will discuss the effect of the predestinating decree.

Brief explanation: the Reformation theologians (and their spiritual heirs today) often used "predestined" in the sense of election, a case of naming the cause from one of its effects. However, it is clear from the scriptures that predestination is not synonymous with election, nor is it the cause of election. Predestination is the result of election. The prior election of those predestined is seen in (1) that the elect were "called according to his purpose," Romans 8:28, before they were predestined, v. 29, and (2) that the elect were chosen, Ephesians 1:4, before they were predestined, v. 5. Predestination is a decree affecting the future of the elect after their salvation.

THE DECREE OF PREDESTINATION

The word "predestined" is a translation of the Greek *proorízō*. Literally this word means to decide beforehand. The word is used six times in four New Testament books. (All uses. I have italicized the translated word.)

> Acts 4:27–28, For truly against Your holy Servant Jesus, whom You anointed, both Herod and Pontius Pilate, with the Gentiles and the people of Israel, were gathered together to do whatever Your hand and Your purpose *determined before* to be done.
>
> Romans 8:29–30. For whom He foreknew, *He* also *predestined* to be conformed to the image of His Son, that He might be the firstborn among many brethren. Moreover whom *He predestined*, these He also called; whom He called, these He also justified; and whom He justified, these He also glorified.
>
> First Corinthians 2:7, But we speak the wisdom of God in a mystery, the hidden wisdom which God *ordained* before the ages

for our glory.

Ephesians 1:5, *having predestined* us to adoption as sons by Jesus Christ to Himself, according to the good pleasure of His will.

Ephesians 1:11, In Him also we have obtained an inheritance, *being predestined* according to the purpose of Him who works all things according to the counsel of His will.

In the Acts 4 passage, *proorízō* indicates God's decrees concerning the crucifixion of Jesus. In eternity-past God made a decision concerning the Redeemer's death. In the fullness of time sinners gathered together to crucify Jesus in accordance with the manner, time, and place God had decreed. God's foreordination permitted men to act freely out of their sin attribute as the means whereby God would accomplish the death of the Redeemer according to his redemptive purposes. This "predestined" purpose affected the Redeemer, not the salvation or reprobation of those who crucified Christ (from the history in Acts we know that many of those who acted to crucify Jesus were later saved).

In 1 Corinthians 2:7 the subject is again the crucifixion of the Christ. Paul says the plan of God to effect salvation in the death and resurrection of a Redeemer was *proorízō*, predestined, ordained, "before the ages," i.e., in eternity-past. This decree of God in eternity-past respecting the means of redemption, resulted in men accomplishing their part of the plan in the historical-present, without knowing or understanding God's plan or their part in God's plan.

In the Acts and Corinthians passages, *proorízō* can rightly be understood as indicating a specific process in God's redemptive plan. In Acts 4, what is being said is that Herod, Pilate, the Gentiles, and Israel gathered together to do that which God had decreed in eternity-past. In 1 Corinthians 2:7–8, the Romans and Jews did not know when they crucified Jesus that they were carrying out God's decree, because it was hidden from their understanding until the act had been accomplished. Let us not expand the decree to crucify the Redeemer beyond that which God has revealed. God decided beforehand (predestined) that these particular sinners would accomplish the crucifixion, and that would act they freely (voluntarily, unforced) out of their own wicked human nature to crucify Jesus. Man freely chooses, and God's sovereignty infallibly causes those choices to be the means whereby his purposes and plans are fulfilled. Take note that the predestinating decree that infallibly accomplished the crucifixion of the Redeemer did not affect the eternal state of those sinners who accomplished the decree. They had a part to play in God's plan. They played their part—not by fate but freely chose to act as they did. What happened to them afterward was not a result of their previous act. Sinful actions do not prevent salvation. Christ's merit is sufficient to forgive any and all who come to him in faith seeking forgiveness and salvation.

In the Romans' and Ephesians' passages, the subject of "predestined" is the believer. Two aspects of the predestinating decrees are respectively the subject of these verses. In Romans the believer is conformed to be like Christ. In Ephesians the believer is predestined to be adopted as an adult son of God, and be made God's heritage. I will address the Romans passage later in the chapter.

In Ephesians 1:5 there are some interpretive issues regarding the relationship between "he chose us" in Ephesians 1:4, and he "predestined us" in Ephesians 1:5. I will repeat the verses, and then discuss the four views.

> Just as he chose us in him before the foundation of the world, that we should be holy and without blame before him in love, having predestined us to adoption as sons by Jesus Christ to himself, according to the good pleasure of his will."

The four views[1] are:

> The expression "predestined us" in v. 5 repeats the same truth of v. 4 but in different words.
>
> "Predestined us" indicates the means by which God "chose us." He chose us by predestinating us.
>
> "Predestined us" is causal: because God predestined us, he therefore chose us.
>
> Paul is opening a new subject, predestination, and is telling us the goal of predestination.

As already noted, predestination is the plan of God to adopt the believer as God's son, heir, and heritage, and to conform the believer to be like Christ. The key here is that these actions affect believers. Election is the decree *effecting* salvation. Predestination is

---

[1] Summarized in O'Brien, *Ephesians*, 102, n. 61.

the decree *affecting* those who are saved. The ends of predestination are subsequent to election. Therefore predestination is not the means nor the cause of election (views two and three). Nor does predestination repeat the truths of v. 4 (view one). The correct view is number four: Paul is opening a new subject, predestination. In the order of God's decrees, predestination occurred after election. What, then, are the effects of predestination? They are adoption, conformance, inheritance, and heritage.

PREDESTINED TO ADOPTION

In Ephesians 1:5, one aspect of adoption is in view, placement as a son (the son as heir is a consequence of adoption). Paul tells us God has decreed that every believer will be adopted into the relationship of "son" to himself. To be a "son" is a position or status for the believer. Adoption is a legal action wherein the believer becomes an adult son in God's household, and God's heir. The term "son" is not gender specific but indicates the believer's status in God's household. He or she is legally an adult child of God by adoption, and treated in the household as though a natural son; thus the adopted sons are also God's heirs.

Paul's reference is to the cultural practice of adopting an individual to be an heir. An heir is usually a natural born child. However, other persons can legally be made an heir. In the Roman law of Paul's day, a man could adopt any person as his heir, including a slave. When so adopted, the old relationship was severed, and in the new relationship the person had the same legal status as a natural born child. God has one natural child, the Son, who is heir of all things. God takes those who are not his natural children, sinners, saves them by grace, and then adopts them into the position of a natural born child. Created personal beings (man, angels) are not God's sons by virtue of their creation. God as Creator and God as Father are two different things. Men and women are sons of God only through their saving relationship with God in Christ. Paul succinctly defines who is a son of God: Romans 8:14, "as many as are led by the Spirit of God, these are sons of God"; Galatians 3:26, "you are all sons of God through faith in Christ Jesus." The decree effecting predestination accomplishes the legal placement, the adoption, of saved sinners into the position of "son."

Predestination

That the decree to adopt is a consequence of election is plain, for unsaved sinners cannot be sons. Throughout the whole of Scripture, only those persons who have a faith-based relationship with God are called the sons of God. Neither unsaved human beings nor fallen angels are called sons of God.

The saved sinner is adopted as a son through (Greek: *diá*) Jesus Christ, meaning salvation is the channel through which adoption occurs. The believer is adopted through Christ "to himself,"[1] meaning that God adopted believers, through salvation in Jesus Christ, to be his sons. The purpose of the decree to adopt the elect as sons is to bring the believer into intimate communion with God: "To HIMSELF we are adopted."[2] God raised saved sinners to the position of "sons of God" for his own purposes. The work Christ has done on behalf of the believer is the basis for his or her adoption as a son.

The adoption as sons was accomplished "according to the good pleasure of God's will." God's "will" is the Greek *thélēma*, the word meaning "that which God has determined he will do," and is a reference to his sovereignty.[3] God decides and acts apart from any exterior influences. This rationally follows from his perfections. A perfect being does not need outside counsel. His knowledge and wisdom result in perfect decisions. God is not, and in the nature of things cannot be, influenced by any will, thought, or action occurring apart from himself. God's omnipotence may also be in view. Negatively, no being can change, hinder, or stop God's actions. Positively, God has the authority and power to do all he decides to do. Whatever God's perfect wisdom decides, his sovereign authority accomplishes through his omnipotent power. In sum, the cause of God's works, whether in election, redemption, or adoption, is his own free will. However, stating this particular doctrinal truth does not seem to be Paul's purpose. Rather, Paul is praising God for having blessed us, chosen us, redeemed us, adopted us, informed us, united us in Christ, sealed us by the Spirit, and given us an inheritance.

The adoption of the believer as a son is a choice of God to bless the sinner beyond the immediate blessing of salvation from

---

[1] These words are in the Greek text of Ephesians 1:5 but not translated by the NIV.
[2] Eadie, *Ephesians*, 33 (emphasis original).
[3] Zodhiates, *WSDNT*, s. v. "2307."

the guilt and penalty of sin. The plan of salvation need not have included adoption; God could have restored what Adam lost, and no more. The adoption as sons is generally forward looking, as at Romans 8, although as with all other spiritual blessings the "now-yet future" component must be considered. In the here and now the believer enjoys fellowship with the Father, access to him as an adult son, spiritual growth to be more like Christ, and all other privileges and blessings his spiritual maturity and finite condition can encompass. In the "yet-future" category, the believer's status as a son looks toward the inheritance (Ephesians 1:11; 1 Peter 1:4) that naturally accompanies that position, and was decreed to be an innate part of God's plan of redemption. The decree of God from eternity-past has reserved a place and inheritance for the saved. One should note that the predestination of the believer to be a son of God was not only God's choice (his will) but also his pleasure, "the delight he takes in his plans."[1] The willingness of God to do good to his people, and his joy in doing good to them, is in view.

PREDESTINED TO BE CONFORMED

We know that the believer is to become more like Christ in his day-to-day life, e.g., Romans 12:2; Philippians 3:10; Ephesians 4:1–2; 5:1–2; 1 Corinthians 1:11; 1 Peter 2:21. To be like Christ is the outworking of God's purpose in the believer's life, as effected in the believer by the day-to-day work of the indwelling Holy Spirit.

In Romans 8:29, Paul says God predestined the believer to be *súmmorphos*[2] ("conformed") to the image of Christ, that is, to have the same form as Christ. In the here-and-now of this mortal life, to be conformed to Christ is to be gradually transformed in spiritual character by the operation of the Holy Spirit. At salvation the believer receives the communicable attributes of God, in a measure suitable to the limits of finite being. Throughout the believer's mortal life, the Holy Spirit uses a combination of these communicable attributes, the Scripture, his own omnipotent power, and cooperation from the believer, to conform the believer to be like Christ. What this means is the believer is to develop a moral and spiritual character that is like Jesus' moral and spiritual character. The believer is to internalize God's values as his or her

---

[1] O'Brien, *Ephesians*, 103.
[2] Zodhiates, *WSDNT*, s. v. "4832."

own, so that he or she thinks and acts like Jesus thought and acted. There is perhaps no better way to explain how the believer is to be like Christ than to apply a phrase from 1 Timothy 3:16 to the believer. "[G]reat is the mystery of godliness: God was manifest in the flesh." The goal of conformation to Christ in this mortal life is for others to see godliness (God-likeness) demonstrated in the believer's thoughts, words, and works. This is a state of spiritual maturity that can be achieved only by dependence on the Holy Spirit; a dependence which also characterized Christ during his mortal life on earth.

Romans 8:29 also looks forward to a believer becoming like Christ physically and spiritually when he or she is glorified. To be "glorified" is to be freed from the presence of sin at physical death (or rapture) and to receive a body without sin at resurrection (or rapture). At 1 Corinthians 15:50–54 Paul speaks of the transformation of the physical body at death or rapture to become incorruptible and immortal. This word *súmmorphos* is also used at Philippians 3:21 (only other use), where Paul speaks of Christ changing "our vile body," that it may *súmmorphos*, have the same form as his own body. The apostle John says the same thing without using this word, 1 John 3:2, "we know that when Jesus is revealed, we shall be like him." These things will happen because God has decreed, Romans 8:29, that the believer will be *súmmorphos* to the image of his Son. Romans 8:30 gives the proper order: called (to salvation), justified (through faith in Jesus) and glorified (conformed). Predestination in Romans 8:29 is the decree that each believer will be conformed to be like Christ on earth and transformed to be fit to live in God's presence in heaven for eternity.

PREDESTINED TO AN INHERITANCE

Christians are predestined to receive an inheritance from God. Their inheritance is the result of their adoption as adult sons and daughters of God. The believer has an inheritance "incorruptible and undefiled and that does not fade away, reserved in heaven for you," 1 Peter 1:4. Paul said that believers are "heirs of God and joint heirs with Christ," Romans 8:17. "Joint-heirs" means what Christ inherits is not divided among the other heirs (believers) but is equally shared by all the heirs. Christ's inheritance is the Davidic-Millennial Kingdom, e.g., Psalm 2:8. Believers share in his rule (in a manner not explained). Believers have an inheritance reserved in heaven: eternal life in the presence of God, worshiping and serving him for eternity. They will be pillars in the temple of God, never going out, marked with his name, Revelation 3:12, worshiping and serving forever.

PREDESTINED TO BE GOD'S HERITAGE

Most Bible students should know that the arrangement of Scripture into chapters and verses was a reference method developed in the mid sixteenth century.[1] The versification is not always helpful to an accurate interpretation. Ephesians 1:7–14 was arranged by Paul under four heads, each introduced by the Greek *en ho*, which should in every instance have been uniformly translated as "in whom."

> vv. 7–10, "in whom we have redemption through His blood, the forgiveness of sins, according to the riches of his grace which he made to abound toward us in all wisdom and prudence, having made known to us the mystery of his will, according to his good pleasure which he purposed in himself, that in the dispensation of the fullness of the times he might gather together in one all things in Christ, both which are in heaven and which are on earth in him;

> vv. 11–12, "in whom also we have obtained an inheritance, being predestined according to the purpose of him who works all things according to the counsel of his will, that we who first trusted in Christ should be to the praise of his glory;

> v. 13a, "in whom you also trusted, after you heard the word of truth, the gospel of your salvation;

> v. 13b–14, "in whom also, having believed, you were sealed by the Holy Spirit of promise, who is the guarantee of our inheritance until the redemption of the purchased possession, to the praise of His glory."

---

[1] Before printing, Scripture was arranged into blocks, loosely corresponding to paragraphs. The oldest Hebrew versions were divided into unnumbered verses. Chapter divisions were introduced in the 13th century AD. The (Latin) Vulgate was divided into unnumbered verses late in the 14th century AD. A French printer named Robert Estienne, more commonly known as Robert Stephens or Stephanus (AD 1503–1559), created the numbered verse divisions now in use. He printed the Greek New Testament in AD 1551 and the Hebrew Old Testament in AD 1571 using the numbered chapter and verse reference system he developed. The Geneva New Testament, AD 1557, used the Stephanus' numbered verse system, and it was this system that became the standard.

Predestination

The structure created by *en ho* arranges the spiritual blessings of election into separate ideas, each to be thoughtfully considered by the reader. One of those ideas is predestination. Not, however, the same aspect of the predestinating decree Paul presented in v. 5. There it was the adoption of sons, which by the very nature of adoption must include the inheritance due all sons from their fathers. Here it is a different kind of inheritance: God's inheritance, or heritage, in his saved people.

Our discussion of predestination continues with Ephesians 1:11, 12. However, I cannot discuss what "predestined" means in v. 11 until I have addressed the interpretive issues posed by translating the Greek *eklerothemen*[1] as "obtained an inheritance." To do this I must also explain the pronouns "we" and "you" in vv. 11–13. To this end, we must first discuss the words in v. 11 describing God's will: "according to the purpose of Him who works all things according to the counsel of His will." The plan of this section will be (1) to discuss God's will in relation to predestination, (2) discuss the meaning of *eklerothemen*, (3) explain the interplay between the pronouns "we", "you", and "our" in vv. 11–13, and then (4) explain the meaning of v. 11.

According to the Counsel of his Will

The word translated "purpose" in Ephesians 1:11 is *próthesis*,[2] indicating intent and design. The word can be translated as method, purpose, or plan. The word translated "counsel" is *boulé*, a word meaning the deliberation and reflection underlying a decision. The word "will" is *thélēma*. God's *thélēma* is his decision, what he has determined he will do. The predestination of the believer is,

> According to the method/plan (*próthesis*) of him who works all things according to the deliberation/purpose (*boulé*) of what he has determined/decided to do (*thélēma*).

Though this seems complex, it is similar to the process man engages in. Man deliberates, plans, and acts. Men think about a matter, determine their purpose, make a decision, form a plan, then put the plan into action. The Scripture uses words like *próthesis*,

---
[1] This is the grammatical form in the Greek text. The root is, Zodhiates, *WSDNT*, s. v. "2820."
[2] Ibid., s. v. "4286."

Predestination

boulé, and *thélēma* to help believers understand God's decision making process. Hoehner writes, "*boulé* describes the intelligent deliberation of God and *thélēma* expresses the will of God which proceeds from his deliberation . . . thus, God's will comes from the deliberation."[1] The choice that results from God's deliberation/ purpose (in this verse) is that believers are *ekleróthemen*, translated by the NKJV as "obtained an inheritance." Believers, having been predestined according to the purpose of him who works all things according to the counsel of His will, are *ekleróthemen*.

The Meaning of *eklerόthemen* in Context

The word *eklerόthemen* occurs only here in the New Testament. The root word is *klēróō*, meaning to determine or make a choice by casting lots. However, in God's will there is deliberate decision, not random chance, so the meaning is that the believer has been predestined according to the *próthesis* (intent-design/method-plan) of God in order to be *eklerόthemen*. Eadie believes that *eklerόthemen* does not refer "to the manner of our getting the possession, but to the possession itself—not to the lot, but to the allotment."[2] The use of *eklerόthemen* may mean the believer himself is God's possession/allotment. The meaning of *eklerόthemen* in context is not easily decided. There are four possibilities:[3]

> To obtain a portion/share.
>
> God chose us by lot. This does not mean God chose by chance, but is the same as election in v. 4.
>
> We were assigned or appointed a portion or share of what God has; we were appointed an inheritance.
>
> The believer is viewed as God's heritage, "we were made an inheritance."

The NKJV follows view three, linking God's appointing the believer a share in the inheritance, v. 11, to the inheritance in v. 14. This seems a reasonable view that coordinates the uses of "predestined." The believer is predestined as a son, v. 5, part of

---

[1] Hoehner, *Ephesians*, 230.
[2] Eadie, *Ephesians*, 58.
[3] Hoehner, *Ephesians*, 226–227.

Predestination

sonship is inheritance, v. 14, therefore the believer is appointed (*eklerόthemen*) a portion of the inheritance, v. 11. In this view the lot/allotment falls to the believer as the inheritance due him as a son. The NIV follows view two, and translates "in him we were also chosen." This view requires that the "we" of vv. 11–12 be a different group than the "you" of v. 13. However, as I will show below, the better view is that "we" and "you" refer to the same group.

A discussion of "we," "you," and "our" in vv. 11–14

Deciding which view is best is in part dependent on which group or groups of believers the "we", "you", and "our" of vv. 11–14 refer to.

> v. 11, In whom also *we* have obtained an inheritance, being predestined according to the purpose of him who works all things according to the counsel of his will,
>
> v. 12, that *we* who first trusted in Christ should be to the praise of his glory.
>
> v. 13, In whom *you* also trusted, after *you* heard the word of truth, the gospel of your salvation; in whom also, having believed, *you* were sealed by the Holy Spirit of promise,
>
> v. 14, who is the guarantee of *our* inheritance until the redemption of the purchased possession, to the praise of his glory.

Do these pronouns refer to different groups? Some believe the "we" of vv. 11–12 refer to Paul and the first Jewish converts, in keeping with such Old Testament passages as Deuteronomy 32:9, "For the Lord's portion is his people, Jacob is the place of his inheritance." The "you" of v. 13 would then be the later Gentile converts to whom Paul is writing. The combining of "we" and "you" produces the "our" of v. 14. Others believe the "we" of v. 12 is Paul the letter writer, and the "we" of v. 11 is Paul and the Ephesians.

However, the better view is that the "we" of vv. 11 and 12 refers to the same people as all prior verses, and the "you" of v. 13 refers to the Ephesians. Hoehner gives a long list of ancient documents to demonstrate that the interchange of "we" and "you" was a normal epistolary style.[1] A review of the previous verses supports this view. The "we" of vv. 11 must refer to the same group

---

[1] Ibid., 232.

117

Predestination

of people as the "us" and "we" of vv. 3–9, which in context is Paul and the Ephesian church.

> v. 3, blessed *us* with every spiritual blessing
>
> v. 4, chose *us* in Christ
>
> v. 4, that *we* should be holy and without blame
>
> v. 5, predestined *us* to adoption as sons
>
> v. 6, made *us* accepted in the beloved
>
> v. 7, *we* have redemption
>
> v. 8, made [the riches of his grace] to abound toward *us*
>
> v. 9, made known to *us* the mystery of his will
>
> v. 11 in whom also *we* have obtained an inheritance

Consistent with this use, the "all things" united in Christ, v. 10, includes Paul and the Ephesian church. The "we" of v. 11, then, must refer to both Paul and the Ephesians, in order to be consistent with the preceding verses. Being God's *ekleróthemen*, v. 11, and being predestinated to praise God's glory, v. 6, applies to Paul and all the Ephesian believers.

What about the "we" of v. 12, "that *we* who first trusted in Christ should be to the praise of his glory"? The immediate referent of this "we" are those "who first trusted in Christ." That phrase is the translation of *proelpízō* and occurs only here in the New Testament, never in the LXX (Greek version of the Old Testament), and rarely in Greek classical literature. The problem is not the meaning of the word, "to hope in advance," but to whom it refers.[2] Two views have been advanced:

> 1. The "we" in v. 12 refers to Jews and the "you" in v. 13 refers to Gentiles. There are two options.
>
>> a. Jews living before Christ believing in the Messiah.
>>
>> b. Hebrew Christians living after Christ who believed in Christ before Gentile Christians believed.
>
> 2. The "we" in v. 12 refers to Paul and the "you" in v. 13 refers to the Ephesian believers. There are two options.

---

[1] Zodhiates, *WSDNT*, s. v. "4276."
[2] Hoehner, *Ephesians*, 231–232.

Predestination

    a. "We" is Paul and his fellow workers: a "we" of leaders addressing followers.

    b. The "we-you" is a normal variation in ancient epistolary writing and "we" refers to Paul in distinction from the Ephesians.

If I was forced to choose between these views, then the second option is the more plausible. It allows *eklerōthemen* to be translated as "we were chosen" aligning the "we" of v. 11 with the "us" of previous verses. It accounts for the *proelpízō* in v. 12 as indicating a person or persons who believed prior to the Ephesians.

Frankly, I don't like either of these views, because these views create the issue of why Paul chose to refer to himself as distinct from the Ephesians when speaking of things common to both him and them in vv. 11–12. I don't believe Paul is making that distinction, and *proelpízō* does not require him to do so. And neither does the Greek text.

The "we" of v. 12 is the word *hēmás*,[1] used in vv. 3–6, 8 where it is translated "us": God blessed *hēmás*, chose *hēmás*, predestined *hēmás* to adoption as sons, made *hēmás* accepted in the beloved, and abounded toward *hēmás* in wisdom and prudence. The personal pronoun *hēmás* was used to distinguish "our, us, we" from *humeís*,[2] "you, your." The *hēmás* of v. 12 is interpreted by most commentators as referring to Paul alone, solely because of the "you," *humeís*, in v. 13. However, in every other place in vv. 3–14 *hēmás* always refers to Paul and the Ephesians together.

It is more consistent with the aims and doctrines taught in the passage to view *hēmás* in v. 12 as also referring to Paul and the Ephesians. Paul is saying that we—you and me—were chosen, were predestined, have redemption, that we—you and me, says Paul—who first trusted in Christ should be to the praise of his glory. This view applies to *eklerōthemen* and predestined, and applies the phrase "to the praise of his glory," to both Paul and the Ephesians. This view also incorporates all subsequent believers—you and me—into the spiritual blessings indicated by these phrases. The "blessed us" in v. 3 means not only Paul and the Ephesian church body, but that all subsequent believers are included in God's blessing in the

---

[1] Zodhiates, *WSDNT*, s. v. "2248."
[2] Ibid., s. v. "5210."

heavenlies in Christ. That is because the blessing is intended for those "in Christ." The same is true of every "us" and "we" passage.

More simply, if the "we" who *first* believed in Christ were predestined to be the praise of God's glory, then those who *afterward* believed were also predestined to the same end, because all believers are "in Christ," and therefore are recipients of divine blessing, no matter when they might have believed. In an illustration, Paul and the first believers in Christ were the firstfruits that are indicative of the full harvest. The conclusion of this issue is that the "we" of vv. 11–12 refers to Paul and the Ephesian Christians, and to every subsequent believer. Applying these conclusions to the passage:

> v. 11, In whom also *we* [every believer] have obtained an inheritance, being predestined according to the purpose of him who works all things according to the counsel of his will,

> v. 12, that *we* [Paul, Ephesians] who first trusted in Christ should be to the praise of his glory.

> v. 13, In whom *you* [every believer] also trusted, after *you* [every believer] heard the word of truth, the gospel of your salvation; in whom also, having believed, *you* [every believer] were sealed by the Holy Spirit of promise,

> v. 14, who is the guarantee of *our* [every believer's] inheritance until the redemption of the purchased possession, to the praise of his glory.

It is clear then, that whatever view we take of *ekleróthemen*, it applies to Paul, the Ephesians, and all believers in the body of Christ.

Believers are God's Heritage

Having resolved that the *ekleróthemen* of v. 11 applies to every believer, does it mean that believers receive an inheritance, or that believers are God's heritage? In deciding this interpretive issue, one must consider that *ekleróthemen* is associated with the believer being predestined to the praise of God's glory. In a special and unique way, a redeemed sinner is cause for applause and declaration of the superlative worth of God's grace. The predestined aspect of *ekleróthemen* makes it more likely that what Paul had in view was the believer chosen as God's heritage, through whom God's glory is praised. The biblical sense of this concept (God's

Predestination

heritage), as we saw earlier from Deuteronomy 32:9, is that out of everything the world has to offer, God predestined the believer to be his portion, his heritage. Everything belongs to God as Creator, and everything is under his control as Governor. The believer, however, is that portion of creation which God the Father and Redeemer chose (elected and predestined) to belong to him as his heritage. We are his heritage because he predestined us to be his portion out of the whole world. He is our Father because he redeemed us and adopted us to be his sons. The translation of v. 11, 12 should be: "in whom also we are God's heritage, being predestined . . . to the praise of his glory." This was the view of at least one church father, Chrysostom, "'In whom we were made a heritage,' [t]hat is to say, not merely have we been made a heritage, as, again, we have not merely been chosen, (for it is God who chooses,) and so neither have we merely been allotted, (for it is God who allots,) but it is 'according to a purpose.' "[1] Compare Buswell, "We have been made an heritage in Christ."[2]

In eternity-past, as part of his decrees respecting redemption, God decided that his portion out of the world would be those upon whom he chose to exercise his grace to their salvation. A homely example will illustrate the meaning. I have created books and videos that contain all I know about the Bible. Out of these, I will select a few to pass on to my children when I die. Those few will be selected because they will reveal who I was as a Christian. They are my heritage to my children—their inheritance—that will reveal my glory to them.

God, having all the universe, all his works, and all his creatures to select from, chose a few human beings to demonstrate for all eternity what his glory was in the first creation (for there will be a new creation, Revelation 21:1). Those elect persons are God's *eklerόthemen*, the ones he chose to be his lot, allotment, portion, heritage in the world. They are the praise of God's glory, the pinnacle and epitome of his works, the one's whose very presence causes others to spontaneously give God praise and glory for his mighty works in them. Throughout eternity-future, when they are seen in heaven, what others will see in them is not the person whom God saved, but the glory and magnificence and superlative

---

[1] Schaff, *Nicene and Post-Nicene Fathers*, First Series. 13:55.
[2] Buswell, *Theology*, 2:163.

worth of their God and Savior. That is the ultimate glory of the creature: to so reflect and demonstrate the glory of God, that what is seen is not the creature, but the image and glory of the Creator in the creature.

The believer, then, is predestined to adoption as God's son, in order to be to be conformed to Christ, to receive an inheritance, and to be the heritage of God; and as a result of these things, to be the praise—the applause and declaration—of God's glory, vv. 6, 12, 14.

Looking further into the passage, we, said Paul, are part of the "all things" to be united in Christ, because God chose us to be his heritage (*eklerόthemen*), and predestined his heritage to be the praise of his glory. The "also" of v. 11 connects heritage and predestined to vv. 9–10. God made known to "us" the mystery, which is that all things are to be united in Christ, in whom "we were also 'chosen as God's heritage,' being predestined . . . for the praise of his glory." The "we" in vv. 11–12 are those who heard the gospel, believed, and were sealed by the Spirit.

Putting all these things together in the context of the entire vv. 3–14 passage, Paul is saying that God chose you Ephesians, and has a purpose for you, just as he chose me, Paul, and has a purpose for me. God predestined Paul and the Ephesians to be his sons and heirs. God predestined Paul and the Ephesians to be his portion out of all his works. God predestined them to be the praise of his glory for all eternity. Through the example of those who first believed, i.e., Paul and the Ephesians, all believers are to understand that every person who believes in Christ is chosen and predestined to be God's sons and heirs, to be God's heritage, and to be the praise of God's glory. This is the full meaning and end result of the doctrine of predestination.

PRACTICAL CONSEQUENCES OF THE DOCTRINE

Cooperation with the Holy Spirit

There are several practical consequences to the doctrine of predestination. At the top of the list must be the believer's disposition to cooperate with the Spirit in being conformed to Christ. In Psalm 110:3 it is said, "Your people," that is, Messiah's people, "shall be volunteers in the day of your power." The word translated "volunteers" is the Hebrew *nᵉdābâ*, a word indicating something offered willingly.[1] A more literal translation would be "Your people are free-will offerings in the day of your power,"[2] the sense of which is Christ's people most willingly devote themselves to his cause, conforming their own needs and desires to serve him. Paul succinctly expressed the attitude necessary for cooperation with the Spirit: "we judge thus: that if One [Christ] died for all, then all died; and he died for all, that those who live should live no longer for themselves, but for him who died for them and rose again" (2 Corinthians 5:14–15).

Cooperation with the Spirit is emphasized by its negative, "Do not grieve the Holy Spirit," Ephesians 4:30, and "Do not quench the Spirit," 1 Thessalonians 5:19, either of which is possible when the believer makes a choice to act on temptation and commit sin.

Looking to "grieve," the believer is to live a life that is compatible with the holiness of the divine Person indwelling the saved soul, a quality of life that contributes to the Spirit's work of conforming the believer to be like Christ. The word translated "grieve," means grief, pain, sorrow, distress. The grammatical form used here means to cause grief, to offend. How can one offend the Holy Spirit? By doing the works of sin. In context, the works of sin Paul warns against are those that promote disunity in the body. The Spirit seals and indwells New Testament believers, forming them into one body in Christ. When the body is divided against itself, the Spirit grieves, because his body, that is, the church, is in conflict.

Looking to "quench," the word means to put out a fire. The sense in the 1 Thessalonians passage is metaphorical, and is perhaps best understood in its opposite, "Stir up the gift of God," at 2 Timothy 1:6, where the context is Timothy's spiritual gift of pastor-teacher. Timothy is to actively, willingly, and deliberately pursue a course that uses and improves his spiritual gift, in dependence on the Spirit for understanding and power in ministry. In relation to our subject (the work of the Spirit to fulfill the believer's predestinated character to be like Christ) to quench the Spirit is to stop cooperating; not merely to commit acts of sin, but to stop living the kind of Christian life the Spirit desires and commands of the believer. At the least, to quench the Spirit is to stop depending on his teaching, guidance, and power to understand

---

[1] Harris et al., *TWOT*, s. v. "5071."
[2] Perowne, *Psalms*, 5:306.

and apply one's self to live according to God's values. The believer is to persevere in the Christian life at all times, in all circumstances, all the way through the end of life. To grieve the Spirit is to sin along the way. To quench the Spirit is to stop living the Christian life. Both are temporary conditions in the believer (the Spirit will not lose one of his lambs), but neither should happen, as the exhortations require. Nor can the believer continue in sin. By the predestinating decree of God the believer must be conformed to be like Christ, and therefore chastisement will follow sin until the sinning believer repents, confesses, is forgiven, and cleansed (1 John 1:9), and begins again to cooperate with the Holy Spirit. However, there is good reason to believe that the believer who refuses to respond in a positive manner to chastisement (through conviction, repentance, confession, and return to fellowship), will have his sinning stopped by death, 1 John 5:16. Being taken to heaven for quenching the Spirit is not the best way to meet Jesus.

Experiential sanctification

Experiential sanctification was discussed earlier, but let me describe it in relation to the doctrine of predestination. Experiential sanctification is the progressive outworking of the believer's moral character in his or her daily life, as he or she becomes more like Christ. As the Spirit works day by day in the believer through his teaching, guiding, and empowering ministries, the believer's character becomes more like Christ's. This means the believer's behavior changes. Behavior is the demonstration of who we are as a person—our beliefs and values put into action. To use more biblical terms, as the Spirit conforms us to be like Christ, our behavior becomes less sinful and more righteous. The course of the believer's life in righteousness should be a process of learning and doing. To use stairs as an illustration, one learns on the riser and practices on the step. When the lessons have been internalized through practice, then the Spirit teaches more about Christ (the riser on the stairs), until the new lessons have been learned, and then one stays awhile in that place and practices what has been learned (the step on the stairs), until the Spirit decides it is time to "learn and do" again. So the Christian life is a series of successive steps of learning and doing. Sometimes we grieve the Spirit: we sin and go down a step or two. He recovers us through conviction, confession, repentance, and forgiveness, and we continue the upward process.

Paul's exhortation to "work out your own salvation," Philippians 2:12, is preceded by a description of the Christ-like character the believer is to develop. The phrase "work out" means to bring to a reasonable conclusion or goal. The goal of the Christian life, the goal of one's own salvation, is to be like Christ. Stated in the context of the Holy Spirit's work, Romans 8:29, the believer is to cooperate with the Spirit in his work of conforming the believer to be like Christ. Other exhortations reveal the character of the believer's effort to be like Christ; which is to say that there is a God-ward side to living a Christian life—God gives grace—but there is also a man-ward side: the believer works out the natural and expected consequences of being saved. Some of the exhortations to this end are at Colossians 3:1–17; Philippians 4:4–9; Romans 6:12–13; 12:9–21; 13:8–14; James 1:21–22; 1 Peter 2:11–12; 3:8–17; Jude 20–21, to name but a few. The believer is predestined to be like Christ, and is to work with the Holy Spirit to accomplish that goal in daily life.

God's Representative to Sinful Man

If, as is the case, the believer is predestined to be like Christ, then one of the believer's duties is to model Christ to an unbelieving world. This is more than overt evangelism. The Christian's behavior is to be the testimony of a life lived according to godly values, principles and precepts. Jesus could say that seeing him was the same as seeing the Father, because he possessed the one same divine essence as the Father, and therefore his character and behavior were the same as the Father's. See, for example, John 5:19; 10:30; 14:9. The Christian should be able to say, "He who has seen me has a witness of Christ," because the believer's character and behavior should be like Christ's, 1 Peter 2:21–23. See also Philippians 3:17; 2 Thessalonians 3:9; 1 Timothy 4:12. God is not going to appear in a burning bush to every sinner. Christ is not going to crucify himself afresh for every generation. Believers are called upon to give a verbal witness and living testimony of the salvation available in Jesus the Christ.

A Life of Worship & Praise.

Worship and praise of God are required of every creature: "Let everything that has breath praise the Lord," Psalm 150:6, compare

Revelation 5:13. Someday every person will be made to submit to Christ, Philippians 2:10, but it is the believer's privilege and duty in the here and now to willingly offer worship and praise. Believers are predestined to be the praise of God's glory, Ephesians 1:12. The believer is to live his or her life in such a manner that their words and works are the applause[1] that draws attention to the grace and glory of God in Christ the Savior.

Perseverance in the Christian life.

Perseverance is continuance in one's salvation all the way through life and death. Perseverance is maintaining one's faith all the way through life and death. Perseverance is the continuous practice of the dos and don'ts of Christianity, all the way through life and death. Perseverance is also the grace God gives to guarantee the believer will continue in salvation, faith, and the Christian life, all the way through life and death. Both God-ward and man-ward sides are important. The Christian life and the Christian's life are the product of God's grace, but a lot of personal effort must be expended in living that life. There is a cost to Christian living: putting off the values and works of the old sin attribute and putting on the values and works of the new person the believer has become, and is becoming, in Christ. When the believer begins his or her Christian life—when he or she is saved—sin has already influenced one's values, character, and behavior. It is to the glory of God that these things of the sin attribute are not eliminated, but must be overcome by God's grace and the believer's efforts. God gives grace and the believer uses that grace to put away sin and put on Christ. That cooperation between God and the believer is perseverance.

Perseverance is the natural and expected outcome of the believer's predestination. Let us reason together. If, as is the case, God has decreed each believer will be his legal son and heir, and be conformed to the image of Christ, and be God's heritage out of the world, then the sovereign decree of a sovereign God must come to pass: the believer must and will persevere in his or her salvation, faith, and Christian life. He or she may stumble along the way—that happens when one succumbs to temptation—but the habitual

---

[1] To "praise" is to give approval, so to translate "applause" effectively expresses the meaning. Praise as "approval" is understanding the worth or value of God and his works, that one may properly appreciate, acknowledge, and declare that value.

Predestination

course of his or her life will be to "forget those things which are behind, and reach forward to those things which are ahead, and press toward the goal for the prize of the upward call of God in Christ Jesus," Philippians 3:13, 14. Believers persevere.

Preparation for Christ's return (1 John 3:2)

The believer's cooperation with the Holy Spirit, and his or her personal effort to persevere in the faith, are the necessary preparation for Christ's return. As I have argued elsewhere,[1] in relation to Christ's return the believer is to be expectant and prepared. He (or she) is to be expectant because Christ's return is imminent (occurring at any moment). Therefore the believer is not to be looking for Christ, but is to be always prepared to meet with Christ at any moment. First John 3:2–3 is perhaps the clearest Scripture requiring the believer to be expectant and prepared.

> Beloved, now we are children of God; and it has not yet been revealed what we shall be, but we know that when He is revealed, we shall be like Him, for we shall see Him as He is. And everyone who has this hope in Him purifies himself, just as He is pure.

The Apostle is not saying that the hope of Christ's return is purifying, he is saying that those who have this hope keep themselves pure. The pronoun is reflexive, "purifies himself." Those persons who have the steadfast assurance—the conviction of certainty in their soul—that Jesus is returning for his church, will (in terms previously used) cooperate with the Holy Spirit to become conformed to be like Christ, and will exercise righteousness to become as holy in this life (experiential sanctification) as they will become when transformed and glorified (1 Corinthians 15:51–53) at the rapture of the church. For "we shall be like him" and "we shall see him as he is," expresses the work of Holy Spirit, which is to conform the believer to be like Christ. To "purify him [or her] self" is to cooperate with the Spirit by living a righteous life and perseverance in the same. Since these things, conformance to Christ, living a righteous life, and perseverance in the faith, are the goal of the predestinating decree, then predestination prepares believers for Christ's return.

This mortal life is preparation for the eternal life to come. Our manner of living and our works will be judged by Christ, 2

---

[1] Quiggle, *Antichrist*, appendix 1.

Corinthians 5:9–10, at his return. The focus of that judgment is to reward the believer for his righteous works, and cleanse him from unrighteous works, 1 Corinthians 3:5–17. The issue is not salvation. Works come after salvation. Ephesians 2:10, "created in Christ Jesus for good works," comes after "for by grace you have been saved through faith . . . not of works." The works one does as a believer will be judged by Christ. Those works that tended to conform the believer to be like Christ, and those works that resulted in the experiential sanctification that made the believer live, act, and speak like Christ—in other words, righteous and holy works—those works will be rewarded. Those righteous works will have formed the believer's character. The result of those works—the reward—will accompany the believer into and throughout eternity.

Preparation for heaven

The predestinating decree makes the believer fully qualified to be in heaven in God's presence. The believer is changed to be like Christ, through that combination God-ward and man-ward responsibilities that shape the outworking of every decree of God concerning man. Jesus said that believers would be "a pillar in the temple of my God [in heaven], and he [and she] shall go out no more," Revelation 3:12. Two things are intended by this declaration. One, the believer will always be fully qualified to worship God; two, the believer will always be fully qualified to serve God. The work of the Spirit and the believer's works in the here-and-now are set in motion by the decree of predestination, to be fully realized in an eternity of worship and service.

OBJECTIONS TO THE DOCTRINE

There are no specific objections to the doctrine of predestination when rightly understood as not being the decree of election to salvation, but the decree affecting those who have been saved.

PART THREE

The doctrines previously discussed, especially the doctrine of election, seem contrary to a view of man's will as free to make choices affecting his (or her) personal destiny. For this reason an extended discussion of divine sovereignty, the freedom of the human will to make moral choices, the doctrine of sin, a person's culpability for sin, the effect of sin on human nature, and how saving faith is achieved and exercised, are discussed from the Scriptures.

6. DIVINE SOVEREIGNTY AND HUMAN FREEDOM

GOD'S SOVEREIGNTY

God's authority is sovereign, his power is all-powerful (omnipotent), his knowledge and wisdom are all-knowing and all-understanding (omniscient), his presence is ubiquitous (omnipresent), and he is infinite in every aspect of his being. Our limits as finite beings cause us to think of infinity as the boundary of an ever expanding universe where space and time are created. God has no boundary, his essence and attributes have no limits. God's infinity means he is immeasurable because he has no material dimension; he is incomprehensible because he has no all-encompassing boundary; he is everywhere because there is no place from which he is excluded and no place to which he is limited.[1]

In eternity-past, before God created anything, when he alone existed, he decided on a purpose. To fulfill that purpose God decreed the creation of the universe and everything in it, as well as the plans and processes to accomplish his purpose through the creatures he had created. He decreed to allow sin, decreed the election of some sinners to salvation, and decreed the means to their salvation. He did all this sovereignly, i.e., uninfluenced by any will other than his own.

> Isaiah 40:13–14, Who has directed the Spirit of the LORD, or as His counselor has taught Him? With whom did He take counsel, and who instructed Him, and taught Him in the path of justice? Who taught Him knowledge, and showed Him the way of understanding?
>
> Isaiah 44:24, I am the LORD, who makes all things, who stretches out the heavens all alone, who spreads abroad the earth by Myself.
>
> Isaiah 48:4, My hand has laid the foundation of the earth, and My right hand has stretched out the heavens; when I call to them, they stand up together.
>
> Isaiah 43:13, I am He; and there is no one who can deliver out of

---

[1] Ames, *Marrow*, 86.

My hand; I work, and who will reverse it?"

Isaiah 45:18, For thus says the LORD, who created the heavens, who is God, who formed the earth and made it, who has established it, who did not create it in vain, who formed it to be inhabited: "I am the LORD, and there is no other."

Romans 11:34–35, For who has known the mind of the LORD? Or who has become His counselor? Or who has first given to Him and it shall be repaid to him?

God's sovereignty is his omnipotence, omniscience, omnipresence, holiness, and love working together to infallibly accomplish his purpose, plans, and processes. The sovereignty of God over his creation is a rational conclusion reached by a consideration of his perfection. God is increate, a self-existent being. Before he created the universe and all that it is, God existed alone in his perfections, including a perfect love and fellowship between the three Persons of his essential being. God had no need for any other being to perfect or complete him. His decision to create was therefore a perfect plan designed to fulfill a perfect purpose. The Scripture revelation is that the purpose of the creation was to manifest God's glory to sentient creatures, e.g., Isaiah 6:3; 43:7; Luke 2:14; Ephesians 1:6, 12, 14. All things concerning the creation, including its creatures, center in God and were created to fulfill his purpose.

God's decision to create was singular, incorporating all means and ends, and effected through a series of creative acts (i.e., the six days of creation). In trying to understand God's singular creative decision, theologians imagine the decision to create as being enacted according to several decrees. These decrees express the many means necessary to fulfill the purpose of God in creating. These decrees caused the existence of all the parts necessary to the whole, and caused the integration of those parts into a whole. For example, the determination of a purpose led to the decision to create, followed by the decree of foreordination; then other decrees, including those directly affecting man: the decrees of permission (to permit the fall), election, and predestination. If one focuses on man only, and lists only a few of the more significant decrees, there was the decree to create mankind, the decree to permit sin, and the decree to redeem. In the decision to redeem, there was not only the choice of who would be redeemed (election) but also the decree to allow men to exercise their faculty of choice, and a decree to incorporate the choices men make as part of the means to accomplish their redemption.

Under the doctrine of foreordination we discussed that God's sovereignty in decreeing means and ends is not fate. God's sovereignty incorporates freely made choices, by effectuating those choices that form the processes to accomplish the plans that fulfill his purpose. Every person has a choice to go to the left hand or the right, to sin or be holy, to be moral or immoral, to believe or not believe. If there were no real choices, then there would not be real responsibility to choose rightly, no culpability for choosing wrongly, and no rewards for choosing rightly. God's decrees sovereignly, omnipotently, and omnisciently incorporate man's choices as means to ends, but man does the choosing. We see this as patently true in that the Scripture commands, exhorts, encourages, and rewards right actions. We see this as patently true in that man is culpable when he chooses sin. God's sovereignty is his omnipotence, omniscience, omnipresence, holiness, and love working together and incorporating man's freely made choices to infallibly accomplish God's purpose, plans, and processes.

THE DECREE OF A SOVEREIGN GOD

The inclination and disposition of the sin attribute—of unsaved human nature—means a person does not voluntarily seek after God for salvation from the guilt and penalty of their sin, Romans 3:10–18. God must act to overcome the influence of the sin attribute. The work of God to save sinners began with his decree of election. The decree of a sovereign God to redeem sinners must include all the means necessary to effect salvation. God is perfect. Therefore the decrees to accomplish his purpose and plans, including all things related to the decree to redeem sinners, must perfectly include all necessary means. The action of God toward every person involves the outworking of God's sovereignty through man's responsibility. This is the interaction between God and man that allows man to choose freely, but infallibly brings about God's decrees respecting his purposes in the world. Man, acting out of his human nature, chooses to sin until God frees him from sin's dominance, reveals salvation in the Redeemer, and infallibly leads him to choose Christ. I must say "infallibly," because the perfect decrees of a sovereign perfect God must include all the means (processes) necessary to accomplish the ends established by his perfect purpose. If God were not sovereign he would be surprised by the choices of his creatures and must constantly revise his plans to incorporate their choices. God is never surprised, because as the sovereign God he foreordained beginning, end, and all in between. God's sovereignty means he is the active agent in accomplishing his plans, not the passive recipient of man's choices.

MAN CREATED WITH FREE WILL

Despite what has been said about free will as a component of foreordination (chapter 3), some might question how the sin attribute and the decree of election affect a person's choice for or against salvation. Are those elected to salvation truly making a free choice to believe in Jesus as their Savior? In relation to those not elected, is their rejection of salvation in Jesus Christ a free choice of their will, or is their choice determined by the fact they were not elected? The next two chapters explore the consequences of being a sinner in relation to God's sovereignty and man's sin. The remainder of this chapter discusses the effect of sin on man's free will, and the relationship between man's sin and God's sovereignty.

In a discussion of free will and freely made choices, one must remember that free will is the ability of sentient creatures to make decisions within the boundaries of their nature. If that nature is holy, as in the unfallen angels, then free will decides for holiness and righteousness, because the boundaries of the unfallen angelic nature are holiness and righteousness. If that nature is sinful, as in the fallen angels and human beings, then free will decides for sin and rebellion against God, because the boundaries of the fallen nature are autonomy and self-reliance opposed to dependence and obedience to God.

Mankind (Adam) was not created innocent. Creation in a state of innocence would mean Adam knew neither right nor wrong, implying that he was indifferent to one or the other.[1] He was not indifferent but was inclined to righteousness. Holiness was the grace God added to Adam's human nature so he could maintain himself in a state of righteousness. Adam knew that it was right to obey God, and was created with the desire to obey (inclination) and the moral ability (disposition) to live righteously within the moral

---

[1] Shedd, *Theology*, 2:96–97.

boundaries of God's authority. His moral purity inclined him to live under God's authority by conforming his thoughts and actions to God's will (expressed in his commandments). Every part of Adam's complex humanity was disposed to glorify God and experience fellowship with God. Put a little differently, Adam's human nature, pre-sin, was of such a quality that he could freely choose his path in life, and did freely exercise his power of choice to worship, serve, and obey God, and thereby he maintained his fellowship with God. He had every moral, spiritual, and intellectual equipage to be holy as God is holy. To Adam, God's commandments were not a restraint, nor a taskmaster, but were in perfect harmony with his own nature. "The positive holiness, then, with which man was endowed, consisted in an understanding enlightened in the spiritual knowledge of God and divine things, and a will wholly inclined to them."[1] Adam possessed the spiritual perception necessary to fully comprehend God's will as it applied to him and Eve. To submit and obey was what he desired. He was given grace and had every spiritual, moral, and intellectual aspect of personality and character he needed to fulfill his desire. Since Adam's will was inclined to glorify God and participate in fellowship with God as the ultimate goal of his life, there was no defect in Adam's humanity. He had free will and he exercised that will to obey God.

Mankind, Adam, was created with sentience. Sentience is a quality of self-perception or self-awareness that only God, mankind, and angels possess. Man consciously perceives himself and his environment, and interacts with his environment in a way that reflects and demonstrates his self-awareness. Man learns and then grows mentally and emotionally as a result of learning and experience. Man purposefully seeks out knowledge. Man deliberately learns and on his own initiative uses that knowledge to learn more. No other creature does these things. A human being is able to think abstractly, and is able to make choices based on rational thought processes that are more than the sum of instinct and experience. A human being is aware of himself as a being that is separate from all that is not him. The human soul is the only soul said to be created in God's image. Every human being is capable of individual and independent growth, thought, choice, and action.

Man was created with sentience that he might actively seek

---

[1] Ibid., *Theology*, 2:99.

God; spiritual perception that he might know and worship God; intellect that he might understand and obey God; the capacity to exercise love that he might have intimate fellowship with God; and the authority to freely choose, that he might willingly serve God.[1] God desired his creature man to make a choice to worship God freely and not by necessity. All other material creatures worship God by instinct. Where there is no sentience there is no choice. Non-sentient creatures do worship, e.g., Revelation 5:13, every creature in heaven, on the earth, under the earth, and in the sea, praise and worship the Lord, cf. Psalm 148. The inanimate things worship by displaying God's works, the animate non-sentient creatures by instinct. Man, however, being a sentient being, was (and is) given a choice.

Adam was a sentient creature with free will, made in the image of God to exercise discernment, make rational decisions, and choose which way of life he would follow. He could choose willing submission to God's authority, or make a wrong choice to autonomously determine his own way in defiance of God's authority. God wants voluntary worship, fellowship, service, and obedience from his sentient creatures. Adam had every advantage to make his choice the right choice. He had a sinless, righteous nature strengthened by the added grace of holiness. He had a personal relationship with God, so he could ask for help in a time of temptation or other need. The test posed by the tree of knowledge good and evil was designed to force Adam to make the choice between God and self, by giving the Tempter an opportunity to tempt, and Adam an opportunity to exercise his righteous nature and say "No" to the temptation, thereby choosing God over self. Adam was created free to choose, abetted by his holiness, unfettered by a non-existent sin attribute. His human nature was designed to show the glory of the Creator. Adam should not have failed and sinned since he had every ability and desire to succeed. In his holy nature God had supplied him with that measure of grace necessary to continue to be inclined toward obedience. His choice to sin—to voluntarily self-originate sin—was wholly the result of his deliberate misuse of his power to choose.

Adam's sin changed his human nature by adding to it a sin attribute: an evil principle of moral autonomy, which is the

---

[1] Quiggle, *Adam and Eve*, 73.

inclination and disposition to choose one's path in life wholly apart from God's will, by rebellion against and disobedience toward God and his commandments. Because God's law of reproduction is that every kind of creature reproduces children in the image and likeness of their parents, after their sin Adam and Eve propagated their now sinful human nature to their children. The nature of every human being is to rebel against God and disobey his commandments. A person's choice to rebel and disobey is a choice freely made. Sin influences that choice but does not determine it. The sinner freely chooses sinning because his will is of itself always inclined by the sin attribute to choose sinning, and as being rebellious and disobedient toward God never desires to change its inclination to choose sinning. Because the sin attribute influences the will against God, no person voluntarily seeks God or salvation. It is not the absence of election that disposes a person not to seek God, but the presence of the sin attribute that inclines the sinner not to seek God. Election means God supplies the gift of grace-faith-salvation that irresistibly leads the sinner to willingly repent of his or her sin and exercise personal faith to receive/accept Christ as his or her Savior.

THE SIN NATURE

The issue of man's freedom of will is complicated by the sin attribute. Sin is a principle of evil, one of several principles, or attributes, that together make the human nature. Man was not created with a sin attribute. This principle of evil, the sin attribute, became an innate part of human nature through Adam's choice to commit an act of sin. The result of Adam's sin is that self-determination (choices made in defiance of God), became an innate attribute of human nature. Rebellion against God and disobedience to his commandments are the expressive characteristics of the sin attribute. How did Adam's sin affect all the human race? The Scripture teaches the essential unity of the human race in and with Adam (Romans 5:12–21; 1 Corinthians 15:22): all human beings are legally part of the covenant God made with Adam, and all human beings are physically from Adam. As to being physically from Adam, the addition of sin to Adam's human nature means the principle of evil became innate to the nature of the human race through Adam's propagation. The sin attribute, therefore, is present in every person, influencing the will. Man's will is the power of human nature determining behavior, and sin is an innate part of human nature. The unsaved human nature is always defiant against God because the sin attribute is not a separate nature, it is an innate part of the whole person, and it is the whole person that "wills" the choice of behavior. Therefore, the unsaved person freely chooses to follow his or her sinful human nature and self-determine in defiance of God. Since the choice of behavior is free and natural to human nature, the person is responsible and accountable for his choices. All persons are culpable for their sin attribute and for their acts of sin. A person can choose to sin or not, but he or she chooses sin because it is their nature to sin.

The strength of sin in human nature is that it actively opposes God and promotes the satisfaction of self over all else. As a fundamental law of life the sin attribute is an immoral force in human nature that influences the will to choose sinning over righteousness.

All persons are, on some level of consciousness, aware of all the principles of life in their human nature, including sin, but tend to focus the mind on the actions those principles generate. Sin (the sin attribute) is the word used to denote the principle of evil in human nature. Sin (sins, sinning) is also the word used to identify individual acts of moral evil. We tend to focus on the acts, not the nature, but it is the nature that generates the acts. The will is the power of the person choosing which principles of life (good, evil) will govern his or her behavior in general and in any particular circumstance. Volition is the expressive faculty used by the will to carry out its choices through actions in thoughts and deeds. The will chooses the principles determining the how and why of action, volition carries out those choices through individual actions. In other words, the outward act, volition, is not the source of who we are, it is the result of who we are. The outward act is the result of the will choosing which principles of life will govern behavior.

An illustration may be helpful. A person buys a house with mature landscaping. There is a tree he cannot identify. In the process of time the tree produces oranges. An ordinance forbids fruit trees within city limits. The man is unwilling to remove the tree, so he removes the fruit—and continues to remove the fruit, year after year—to hide its nature. However, the tree has not changed its nature. The oranges do not make it a fruit tree; it produces oranges because it is a fruit tree. The outward act of sin does not make one a sinner; one sins because the evil life-principle of sin is part of his or her human nature.

The principles of life are the human nature. Since sin is an innate principle of the human nature, when a person chooses to commit an act of sin, he or she has acted out of their human nature. Man is culpable for sin because the act of the will to govern behavior by the sin attribute reflects the choice of the whole person. Sin is said to dominate man's will, not because sin is some sort of overlord imposing itself on man, but because it is innate to man's nature, and continuously influences the will to choose rebellion and disobedience; therefore the choice to sin is freely committed.

Man is responsible for all his choices. The influence of sin in human nature does not mean that unsaved man does not possess any freedom of will, but because sin is an innate principle of life in man's nature, his will is of itself always inclined to choose to sin and, as being rebellious and disobedient toward God, never desires to change its inclination to choose sin. Therefore, the sin attribute may be accurately defined as an evil life-principle of human nature that, in harmonious interaction with other life-principles in one's human nature, influences a person to self-determine his or her course in the world in opposition to God's revealed will, whether that will of God is discovered in Scripture, or in that revelation of himself God has made in human conscience. Sin is accomplished in acts of rebellion against God and disobedience to his commandments.

We should not think of sin as forcing a person to make a decision for evil. The whole person wills the choice of behavior. Sin is only one part of human nature involved in making a decision, but sin's part in the decision-making process is to exert an influence against deciding for righteousness. When the whole human nature decides to follow sin's influence the person has freely chosen to be rebellious and disobedient toward God. That any one person is not as bad as he or she might be indicates the will can make choices to resist some acts of sin. That men and women do commit acts of sin indicates man freely chooses to follow his innate sin attribute into rebellion and disobedience toward God. Since the choice of behavior is free and natural to human nature, the person is responsible and accountable for the choice to commit an act of sin. Adam was created without sin, and therefore was naturally inclined to obey

God. Sin became part of Adam's humanity when by a freely made choice he originated an evil inclination to disobey God. The action of sin, which was the volition to act on the inclination and eat the fruit, was the result of the self-origination of the evil inclination in the will. The fall of man into sin was caused by the change in inclination, not the exertion of the volition. The same is true for Adam's descendants. What makes a person a sinner is the inclination to evil—the sin attribute—not the volition, the actions of sin, that the inclination causes. Man's free will continues to operate and make choices, just as Adam did, but his free will is inclined away from God by his sin attribute. It is this evil inclination and disposition—the desire to sin and the immoral life-principle that generates the desire—that makes election necessary. Left on his own, even with knowledge of what will happen, a sinner will choose to remain in the river of sin emptying into the lake of fire.

With these thoughts in mind, we will in turn (chapter 7) discuss man's culpability for sin and the inability to seek God that sin causes, which together make an election to salvation necessary. We will then turn to a discussion of saving faith (chapter 8), wherein the voluntary acts of God and man are required for the decree of election in eternity-past to become effective in the historical-present.

7. CULPABILITY AND INABILITY

CULPABILITY

Statement of the doctrine: to be deserving of condemnation because guilty of the crime as charged. The legal status of the unsaved sinner standing before God the Judge is, "guilty of the crime of being a sinner and therefore deserving of condemnation."

The unsaved sinner is guilty and therefore deserving of eternal condemnation for three reasons. One, his (or her) imputed guilt from Adam's sin, because every human being is a participant in the covenant God made with mankind through Adam. Two, moral failure to be conformed to the image in which God created man (because the sin attribute has corrupted human nature). Three, legal disobedience toward God through the commission of acts of sin.

The Scripture teaches the sin attribute dominates the unsaved person's will by inclining the will away from God and toward acts of sin. How can a person be culpable (deserving condemnation or blame as wrong or harmful[1]) for his or her choices to sin when the sin attribute dominates the person's will? I very briefly discussed above that sin's part in the decision-making process is to exert an influence against deciding for righteousness. Sin does not dominate man's will as some sort of overlord, but as an innate part of his nature constructively working with all the other life-principles to incline the will to choose sinning. The sinner freely chooses sinning because his will is of itself always inclined by the sin attribute to choose sinning, and as being rebellious and disobedient toward God never desires to change its inclination to choose sinning. Therefore, since sinning is a freely-made choice of the whole human nature, a person is culpable for his or her acts of sin. What follows in the next paragraph is a more technical discussion of culpability for sin.

The will is the decision-making faculty of the soul, the power of choice freely choosing thought and action as the expression of the whole person. The will is "that voluntary power of human nature which determines the continuous movement of the soul toward its ultimate reason for living, according to those principles of life which together make up human nature."[2] A person uses his or her will to

---

[1] Dictionary.com. "Culpable."
[2] Shedd, *Essays*, 233–234.

Culpability and Inability

choose a course of behavior according to the various and competing principles of life innate to human nature. A principle of life is a fundamental law governing behavior. Holiness is a principle of good. Love is a principle of selflessness. Sin is a principle of evil. Adam's choice to commit an act of sin changed the human essence by adding to it the principle of sin (a sin attribute). The entire person is corrupted by his or her sin attribute—not that a person is as bad as he or she might be, but that there is an entire absence of holiness in the sinner, and a complete absence of love for God.[1] Thus: man's will is the power of human nature determining behavior; sin is an innate part of human nature and thus influences the decision-making process; man freely chooses to follow his human nature and commit acts of sin. Since the choice of behavior is free and natural to human nature, the person is culpable for his or her wrong choices. Therefore, since sinning is a freely-made choice of the whole human nature, a person is culpable for his or her acts of sin.

How does foreordination fit into this understanding of sin? That God foreordained the circumstances leading to Adam's freely made choice to sin does not make God culpable for sin. Foreordination assumes four conditions concerning sin.

> An essential characteristic of Adam's sentience was the ability to make choices in response to circumstances.
>
> Foreordination effectuated the Adam's freely made choice to sin, but did not require him to sin.
>
> All possible circumstances and choices subsequent to Adam's sin were within the context of the sin attribute present in every human being as a result of Adam's sin.
>
> Therefore, sin is a circumstance of the historical-present.

In the historical-present every person makes a free choice out of his or her sinful nature to react in a certain way to circumstances. Each can choose to sin, or not. God's foreordination in eternity-past effectuated possible choices made within the context of man's sin attribute, into actual choices in historical-present. To effectuate only those choices which were not sinful would have been to cancel man's sentience, for choice is essential to sentience. Therefore, God's foreordaining decree effectuated freely made choices to sin or not sin. One must accept by faith that God's choice to make man a

---

[1] Shedd, *Theology*, 2:257.

Culpability and Inability

sentient being, and God's choice to permit his sentient being to choose sin, were made in the context of manifesting his glory in both the salvation and the judgment of his erring creatures. People choose to sin, and people act in accordance with God's foreordination.

Adam's choice to sin gave him a sin attribute which he propagated to his descendants. Therefore, every person has a sin attribute. Is a person culpable for having a sin attribute, or only culpable after committing an act of sin? The Genesis account seems to imply that Adam became guilty by eating the fruit; that it is the act of sin that makes one a sinner. However, the act of sin merely manifested the pre-existing sin attribute and gave focus to its guilt. Adam became guilty of sin the moment he decided to disobey the commandment; at the moment of his decision to disobey, a sin attribute became part of his human nature. Remember, the will is the cause of volition. Adam's will, his human nature, had to have been corrupted by sin prior to the act of sin, otherwise there would not have been volition to commit the act. Therefore, Adam was guilty of having a sin attribute before he became guilty of committing an act of sin. Adam became culpable for his sin attribute the moment he self-originated the inclination to sin, although the consequences were held in abeyance until he ate the fruit—for he might have changed his mind and turned to God to save him from temptation and sin in his time of need. But he did eat, and thereby reaped the consequences, becoming culpable for the act as well as the inclination.

The conclusion is that it is the sin attribute itself that makes a person a sinner. The argument derived from this conclusion is that all persons are judicially guilty for having a sin attribute, as well as for acts of sin. Sin-corrupted human nature is no longer in the image and likeness in which it was created. Therefore, human nature is itself a violation of God's character and law. What follows in the next four paragraphs is a more technical discussion of culpability for the sin attribute.

Many would say a person becomes guilty for sin only as they become capable of distinguishing between right and wrong. This argument says there is no culpability for the sin attribute itself. It also says culpability exists only when a person knows they are doing wrong. Although many responses may be made for or against this view, the circumstances of life and the testimony of Scripture

Culpability and Inability

present a conclusive argument: death. Death is sin's result, the sign that each person is culpable for the judicial guilt of having a sin attribute. The fact of death reveals man's culpability for sin at every stage of human personal existence from conception to expiration. "All mankind are exposed to death in consequence of the first sin of the first man; all men are treated as guilty on account of that one offence."[1] Whether a person dies moments after conception or dies from old age, death says "this person was a sinner, guilty of and culpable for his or her sin." Paul said in Romans 5, "through the one man's offense death reigned"; "through one offence all men were condemned so as to die"[2]; "through one man's disobedience many were made sinners."[3] Adam's sin changed his human nature by adding to it a sin attribute; he propagated his changed human nature to his descendants; he died because of sin and his descendants die because of sin. Therefore, as death is the punishment for sin, and as death can occur at any stage of human (physical) existence, then every person has a sin attribute from the moment of conception, and every person is culpable for having a sin attribute, regardless of their moral capacity or actions.

Scripture therefore clearly teaches Adam's act of sin corrupted human nature with a sin attribute. Adam propagated that corrupted human nature to his descendants. Therefore all human beings are sinners because they have a sin-corrupted human nature; i.e., they are personally guilty of having a nature that violates God's character by failing to maintain the image in which human nature was created (the moral definition of sin).

Scripture also teaches every human being is a sinner because Adam's sin-guilt is imputed to his descendants, because he was their legal representative (because their seminal head) in the covenant God made with Adam. In Romans 5:14–21 Paul said through Adam sin entered the world, death entered through sin, and thus death spread to all men, because all sinned. How is it that all sinned? In v. 13 Paul made what seems a contradictory statement, that "until the law sin was in the world, but sin is not

---

[1] Brown, *Romans*, 74.
[2] Ibid., 79
[3] The text is literally, "through one offence toward all men to condemnation." To make sense in English something must be supplied. Brown's translation puts Paul's idea in the English idiom: "Through one offence all men were condemned so as to die; through one man's disobedience many were made sinners."

Culpability and Inability

imputed when there is no law." However, what Paul was saying is that the fact of death proves all who die are guilty for sin. By "law" Paul meant the Law of Moses, and his argument was that even though there was no stated or written legal code, such as given to Moses, yet there was always a law which sin transgressed. "Sin supposes that there is a law in being, for where there is no law there is no transgression (Romans 4:15). But where there is sin, there is a law, and a transgression of the law, 1 John 3:4."[1] Therefore, death reigned from Adam forward because all were guilty of breaking God's law. Adam broke God's law (the legal definition of sin) when he disobeyed the prohibition in the covenant. That sin-guilt was imputed to his descendants because Adam was the legal representative of the human race in his covenant with God, Genesis 1:26–29; 2:15; 2:17. Today's readers may not be familiar with the biblical concept of representation, but the idea of family connections through multiple generations, of man's indebtedness to his past, and his responsibility to future generations, are cultural norms throughout the Bible. For example, Abraham represented his descendants, Hebrews 7:9–10. Christ represents all his spiritual posterity—all saved persons: Romans 5:18, 19. The guilt of Adam's transgression against the covenant was therefore imputed to his posterity, making them guilty of the transgression, and so they died. "There is a causal relation between the sin of Adam and the condemnation of his race . . . To say that condemnation is *through*, or by means of an offence, is to say that the offence is the rational or judicial means, i.e., the ground of that condemnation."[2] "On account of the offense of Adam, sentence of death was pronounced upon *all* whom he represented . . . If Christ's obedience is the ground of our justification [which it is], then Adam's disobedience must, by contrast, be the ground of our condemnation."[3] Every person is culpable from conception because every person shares in the imputed guilt of Adam's transgression.

Therefore, both legally and morally, i.e., by imputation of Adam's sin-guilt and by possessing a sin-corrupted human nature, human beings are guilty of sin and culpable for their sin from the moment of conception: they participate in Adam's sin-guilt and are

---

[1] Venning, *Sinfulness*, 25.
[2] Hodge, *Romans*, 170 (emphasis original).
[3] Haldane, *Romans*, 217, 219 (emphasis original).

personally guilty of having a sin attribute.

The doctrine of personal culpability for sin from the first moment of the soul's existence is difficult to accept, because man wants to believe that if any are free from sin's guilt and punishment it is those who have not yet committed an act of sin. Believers know that the death of a sinner is not only physical but also spiritual, and therefore desire those who have not committed an act of sin go to heaven upon their death. Yet Paul's argument and conclusion are inescapable: death proves all who die are sinners, therefore all are guilty and need salvation. The issues of culpability and salvation in those persons who are mentally incompetent to make a faith-based decision—the unborn, infants, small children, adults who never became mentally competent—is addressed below in the section, "Culpability for Sin from Conception."

There is one other issue in a discussion of culpability: God's sovereignty. God knows the end from the beginning because by his foreordination of agents, events and outcomes he has decreed the means to accomplish the ends. How does the sovereignty of God affect man's culpability? God's sovereignty is his omnipotence, omniscience, omnipresence, holiness, and love working together to infallibly accomplish his purposes, plans, and processes through a person's *freely made* choices to do right or do wrong. God's sovereignty in foreordaining means and ends is not fate. Every person has a choice to go to the left hand or the right, to sin or be holy, to be moral or immoral, to believe or not believe. If there were no real choices, then there would not be real responsibility to choose rightly, no culpability for choosing wrongly, and no rewards for choosing rightly.

A person lives in the historical-present, not the foreordaining eternity-past. A person makes decisions based on experience and circumstances in his or her historical-present. God's decrees have incorporated a person's choices as means and ends, but the person does the choosing. We see this as patently true in that the Scripture commands, exhorts, encourages, and rewards right actions. We see this as patently true in that a person is culpable when he or she chooses to commit an act of sin. God is just, he rewards and punishes based on actual choices, and therefore a person's choices are not fate but are their genuine response to immediate circumstances. Those choices were available to be foreordained in eternity-past just because they were the person's genuine response

Culpability and Inability

to circumstances. Who can say if other circumstances and choices would have been better? Is God just, and holy, and wise? Yes, he is all these things and more. The events and choices and circumstances God chose to effectuate from possible to actual were the best, most perfect choices that would accomplish his purpose—a perfect, holy, just, and wise purpose. The choices you make today are not fate; they are your response to life's circumstances. Today's circumstance is that "now is the accepted time; behold now is the day of salvation," 2 Corinthians 6:2. Choose faith, choose Christ, choose to be saved.

God's sovereignty in the world as it relates to sin may be summed under two heads. One, God restrains sin or extends grace so that a person does not always act according to his or her sin attribute. Therefore, there is a measure of justice, kindness, goodness, mercy, and benevolence in the world. Second, God's sovereignty is so all-encompassing that he is able to incorporate a person's freely made choices into his plans and processes. The Scripture gives several examples. In eternity-past God made a choice (election) to save some. Yet those elected must make a choice to "Believe on the Lord Jesus Christ" in order to be saved (Acts 16:31). Though "chosen to salvation through sanctification by the Holy Spirit," yet they must also "believe in the truth" to be saved, 2 Thessalonians 2:13. I will address the compatibility of God's choice and man believing in chapter 8.

In another example, in eternity-past God decreed Jesus would be crucified as part of the decree to redeem mankind. In the historical-present people made morally wrong choices and crucified Jesus. The Scripture expresses God's sovereignty working with their choices. Acts 2:23, "Him, being delivered by the determined purpose and foreknowledge of God, you have taken by lawless hands, have crucified, and put to death." God decreed that redemption would be accomplished through the death (crucifixion) of the Redeemer. God decreed that freely made choices would be the processes that would accomplish the crucifixion. People decided to crucify Jesus through their freely made choices to sin. God neither inhibited nor encouraged the expression of their sin attribute—he let their human nature take its course and decide what to do. Therefore they were culpable for their choices and actions. Another example, Pilate wrote Jesus' crime, "King of the Jews," on a plaque and hung it on the cross. Pilate made his own choices as to what to write, and the Holy Spirit superintended his choices so that he wrote exactly what God wanted written. The Jews did not like what had been written, but Pilate would not change it. His decision was the outworking of his sin attribute in pride and arrogance toward a people he despised, but God sovereignly incorporated Pilate's choices as part of the processes to accomplish God's plan of redemption. One more example: Judas betrayed Jesus because he made choices that centered in his own greed and ambitions. God's sovereignty ensured Judas must accomplish the decree that prophesied his betrayal. However, the decree was not fate; Judas was free to make his choices. He could have chosen otherwise, but he didn't. The choices Judas freely made were incorporated by God's sovereignty into his plans as the means (the processes) to accomplish the betrayal of Jesus. God's sovereignty does not forcibly change a person's nature and does not force any person to act contrary to their nature. Therefore, a person is culpable for his or her sin attribute and acts of sin.

INABILITY

Statement of the doctrine. Inability is that condition of human nature wherein the sin attribute has rendered spiritual perception so grossly insensitive that the unsaved person does not have the spiritual discernment to receive or understand the things of the Spirit of God, 1 Corinthians 2:14.

Because the sin attribute is one of the principles of life in human nature (through Adam's sin and propagation), it is beyond the power of the will to change the condition. The result of the sinner's gross insensitivity to spiritual things is the lack of all ability to will any spiritual good leading to or accompanying salvation, such that the sinner is not able, by his or her own strength of will, to save him or herself, or to prepare for salvation, apart from the work of God the Holy Spirit.

"The Scriptures nowhere attribute to fallen men ability to change their own hearts or turn themselves unto God. As their salvation depends on their regeneration, if that work was within the compass of their own powers, it is incredible that the Bible should never rest the obligation of effecting it upon the sinner's ability. If he had the power to regenerate himself, we should expect to find the Scriptures affirming his possession of this ability, and calling on

Culpability and Inability

him to exercise it."[1] Does the command to repent imply men can save themselves? "The very command to repent and believe implies . . . that those to whom it is addressed are rational creatures, capable of moral obligation, and that they are free moral agents. It implies nothing more. The command [to repent and believe] is nothing more than the authoritative declaration of what is obligatory upon those to whom it is addressed."[2]

The great darkness and misery of sin is that it renders man incapable of initiating communion with God. This follows from man's inability to understand the spiritual things of God due to his grossly dulled faculty of spiritual perception, 1 Corinthians 2:12–14,

> Now we [the believer] have received, not the spirit of the world, but the Spirit who is from God, that we might know the things that have been freely given to us by God. These things we also speak, not in words which man's wisdom teaches but which the Holy Spirit teaches, comparing spiritual things with spiritual. But the natural man [Paul's term for the unsaved person] does not receive the things of the Spirit of God, for they are foolishness to him; nor can he know them, because they are spiritually discerned.

Christ calls the sinner "out of darkness, into his marvelous light," 1 Peter 2:9. God has "delivered his people from the power of darkness and translated them into the kingdom of the Son of his love," Colossians 1:13. If God takes people from darkness into light when he saves them, then those who are in their trespasses and sins must be in spiritual darkness, not the light of spiritual understanding. If God is the only one who can effect the sinner's transition from unforgiven to saved, then the sinner lacks the ability to seek after God ("there is none who seeks after God," Romans 3:11), to understand God ("there is none who understands," Romans 3:11), or to gain a righteous standing with God by their own works ("there is none righteous, no not one," Romans 3:10; "not of works," Ephesians 2:9). All seek after their own things; all seek after a god of their making, Romans 1:19–23. Without faith, it is impossible to please God, Hebrews 11:6. Faith is doing what one is convicted to believe. That is just the point where the sinner fails. He or she lacks the spiritual perception to understand and be convicted to act in faith and be saved.

---

[1] Hodge, *Theology*, 2:267.
[2] Ibid.

Culpability and Inability

Inability is seen in the persistence and obstinance of sin, of which Israel in the wilderness affords a good example. At every turn God blessed them; at every turn they complained. He delivered them from slavery in Egypt; they complained they were in the wilderness, Exodus 14:11; 16:3. He fed them in the wilderness, Exodus 16:35; Numbers 11:31–32; they complained about the food, Numbers 11:4–6, 13. God supplied them with water, Exodus 15:22–27, but they had no faith he would supply more, Exodus 17:2–7; Numbers 20:1–13. God brought them to the border of the promised land, but they had no faith to enter; moreover, when God pronounced their doom, they refused to believe God and tried to enter on their own, Numbers 13–14. Jesus' public ministry also reveals man's inability. He fulfilled every prophecy of the Christ, but they could not, would not, and did not believe on him. He did not meet their expectations, so they rejected his Person and works.

Inability is seen in the order of salvation. We have discussed this in a previous chapter, so I will mention it only briefly. Adam and Eve turned away from God, but God sought them. Jesus said, "No one can come to me except the Father who sent me draws him," John 6:44. Second Thessalonians 2:13 teaches regeneration, then conversion: "Because God from the beginning chose you to salvation [election] through sanctification by the Spirit [regeneration] and belief in the truth [conversion through conviction, faith, and repentance]." Ephesians 2:8–9 teaches salvation through receiving God's gift of grace-faith-salvation which regenerates the soul, giving the sinner perception of spiritual truth, leading to conviction and the exercise of saving faith. God seeks the sinner before the sinner will seek salvation.

The inability to initiate a relationship with God is a result of the effect of sin on the whole person, a principle known in Calvinism as total depravity. Total depravity means sin extends to and corrupts every part and every aspect of man's humanity, including his faculty of spiritual perception. It means that in relation to God there is no spiritual good in the sinner at all. Total depravity does not mean every person is as bad as he or she might possibly become. Nor does it mean the sinner has no innate God-consciousness, nor a conscience that cannot distinguish between good and evil. The doctrine does not teach that every sinner has no interest in virtue, or disinterested affections with his fellow human being. And it does not mean every sinner will indulge in every sin possible.[1] Total depravity means every thought and action of the unsaved sinner is some way conditioned by the sin attribute. It means the faculty of spiritual perception is grossly dulled by sin—so much so that the sinner cannot perceive or understand spiritual things. This lack of perception extends to an inability to recognize one's alienation from God and his (or her) own spiritual needs. Therefore, the sinner's inability encompasses two vital areas: desire and ability. Man does not want to seek God; man does not have the spiritual perception required to seek God. Man can be religious, but religion is an expression of the sin attribute's anything-but-God attitude. Man does not seek God through religion; he uses religion to avoid God. The spiritual truth is that "the carnal [unsaved] mind is enmity against God . . . so then, those who are in the flesh [unsaved] cannot please God," Romans 8:7, 8. "The natural man in his fallen condition is totally unable in the slightest degree to contribute to, or cooperate in his own regeneration."[2] Depravity and inability do not mean man's faculties of reason, will, and conscious are not operational. They are operating, but as conditioned by the sin attribute the reason can come to conclusions not based on fact, the will can make a wrong decision, and the conscience can be damaged to support a wrong conclusion and decision. Man can think, he can make choices, he is capable of discerning between moral good and evil (but the sin attribute prefers evil). "That man is in such a state that he uniformly prefers and chooses evil instead of good, as do the fallen angels, is not inconsistent with his free moral agency."[3] The free moral agency of the sinner is no less free than the same agency in the saved, who choose to make good and holy choices. The saved person's ability is the outworking of his born-again nature and the Holy Spirit's indwelling power and guidance. The unsaved person's inability is because he has the old Adamic nature, no relationship with God, no spiritual power to overcome his sin attribute, and no spiritual perception to initiate a relationship with God.

Total inability, said Hodge, "consists in the want of power to rightly discern spiritual things, and the consequent want of all right

---

[1] The preceding was derived from Berkhoff, *Theology*, 246–247.
[2] Buswell, *Theology*, 2:138.
[3] Hodge, *Theology*, 2:261.

affections toward them. And this want of power of spiritual discernment arises from the corruption of our whole nature [total depravity], by which the reason or understanding is blinded, and the taste and feelings perverted. And as this state of mind is innate, as it is a state or condition of our nature, it lies below the will, and is beyond its power, controlling both our affections and our volitions."[1] What Hodge meant by "below the will" is that sin became one of the fundamental principles of human nature following Adam's sin. All the principles in human nature act on the will, or may be ignored by the will, but because they are fundamental principles of life they are beyond the power of the will. For example, no decision of the will can stop a person from possessing the principle of love; it can only stop a person from acting on the principle. When the will is dominated by sin the moral and selfless principles (holiness, righteousness, love) become less important than the "Me! Me! Me!" principles.

Every person has a God-consciousness: an understanding that there is a God, written into human nature at Adam's creation. Whether man worships the one true God, or worships anything-but-God, or doubts that God exists, or denies the possibility of God, man is responding to the innate consciousness of God put by God into human nature.[2] Yet, sin always inclines the soul against God, so that the soul in and of itself never chooses to seek after God. In some people their experience with sin and their lust after worldly attainments rationalizes their God-consciousness as discontent with worldly circumstances. They work harder to gain the whole world. Others may feel something is not right in their relationship with a non-specific deity. A persistent feeling that "I must get right with god" is the innate God-consciousness at work. Because of this unease, a person may become religious, humanitarian, self-reformed (from anti-social behavior or addiction), seek counseling, or, in the most extreme cases, view life as meaningless and kill themselves through self-destructive behaviors or an immediate suicide. The gospel is the life-line that can rescue these people. A

---

[1] Ibid.
[2] The innate God-consciousness does not save; it is a witness of God as Creator and Ruler that prepares the sinner to receive the gospel of salvation. When the gospel is rejected, or not preached, man attempts to satisfy his God- consciousness with false religions, beliefs, and philosophies. Compare Owen, *Biblical Theology*, 56–57.

gospel proclamation and God's gift of grace-faith-salvation together intervene against sin to make the soul capable of spiritual discernment and faith.

Any person who seeks a relationship with God and deliverance from sin will be saved. I have God's word that this is true. Sinner put aside thoughts of unworthiness: you can never be worthy. Put aside thoughts of your guilt: only God can take away your guilt. Put aside thoughts of becoming better before you seek God: only God can make you better. Put away thoughts of inability: if you call out to Christ to save your soul God will make you able. Put aside thoughts of election: only God knows who is elect, and he saves all who come to him by faith in Christ. Hold to this one thought and pursue it with all your heart: whosoever shall call on the name of the Lord shall be saved (Acts 2:21; Romans 10:13); whosoever will, let him take of the water of life freely (Revelation 22:17); whosoever believes in Christ shall receive remission of sins (Acts 10:43); whoever believes in Christ shall have eternal life. Right now, and once for all, take the keeping of your soul out of your hands and place it in Christ's hands to be kept safe for eternity ("Believe on the Lord Jesus Christ, and you will be saved," Acts 16:31). Do you believe this?

CULPABILITY FOR SIN FROM CONCEPTION[1]

If, as Scripture teaches, all persons are culpable for the legal and moral guilt of sin from the moment of conception, then how are those persons who are mentally incompetent to make a faith-based decision—the unborn (a human being from conception to birth), infants, small children, adults who never became mentally competent—how are they able to express saving faith and be saved from their sin? The answer, as far as can be known, is that they cannot. I am not saying that a person must verbalize his or her faith in order to be saved. The expression of saving faith is not necessarily verbal. Saving faith is the positive response of the soul to God's gift of grace-faith-salvation. However, the way a person's saving faith can be known to others (other than God) is when it is verbalized or actualized. The persons under discussion cannot verbalize faith and they cannot demonstrate their faith by their works. Therefore, we cannot know if these special cases are saved

---

[1] This section is from Quiggle, *Adam and Eve*, 323–328.

because they are not capable of making their salvation (or lack of salvation) known. Since they are culpable for their sin, but, as much as we can observe, are mentally incompetent to make a faith-based decision, can they be saved? Let me firmly answer that the question is *not*, "can these persons be saved" but "how can we know if these persons can be saved?"

The answer is in the efficient cause of salvation, which is the electing choice made by God, and the means God decreed to effect and apply that salvation. The one and only basis of salvation is the propitiating death of Christ, decreed in eternity-past, accomplished in historical-present, and effective from eternity-past through eternity-future. The application of Christ's infinite merit results in the remission of sin's guilt and penalty. In those who are mentally competent to make a choice between faith and no-faith, Christ's merit is applied by their receiving God's gift of grace-faith-salvation through the means of personal faith in God's revealed means (way) of salvation. However, the unborn, infants, small children, and adults who never became mentally competent cannot, as far as is known, grasp or express saving faith. Nor does Scripture deal with their need for salvation. Scripture focuses on those who are able to make a decision for faith or no-faith. Scripture does not directly address the salvific needs of the unborn, infants, small children, and adults who never became mentally competent.

Two Scriptures are often used to defend the salvation of infants and small children (neither of which addresses the unborn or the mentally incompetent adult.) The first is 2 Samuel 12:15–23. The story is familiar to most Christians. David the king committed adultery with Bathsheba and she became pregnant. David recalled her husband from the battlefield so he could have sex with his wife and make it appear he was responsible for the pregnancy. He did not have sex with her, so David had him abandoned on the battlefield so he would die in conflict with the enemy; in God's eyes it was an act of murder. Then David married Bathsheba. The child was born. The child became ill and died. During the illness David prostrated himself in prayer and fasts. After the child died David "arose from the ground, washed and anointed himself, and changed his clothes; and he went into the house of the LORD and worshiped." His servants were amazed he did not mourn. David replied, "While the child was alive, I fasted and wept; for I said, 'Who can tell whether the LORD will be gracious to me, that the child may live?'

But now he is dead; why should I fast? Can I bring him back again? I shall go to him, but he shall not return to me." Was David saying that when he died he would meet this infant in heaven, i.e., that this infant had been saved upon its physical death? To answer this question we must ask, who was speaking? Was it David the prophet or David the grieving father? We must ask, is what David said revelation from God? The words are inspired, which means that what David said was accurately recorded, but was what David said revelation from God the Holy Spirit regarding the spiritual state of all infants? *If* David was speaking as a prophet, and *if* David knew by divine revelation the eternal fate of this one infant, does it apply to all other infants from Adam forward to the end of the world? What David said was a singular statement, meaning that nothing like it, or corresponding to it, or parallel with it, or similar to it in thought or idea, appears anywhere else in Scripture. One of the rules of theology is, do not build a doctrine from a single verse. I will respect that rule in regard to this singular verse. In my view, this one verse answers the question concerning infant salvation only if you bring the answer with you.

The second verse, rather, the incident recorded in Matthew 19, Mark 10, and Luke 18, is Jesus with little children. The passage says nothing conclusive about their salvation. Jesus was displeased that the disciples sought to prevent parents bringing their children to Jesus. However, it was culturally unusual, very unusual, that parents would bring their little children near to any "holy man," such as a rabbi, teacher, or prophet. In the ancient world children were not prized as they are today. In modern times children are evaluated on their assumed adult potential. In the ancient world children were evaluated on what they might contribute to society or family as children. As a result, they were not valued at all (a high mortality rate for infants and children did not help the situation). Christianity is actually one of the impelling reasons the attitude toward children changed. So, it was unusual in those times for parents to bring their children to a teacher, a holy man, a prophet. But they did bring their children to Jesus and he did receive them. He used them as an analogy to teach that saving faith is trusting faith, on the order of the naïve kind of trust expressed by little children: faith without suspicion; faith without doubt. The passage does not say little children will be saved, but it leaves no doubt they can be saved—if they can express saving faith.

Culpability and Inability

So, neither the 2 Samuel passage nor the gospel passages answer the question concerning the salvation of the unborn, infants, small children, and adults who never became mentally competent. To answer the question we must return to the basis of salvation, Christ's propitiation and the application of his merit to the sinner's need, and add in the final point, the choices made by God. What is required to save those who cannot express saving faith, who cannot make a choice between faith and no-faith, is God making application of the merit of Christ to the sinful condition of their soul. To whom God might apply that merit, in the special cases we are discussing, is not stated in Scripture. How God might apply that merit to those who seem incapable of acquiring (let alone expressing) saving faith is unknown in the special cases we are discussing. But that he can is undeniable. God made the soul, so he certainly knows how to communicate with the soul in any of its states from conception forward.

The application of Christ's merit is, in fact, the need of everyone. No one seeks after God, no one understands, all have gone the way of sin. If no person seeks God, if the inclination of the sin attribute is to rebel against God, then how is anyone saved? The answer is Ephesians 1:4, "God chose us in Christ before the foundation of the world." No human being is beyond the reach of God's electing choice. All those whom God has elected will certainly be saved. In this present age between Christ's two advents those persons who are mentally competent to understand and respond in faith will be saved only by hearing the gospel of salvation in Jesus Christ; Scripture gives no other way to their salvation. As to the unborn, infants, and others similarly mentally unable to believe, if they are saved "it cannot be on their own merits, or on the basis of their own righteousness or innocence, but must be entirely on the basis of Christ's redemptive work and regeneration by the work of the Holy Spirit within them."[1] Grudem (looking at Psalm 22:10; Luke 1:15) writes, "It is clear, therefore, that God is able to save infants in an unusual way, apart from their hearing and understanding the gospel, by bringing regeneration to them very early, sometimes even before birth . . . If they are saved, it will be on the basis of Christ's redeeming work; and their regeneration . . . will be by God's

---

[1] Grudem, *Theology*, 500.

mercy and grace."[1]

If God has chosen any one of these mentally incompetent persons to salvation, then God will by grace give them the gift of grace-faith-salvation; and by grace they will positively respond by receiving the gift and applying it to their spiritual circumstances; and by grace God will apply the merit of Christ to their soul and save them. The manner of their positive response—how they might express saving faith—cannot be known, because they cannot tell us by word or deed.

God's electing choice is the primary condition affecting the salvation of all human beings from Adam forward: he saves whom he has chosen; he prevents no one from coming to him to be saved. Beyond this no one can go with certainty. No one can say with scriptural certainty that all, some, or none of the unborn, infants, small children, or adults who never became mentally competent are saved. Perhaps God has elected every single person who dies in the womb, or who is born but dies before developing the mental maturity to decide for faith or no-faith. Perhaps some of these are saved and some not. Is God righteous, holy, and just only when I understand? Certainly not! For then how will God judge the world? Whatever God has decided it is holy, it is righteous, it is just. As Abraham said, "Shall not the Judge of all the earth do right?" If all the unborn, infants, small children, and mentally incompetent adults are saved, God is just; if some, or none, are saved God is just, God is holy. Love and holiness are essential characteristics of God, out of which the communicable attributes (e.g., love, mercy, justice, wisdom) have their beginning and derive their nature. Therefore, God has no sin and takes no action that would be unjust. There is an election according to grace—the blessing of God given to those with no merit. God does make a choice, Romans 9:13, "Jacob I have loved, but Esau have I hated," that (9:11) "the children not yet being born, nor having done any good or evil, that the purpose of God according to election might stand, not of works, but of him who calls." God has chosen not to reveal the why or who of his electing choice. One must either accept that God is holy, righteous, and just in all his ways, or create a soteriology not based on Scripture.

What has been said about the unborn, infants, small children,

---

[1] Ibid.

and others similarly mentally incompetent to understand and make a choice between faith or no-faith cannot be applied to those who have developed the mental competence to make such a decision. All mentally competent people in this age between Christ's two advents are morally required to believe on Jesus the Christ as their Savior. All Christians are required to "go therefore and make disciples of all the nations, baptizing them in the name of the Father and of the Son and of the Holy Spirit." How God deals with the special cases is one of the "secret things [that] belong to the LORD our God, but those things which are revealed belong to us and to our children forever, that we may do all the words of this law" (Deuteronomy 29:29). This also is part of the doctrine of soteriology. Therefore, let us preach the gospel to every soul that has the mental competence to understand and respond to it.

8. SAVING FAITH

STATEMENT OF THE DOCTRINE

A sinner is not enabled to believe, he or she is empowered to believe, John 1:12–13.

> But as many as received Him, to them He gave the right [Greek: *exousía*, "authority"] to become children of God, to those who believe in His name: who were born, not of blood, nor of the will of the flesh, nor of the will of man, but of God.

The sinner is convicted through the work of God the Holy Spirit of the truth of personal sin, the judicial guilt and punishment of sin, the need for salvation by faith not works, and the all-sufficiency of the propitiation made by Jesus Christ the Savior that is required to save his or her soul. On the basis of that conviction the sinner personally appropriates and applies those truths to satisfy his or her spiritual need for salvation. That personal appropriation and application of truth is the exercise of saving faith.

Election is not salvation. Election is the efficient cause of salvation; personal faith is the instrumental cause. The elect are sinners before they are saved: they must seek salvation, must be convicted of their sin, must receive God's gift of grace-faith-salvation, and must exercise saving faith in order for their election in eternity-past to become salvation in their historical-present. In this chapter we will conduct a very thorough investigation of salvation and saving faith.

WHAT IS SALVATION?

Salvation is when God rescues a sinner out of the state of spiritual death and delivers him or her into a permanent state of spiritual life. Salvation is the remission of sin's guilt and penalty by the application of Christ's infinite merit, which is gained by receiving God's gift of grace-faith-salvation, and by means of that gift expressing personal faith in God's revealed way of salvation. In this New Testament age salvation occurs when a sinner repents of his or her sins and believes on Christ as their Savior: Acts 2:38; 3:19–20; 11:18; Romans 3:22–26; 10:9–10, 13; Galatians 3:22; 1 Peter 1:21; 1 John 3:23.

Salvation is an instantaneous act with several results (not given in a specific order of occurrence). God imparts eternal life, John

17:2–3; Romans 6:23b; 1 John 2:25, which is God sharing (in a participatory way) the communicable aspects of his eternal life. It is this sharing of eternal life that causes the believer's spiritual faculty to come to life, creating communion with God and enabling spiritual understanding. The righteousness of Christ is imputed to the now-believing sinner, freeing him or her from the judicial guilt and penalty of sin because Christ has satisfied God's law on behalf of the sinner, Romans 6:23. The now-saved sinner has been reconciled to God, 2 Corinthians 5:18–19. This brings peace with God, Romans 5:1, because with sin forgiven (Ephesians 1:7), and the judicial penalty satisfied through Christ's propitiation (1 John 2:2), there is no more enmity between God and the believer. The Holy Spirit accomplishes the sanctification of the believer, which is to set the believer apart from the defilement caused by sin and dedicate him to God, Ephesians 1:4; 1 Corinthians 1:30; 1 Peter 1:2. In the act of sanctification sin loses its dominating power, Romans 6:14–23, and a new principle of life, holiness, is added to the believer, Ephesians 4:24, becoming the dominating principle in his human nature, 1 Thessalonians 4:7; 1 Corinthians 3:17b; Colossians 3:12; 1 Peter 1:15. In what might be called both the initiating and culminating event, the Holy Spirit takes up permanent residence in the believer's soul, John 14:17; Acts 10:44–48; 1 Corinthians 6:19. The believer now stands before God in Christ as forgiven, sanctified, justified, regenerated, filled with eternal life, and indwelt by the Holy Spirit. He is freed from the penalty, power, and pleasure of sin, with absolute assurance of the future transformation and glorification of his human nature and body, so that he will be freed eternally from the presence of sin. He is empowered to resist sin's temptations, live a holy life, understand the Scripture, worship, obey, fellowship with, and serve God. God hears and answers his prayers, and he (or she) perseveres in the faith to lead a holy life, looking toward resurrection and an eternal life in God's presence.

What is righteousness? The term "righteous" means to be right, fair, and just. At its heart it is a description of moral character. "Righteousness is that attribute by which God's nature is seen to be the perfect standard of what is right."[1] The term "righteous" is used in two contexts in the Scripture. The first relates to the state of the

---

[1] Elwell, *Dictionary*, s. v. "righteousness."

soul in regard to salvation and thus applies to this discussion.[1] The soul is either in a state of sin or a state of righteousness. When the sinner has faith in the saving work of Jesus Christ, God pronounces the sinner just or righteous: the righteousness of Christ is imputed to the believer. Just as Adam's sin-guilt was imputed to those who were condemned by him (by his sin), even so Christ's righteousness is imputed to those who are saved by him (by faith in him as Savior). When Christ's righteousness is imputed to the believer God declares that the claims of justice against the sinner, so far as God is concerned, are satisfied on behalf of the sinner by the death and resurrection of Christ, so that the saved sinner cannot now be justly condemned.[2] The righteousness of salvation is that moral standing in which the saved sinner stands uncondemned before God by reason of saving faith in Christ.

What is propitiation? Propitiation is the full and complete satisfaction Christ made to God for man's crime of sin. He did this by suffering God's wrath and dying on the cross while bearing the imputed guilt of man's sin, and then resurrecting out from death. His resurrection demonstrated the punishment due the crime of sin had been fully satisfied, i.e., God had been propitiated. Christ did not make it possible for a person to earn salvation through good works; Christ's propitiation is applied to the sinner's condition by God's grace alone (not gained by works, lest we should boast) through personal faith alone. The propitiation he made fully satisfied God's holiness and justice for the crime of sin. Christ's propitiation was of infinite merit, because his Person is of infinite worth. The application of that merit is personally applied by the sinner to his or her sin through faith in Christ.

WHAT IS SAVING FAITH?

Saving faith is both rational and super-natural (above-nature: greater than and not bound by the natural laws of the universe):

---

[1] Ibid. The second context is moral acts. In the context of actions, righteousness is behavior toward God and man that is in keeping with the moral standard set by God's character. One must realize that righteous acts arise out of a righteous nature. "It is not we who possess righteousness but righteousness which possesses us; we are its servants" (Romans 6:18; 2 Corinthians 2:9). The moral opposite of righteousness (righteous actions) is lawlessness: to oppose or to have contempt for God and his law.

[2] Ibid.

there is a super-natural God-ward perspective and there is a rational man-ward perspective. In the super-natural God-ward perspective, faith is when God gives conviction of truth in the inner experience of the soul. God-given conviction is the absolute, undeniable, unquestioned, certain, and sure receipt of truth as originating in and communicated from God. No person—saved or unsaved—can obtain this certainty through his or her rational faculties. Only God, by his Holy Spirit, can give absolute certainty, unwavering conviction.[1] This is the part of faith that is God's gift in salvation. In the God-ward perspective, God-given conviction of truth infallibly results in the sinner's positive response of faith to the testimony of God (given in the gospel).

From the rational man-ward perspective, man considers the facts of salvation as to their authenticity, credibility, and accuracy. Did these facts originate in God? Can they be believed? Is the information true as opposed to false? A person may come to a rational conclusion that the facts are authentic, credible, and accurate. The rational conclusion may be persuasive, perhaps even life-changing, but it cannot effect change in the soul's sinful state. A rational conclusion cannot change the state of the soul because such a conclusion is part of man's human essence, which is corrupted and dominated by sin. A rational conclusion may be accepted, modified, or rejected, according to the disposition of a person's nature. Only a super-natural intervention—God's gift of conviction, given by his grace, and thus infallibly leading to faith, can turn a rational conclusion into saving faith and change the state of the soul from sinner to saved. Without the certainty of God-given conviction, rationally accepted facts are not saving faith, they are not soul-changing. When the sinner considers the facts of the gospel and expresses saving faith it is because 1) he has come to a rational conclusion the facts are true and apply to his (or her) specific spiritual needs, and 2) God gave the conviction they are true and the faith to apply them: the gift of grace-faith-salvation. In the man-ward perspective faith is the necessary positive response to God's convicting testimony given in the Scripture.

Allow me to explain this dual perspective on faith in more

---

[1] As in all things spiritual, Satan has his counterfeit, a fanatical zeal. Satan's counterfeit is always in some manner destructive. God's conviction is a life-changing, positive, constructive force for the good of the soul.

technical terms. God's part in saving faith is to give a sinner personal understanding and infallible conviction that the facts concerning his spiritual state are true. Those facts are his personal sin, the eternal punishment due his sin, that Jesus suffered the penalty for his sin, and that faith in Jesus will save him from his sin. The sinner's part is to exercise his or her rational faculties in the certainty of spiritual truth and respond with saving faith. The sinner who receives God's gift will respond to the inner experience of God-given conviction of truth (God's gift of faith) with an outward response (man's responsive faith) that conforms his thoughts and actions to the truth conveyed in that inner, God-given conviction of truth. Thus, the conviction-faith that I am a sinner and Jesus is my only Savior has its origin and source in God alone. That conviction is regenerative in that it restores the spiritual perception required to make a faith decision to believe on Jesus Christ for personal salvation. The soul's response to God given conviction-faith is the personal faith that "Jesus is the only Savior for me!" Therefore, saving faith always consists of God's gift and man's response. The sinner is not "enabled" to believe; he is convicted of the truth and on the basis of that conviction he personally appropriates the truth to his specific circumstances. He receives God's gift of salvation by means of faith: he believes-accepts-receives-responds to Jesus as "My Savior." This is God's sovereignty, working through man's responsibility, to infallibly accomplish God's purposes and plans in his election of sinners in Christ to salvation, in love by grace through faith.

Saving faith, then, has two complementary components. God convicts men about the state of their soul and men reason about the state of their soul. God gives the means to salvation and men use the means to salvation. God elects men to salvation in Christ and men have faith in Christ as their Savior. The Scripture teaches God giving the gift and man's duty to believe as equally true and necessary. Therefore, one must accept these truths as complementary not contradictory. In his sermon "Faith and Regeneration," Charles Spurgeon addressed faith both as man's duty to believe and as the gift of God. In summarizing his argument he said,

> Brethren be willing to see both sides of the shield of truth. Rise above the babyhood which cannot believe two doctrines until it sees the connecting link. Have you not two eyes, man? Must you

needs put one of them out in order to see clearly? Is it impossible to you to use a spiritual stereoscope, and look at two views of truth until they melt into one, and that one becomes more real and actual because it is made up of two? Many men refuse to see more than one side of a doctrine, and persistently fight against anything which is not on its very surface consistent with their own idea. In the present case I do not find it difficult to believe faith to be at the same time the duty of man and the gift of God; and if others cannot accept the two truths, I am not responsible for their rejection of them; my duty is performed when I have honestly borne witness to them.[1]

Faith is the result of God's gift of grace-faith-salvation, which grace includes the conviction concerning man as sinner and Christ as Savior, and faith is man's response to God's gift. Without the gift man is unable to believe. By the gift man is regenerated so as to be able to believe. Through personal faith man is saved.

EVERYONE NEEDS SALVATION

Everyone is a sinner, Romans 3:23, "all have sinned." Since everyone is a sinner then everyone needs salvation. The "wages" of sin is death (Romans 6:23), meaning not just physical death but spiritual death, which is an eternal separation from God and an eternal punishment for sin. Salvation rescues the sinner from the guilt and punishment due his or her sin and places the saved person in a permanent relationship with God.

Ephesians 1:7, 8 states, "In Him we have redemption through His blood, the forgiveness of sins, according to the riches of His grace which He made to abound toward us in all wisdom and prudence." Scripture views all persons as due the penalty of death because of their personal guilt for their crime of sin, Romans 5:12–21. The reference "through his blood" is to the death of Jesus on the cross. Jesus has given his life in substitution for the death due the believer because of the penalty of sin, Romans 6:23. Therefore, the believing sinner is redeemed through Jesus' death and his sins are forgiven. The believing sinner's sins are forgiven because the death of Jesus propitiated God for the crime of sin. "Propitiation" is what God did for himself to satisfy his holiness, righteousness, and his justice for the crime of sin. God personally, in the Person of Jesus the Christ, suffered the penalty he had decreed as due the

---

[1] Spurgeon, *Collection*, Metropolitan Tabernacle, Vol. 17, Sermon No. 979.

crime of sin. When the sinner believes God's testimony that Jesus paid for his sin, then the merit of Jesus' propitiating sacrifice is applied to the believer to redeem him from sin's guilt and penalty, and thereby his sins are forgiven. Saving faith is believing that Jesus assumed to himself the guilt of my sin and suffered sin's penalty due me (Romans 5:8), that my sins could be forgiven and I could be redeemed.

Redemption, *apolútrōsis*, means to set free by paying a ransom, and thus may rightly be viewed as an exchange. I exchange something of value for the item I want to redeem. The item being redeemed is under the control of another. I might redeem a lawbreaker from the possession and control of the police through an exchange of something of equal or greater value: a bail bond. The redemption of a sinner's soul is more serious, and the item of exchange of far greater value: Christ, acting out of his great love, redeems the sinner out of enslavement to sin through the offering of his own soul. In the theology of redemption, sin is (anthropomorphically) viewed as the owner of the sinner's soul; the soul is viewed as the property—the slave—of sin. Sin is constantly "selling" his slave to do evil; to do acts of sin. As a sinner I might say that I am not as bad as the next man—I haven't killed anyone. But the fact is that I am guilty of sin, regardless of what evil acts might or might not be committed. Sin, of course, is not a slave owner, that is simply an illustration of the power of evil in human nature. Sin, as previously discussed, is a principle of evil that is part of human nature. God says every act of sin is the willing choice of human nature to do evil, and the punishment for every sin is death. More than this, unless the soul is redeemed, the eventual destiny of every sinner is an eternal death. The redemption price for the human soul, the thing of greater value that redeems the sinner's soul from sin and death, is the soul of Christ, enduring the punishment of sin and death on the cross. The suffering of his soul—enduring God's wrath, spiritual separation, physical death—was the price required to buy the sinner out of the slave market of sin and eternal death.

How, then, is this transaction of redemption accomplished for the individual sinner? Sin forms a barrier between the sinner and God. The sinner cannot breach that barrier except by the instrument of personal faith in Christ as Savior. God will reach out to the sinner only through the love he has expressed in the

Saving Faith

redemptive death of Christ. God presents this testimony to every sinner: *In my love for you, Christ suffered the penalty due to you for your sin, to redeem you out of sin and death.* That was the redemption price. God's love met the crime of sin by sending his Son to die for your sin. How do you, personally, apply that redemption price to your need? It is there, waiting for you to accept it. God holds it out to you: if you will believe that you are a sinner needing salvation; that no efforts of your own can save your soul; that Jesus Christ died for your sins; then God will save your soul by applying Christ's payment for sin to the spiritual need of your soul. God will forgive your sins and give you eternal life. How can you receive God's gift of salvation in Christ? Faith is believing that God's testimony is true; faith is taking action just because I do believe. Faith is the hand of your soul reaching out to receive God's gift of salvation and apply it to your soul to take away the guilt and penalty of sin. Right now and once for all, take the keeping of your soul out of your hands, and place the eternal destiny and well-being of your soul into the hands of Christ. The wages of sin is death. God's gift is eternal life through Jesus Christ our Lord: let Christ keep your soul safe for eternity. God's holiness and justice demanded that sin's guilt be paid before there could be any relationship between you and God; and then in mercy God's love sent his Son to be the payment, the way of redemption. "In this is love, not that we have loved God but that he loved us and sent his Son to be the propitiation [payment] for [the crime of] our sins" (1 John 4:10).

ACCORDING TO THE RICHES OF HIS GRACE

The greatness of redemption is measured by the riches of God's grace. The defilement of sin affects all parts of a person's human nature, so that he or she willingly sells themselves as sin's slave. The guilt of sin swallows the soul whole, placing the person under the divine sentence of eternal death. The guilt of sin is so vast, and it's defilement so deep, that only the sinless infinite merit of Christ could satisfy God's justice for his broken law and his outraged holiness at sin's defilement. In Christ God satisfied himself for sin. In Christ's propitiation God rescued and cleansed his creation from sin's defilement, creating the basis on which he could act in blessing toward his defiled creation. As to mankind, God could have justly allowed all men to personally suffer the penalty for their sin. Such suffering would be endless, because no person has the intrinsic merit, the innate holiness, with which to satisfy God for the crime. Nothing within a person could cause any man or woman to be deserving of redemption. Everything about a person, about themselves, that people think is righteous, is as an unclean thing in God's sight, Isaiah 64:6; Romans 3:10–18. Only the death of Christ could redeem the sinner from sin's guilt and penalty, for only his death had sufficient merit to pay for all the guilt and penalty due sin, and cleanse the sinner from sin's defilement. How then was the merit of Christ to be applied to sinners for their redemption? The answer is God's grace. No person merits salvation. The richness of God's grace is that although there is abundant demerit on the sinner's part, God applies the full merit of Christ's propitiation to fully forgive a person of the guilt of their sins, and to fully redeem the person from sin's penalty. God made grace "abound," a word (*perisseúō*) meaning the grace God extended to save sinners was much more than needed to effect their redemption. God's grace in salvation overflows man's need; it is more than sufficient to overcome the demerit of every sin.

The demerit of the judicial guilt of sin is eternal in the unsaved, but it is not infinite. The demerit of sin is necessarily confined to the sinner, who is a finite being; therefore the demerit of his sin is finite. But the sinner has no merit with which to satisfy the guilt of sin; thus the guilt, and the sinner's punishment for that guilt, is eternal, because the sinner has no way to satisfy the debt caused by the crime. Only a merit greater than the demerit of sin can overcome the judicial guilt of sin. The greater merit needed is an infinite merit. Christ's merit is infinitely meritorious because 1) he was sinless, suffering unjustly for the sins of others, and 2) because he is the God-man, giving infinite worth to his vicarious death. How then is a sinner saved? The infinite merit of Christ's propitiation must be individually applied to each sinner. The means by which the merit of the propitiation is applied to save the soul from sin, is by faith in God's promise of salvation through Christ's propitiation. The relationship of the demerit of the sinner to the merit of Christ is illustrated by the relationship of a drop of water to all the world's oceans. The merit of Christ's propitiation satisfies all the guilt and all the penalty of all the sinner's sins for eternity.

How can we understand the great blessing of the riches of God's grace? There is a relationship between redemption and forgiveness in Ephesians 1:7, wisdom and prudence in v. 8, and the mystery of his will in v. 9 that will help us understand.

> (7)in Him we have redemption through His blood, the forgiveness of sins, according to the riches of His grace (8)which He made to abound toward us in all wisdom and prudence, (9)having made known to us the mystery of His will, according to His good pleasure which He purposed in Himself,

To understand this relationship we must discern the grammatical and literary connections between the verses. Is v. 8 connected with v. 7 or v. 9? Three possible connections have been proposed and defended.

> The phrase "in all wisdom and prudence" may be connected with the verb, "made to abound," meaning that God has made his grace abound toward men in the exercise of his wisdom and prudence.
>
> The phrase "in all wisdom and prudence" may be connected with what follows, meaning that "in all [his] wisdom and prudence God has made known to us the mystery of his will."
>
> The phrase "in all wisdom and prudence" may be connected with the relative pronoun, meaning that God made his grace, wisdom, and prudence abound toward us.

Many commentators believe the phrase should be connected with verse nine, but this raises the question framed by options two and three: "Does Paul mean that God exercises *his own* wisdom and understanding when he makes known his will, or does Paul refer to the wisdom and understanding *given to human beings* when he makes his will known?"[1] "Prudence" might be defined as insight or discernment, thus in the second view wisdom and prudence are given to men so they can have insight into, or can discern, the mysteries of God's will.[2] This seems contrary to the meaning and use of *mustérion* (mystery, v. 9) in Scripture, as knowledge not discernible by man but knowable when revealed by God.[3] In the third view, to say that God exercises his own wisdom and insight

---

[1] Snodgrass, *Ephesians*, 52.
[2] Hoehner, *Ephesians*, 212.
[3] Colossians 1:9, which seems to be a corresponding use, addresses a different aspect of God's will (not *mustérion*), and does not use the word *phrónēsis* (prudence).

(discernment) in revealing his will seems redundant, and few take this view of the phrase.

The first option, that "God has made his grace abound toward men in the exercise of his wisdom and prudence," seems the one most in keeping with Paul's exaltation of God's sovereignty in giving spiritual blessings: he blessed, chose, predestined, and made us, according to his will, good pleasure, purpose, and counsel. God exercises his own prudence and wisdom in making grace abound. The main objection to this view is that "prudence" is not normally applied to God, although the Greek word (*phrónēsis*) is used of God in the LXX, for example in Jeremiah 10:12, Proverbs 3:19; 8:14. The concept of prudence, however, is quite applicable to God. Prudence is the action of God's wisdom in forming his purposes and decrees.[1] "In the outworking of the plan of redemption, God has wrought on an infinite plane and has disclosed the unsearchable depths of his wisdom and prudence."[2]

God's grace in redeeming men through the blood of Christ was applied to the sinner in the exercise of his wisdom and prudence. I will discuss prudence below. The word translated wisdom is *sophía*. Wisdom is not the cause of God's grace. God's grace is applied according to his wisdom. God's wisdom is more than knowledge, it is God's ability to use his knowledge in a perfect manner to fully meet and satisfy the circumstances. In man, wisdom is the skill to use knowledge rightly: applied appropriate to the need, and used rightly in a moral sense. God used his knowledge in way that maintained and effected his justice, righteousness, and holiness. God's *sophía* applied his grace to meet sin's demerit in such a way that his holiness, justice, and righteousness could be satisfied. God did not merely forgive, he redeemed. He rescued the sinner by giving the ransom of his (God's) personal suffering for sin's guilt and just penalty. In this way God's holy and just sentence of the death due sin was upheld. Love desired the sinner's redemption; holiness demanded the sinner's punishment; wisdom met these requirements in the death of Christ to propitiate God for the debt of sin; grace applies the benefits of Christ's propitiation to the sinner; wisdom and prudence guided (informed) the application of grace to individual sinners. God's wisdom was at work in his election of

---

[1] Eadie, *Ephesians*, 47.
[2] Chafer, *Ephesians*, 47.

sinners to salvation. Election, then, is not capricious, nor biased, nor an unjust choice, but as informed by God's wisdom is fully consistent with God's love, holiness, righteousness, and justice.

The word translated prudence is *phrónēsis*. The connection of "wisdom and prudence" is by some commentators[1] identified as a figure of speech known as a hendiadys, where two words express the same idea, that is, they have similar meanings and function synonymously. However, there is a complementary difference in the way the Scripture uses *sophía* and *phrónēsis*. The Greek *phrónēsis* means "understanding," which is the proper use of knowledge (*ginóskō*) and wisdom (*sophía*) that leads to self-guidance. The person with understanding (*phrónēsis*) is able to make appropriate decisions for life's choices. God is fully capable of perfectly applying grace to meet the circumstances. He is a God of integrity who makes choices according to his character. Grace is not God's favor blindly applied, nor is it blessing indiscriminately applied; grace is blessing extended to the undeserving in a manner that is consistent with God's sovereignty, wisdom, love, and holiness.

SAVED BY GRACE THROUGH FAITH

Saved by God's Great Love and Rich Mercy

The reasoning process that leads to Ephesians 2:8–9, salvation by grace alone through faith alone, begins at 2:1, the saved sinner was dead in his or her sins, but God has made the sinner alive, v. 5, through salvation by grace through faith, vv. 8–9. Salvation fulfills more than one purpose, but Paul states the ultimate purpose, which is to display the riches of God's grace, v. 7, which agrees with God's purposes in creating and electing, which was to manifest his glory. Here, we will pick up Paul's discussion in vv. 4–5, then jump to vv. 8–9. Ephesians 2:4–5 read,

> (4)But God, who is rich in mercy, because of His great love with which He loved us, (5)even when we were dead in trespasses, made us alive together with Christ (by grace you have been saved),

A more literal translation according to the Greek text would be:

> (4)But God being rich in mercy, because of his great love with which he loved us, (5)we even being dead in trespasses, made [us]

---

[1] Lincoln, *Ephesians*, 29; Snodgrass, *Ephesians*, 52.

alive together with Christ—by grace you are having been saved—

The word translated "but" in v. 4 is *dé*, an adversative conjunction indicating a contrast. The contrast is with 2:1. You [the sinner] were dead in your trespasses and sins . . . but [v. 4] God is abundant in mercy, [which mercy is] because of his great love . . . and [v. 5] he has made the sinner alive with Christ. The cause of God's abounding mercy is his love.

God's love, as previously noted, does not exclude sentiment but does not originate in sentiment. God's love is the decision of his will to establish a salvific relationship with the sinner, as the beginning of his eternal fellowship with the saved sinner. God's attributes, such as his love, do not function in isolation from his other attributes. Again, as previously discussed, God is not a union, a joining together, of attributes; God is a simple, uncompounded unity. Each attribute of God operates in perfect harmony with all other attributes. For example, Christ's sacrifice on the cross was an expression of God's love for the sinner, but also an expression of his holiness in punishing sin, his justice toward the sinner for the crime of sin, mercy in that Christ suffered in place of the sinner, etc. The great love that caused God to extend his mercy to save certain sinners (election) was a necessary part of his decision in eternity-past to establish a salvific relationship with certain sinners. From God's point of view the decision to elect and the decision to love the elect were not separate decisions but one and the same. His mercy toward his elect was the necessary outworking of his electing love.

Returning to Ephesians 2:4, the words "because of" ("because of his great love") are the translation of *diá*, a preposition meaning through or throughout, depending on whether the noun is in the accusative or genitive case. Here, "with which" (*hèn*) is in the accusative case. God's abounding mercy is extended toward sinners through (on account of, because of) his great love. The word "love" is *agápē*, the selfless love that seeks the best good for another, without thought of recompense or reciprocity, and without consideration of merit or demerit. An *agápē* love recognizes that its object is undeserving. An *agápē* love is given without respect to any merit, for its object has none, and this is the context here, sinners dead in trespasses and sins. God's mercy, *éleos*, is his active pity or compassion. Mercy defers judgment and relieves misery. Both ideas are present. God did not execute the judgment we deserved as sinners, and he relieved our misery by forgiving our sin and delivering us from his wrath. God's mercy is extended toward all mankind, but it accomplishes different ends according to God's purposes. Mercy can relieve suffering, which is an expression of God's goodness toward all. Mercy can also defer, but not stop, deserved judgment, giving sinners an opportunity to respond to the offer of salvation. Mercy can work with grace and love to bring about salvation, and that is Paul's use here. Mercy is God acting compassionately to save his people from their sins. The basis for his mercy is his covenant with Jesus to provide salvation for whosoever will seek salvation by faith in Jesus; specifically for the elect. I am not saying God's mercy in salvation is without sentiment, for what is pity, compassion, and kindness if not sentiment? But all God's actions toward his people begin with "he chose us in Christ" and therefore are consummated through his covenant with Jesus Christ the Redeemer.

God is the One "who is rich in mercy." The participle *on* ("being," "the one who"), translated "who," does not have a causal significance. "Rather, the participle characterizes the general principle under which the divine compassion was exhibited."[1] The better translation is, "but God being rich in mercy." The word "rich" is the Greek *ploúsios*, meaning rich or wealthy. God's character abounds in mercy; mercy flows out from God, so much so that it overflows, exceeding the creature's need. His abundance of mercy is from his "great" love. The Greek translated "great" is *polús*, meaning many, much quantity. The intensity or degree of love is being emphasized. His love encompassed many objects (all those being saved) and provided mercy for them above their needs. The richness and greatness of God's love is commensurate with his omnipotence and omniscience. His love and his holiness equally pervade and define his works.

The word translated "even" in 2:5 ("even when we were dead in trespasses and sins") is *kaí*, which is usually translated "and" or "also" to connect two coordinate ideas. "Even" is the better translation here, because the two ideas that *kaí* connects, "because of his great love with which he loved us," and "we being dead in trespasses," are not coordinate. Nor, although Paul repeats 2:1, is *kaí* a continuation of v. 1. There is lack of harmony between the

---

[1] Hoehner, *Ephesians*, 327.

two main ideas that emphasizes the richness of God's mercy and love and grace, and man's absolute spiritual destitution. God's love was extended in mercy toward those who were incapable of appreciating, accepting, or recompensing such love because they were spiritually dead. Translating *kaí* as "even" indicates the emphasis: God's love is extended toward the spiritually dead, who are uncaring about him and undeserving of his love. There is also a temporal sense.[1] God's love was extended toward those who were in the past spiritually dead, but whom his love has now made spiritually alive. With the temporal sense, the word "being" (*óntas*) which follows "even" (*kaí*) is more properly translated "when." Thus, as the NKJV has it, God loved us "even when" we were dead in trespasses. As John said, (1 John 4:19), we love him because "he first loved us."

Paul repeats "trespasses" (*paráptōma*) from 2:1 but does not repeat "and sins" (*hamartía*) because these Greek words are being used as synonyms. The thought of deliberate transgression is sufficiently summed by *paráptōma* without again adding *hamartía*. The word *paráptōma* means "wrong doing," and in the plural, as it is here, indicates individual acts of sin. Paul is not making a Hebrew-Gentile distinction in switching from "you" in v. 1 to "we" in v. 4. The "we" uses in Ephesians refer to all the Christians: Hebrew, Gentile, and Paul; the "you" uses refer to a smaller group of Christians who are part of the "we." God loved "us" sinners, including "you" Ephesians, when "we" sinners were spiritually dead. When "we" sinners were spiritually dead, God made "us" spiritually alive.

Paul says we were *suzōopoieō*, "made alive together." This is a word Paul has created from two Greek words, *sún*, a preposition meaning "with," and *zōopoieō*, "to make alive." The word *suzōopoieō* is found in Greek literature only here and Colossians 2:13. The meaning is "to make alive together [with someone]." The root word, *zōopoieō*, is used eleven times in the New Testament.[2] The word is used to indicate God giving spiritual life, or to indicate resurrection. Through Christ, who was physically dead and rose physically to new life, God gave new spiritual life to sinners who

---

[1] Ibid., 329.
[2] John 5:21 (X2); 6:63; Romans 4:17; 8:11; 1 Corinthians 15:22, 36, 45; Galatians 3:21; 1 Peter 3:18.

were spiritually dead. The point of *suzōopoieō* is that spiritual life is only in Christ. Paul is not making a reference to the believer's spiritual participation in Christ's death, as he does in Romans 6, but to the contrast of once being spiritually dead outside of Christ but now being spiritually alive in Christ. Spiritual life is found only in the total identification of the sinner with Christ by faith.

This verb *suzōopoieō* is a constative aorist (as are "raised together" and "sit together" in v. 6). The constative aorist views the entire action indicated by the verb without reference to beginning, progress, or end. This tense seems most appropriate to me. Once a sinner is saved his state of spiritual life is constant and unending. Because the sinner became alive when he believed in Christ, his life can be viewed as beginning at that moment of faith; moreover, his spiritual life in Christ never ends; therefore, it is appropriate to view the believer as always being in the state of spiritual life. His life began with Christ and never ends in Christ. Although the believer had a past, that past becomes unimportant to his or her spiritual life.

Paul then makes what appears to be a parenthetical comment: "by grace you are saved." The NKJV and NIV translation, "by grace you have been saved" is wrong. The word *esté*, "are," which these translations translate "have been," is in the present tense, indicative mood, which in Greek speaks of contemporaneous action. The word "saved," *sózō*, is a participle in the perfect tense, which speaks of a past completed action with continuing results in the present time. God saved the believer by his grace in the past, and by his grace God maintains the believer's salvation in the present.

The combination of present and perfect tenses is difficult to express in English. A more appropriate translation would be "by grace you are having been saved," which is clumsy English, but indicates the present continuing result of a past completed action. A less clumsy translation would be "by grace you are being saved," but in English "are being saved" implies a not yet completed process. The NKJV, NIV "you have been saved" communicates the past completed action, but fails to indicate clearly the present continuing result. Therefore, the better translation in English is "by grace you are saved," since the verb "are" indicates a present state of being, and the verb "saved" indicates a past completed action with continuing present results.

Grace is often defined as unmerited blessing, which it is, but the thought of positive demerit in the recipient must be incorporated if one is to properly understand grace. By "positive demerit" I mean active opposition toward God. Even the most moral and kind person one might imagine is a sinner actively opposing God: because Christ is not his Savior; because God is not the god he worships, obeys, serves, and has fellowship with; because the one true God is not the one and only God for whose glory he lives and acts. Without a saving relationship with God in Christ, all a person might do originates in a human nature defiled and dominated by sin, therefore unacceptable to God, who hates sin and must punish sinners. Toward such persons blessing is extended by grace. Toward such persons, God's grace is the means whereby his gift of saving faith is given to those who rebel against him, and disobey him, and cannot originate a desire to be saved by him. It is on the basis of grace that God saves, *sózō*, those who deserve nothing but wrath. The word *sózō* has a general meaning of "to rescue," with a broad variety of applications. Here, because the context is spiritual life, *sózō* means to rescue from spiritual death. That the rescue was performed against the opposition of the sinner's positive demerit reveals the desperate case of the sinner: there is no innate merit in the sinner to be the basis of salvation; grace alone can overcome sin's demerit.

Why Paul makes this parenthetical statement in v. 4 cannot be known with certainty. That it is not an insertion made by a copyist seems certain from the manuscript evidence. The thought he inserts here is further developed in vv. 8–10. It may be Paul wanted to emphasize that the difference between spiritual death and spiritual life is never the result of any innate merit in the sinner; that the richness of God's mercy, and the greatness of his love, sufficient as it is to wipe away all sin, is effective only on the basis of his grace.

Saved by God's Grace

We now turn to Ephesians 2:8–9, which reads, "For by grace you have been saved through faith, and that not of yourselves; it is the gift of God, not of works, lest anyone should boast." A more literal translation according to the Greek text is:

> For by [the] grace you are having been saved through [the] faith; and this not of you, of God the gift; not of works, that not anyone should boast.

Saving Faith

The Greek text opens with an untranslated article, "the," which I have shown in brackets, above. The article refers back to the grace mentioned in v. 5, indicating Paul is going to further develop and explain that statement. The opening *gár*, "for," indicates Paul is going to explain that salvation is of God alone, i.e., by means of his grace, and therefore does not originate in or result from the efforts of the unsaved sinner. The NKJV and NIV translation, "you have been saved" is, as in v. 5, an attempt to render the Greek present tense of *esté* (are; have been) and the perfect tense of the verb *sózō* (saved). However, as explained above, this is not the best translation. The better translation is "you are saved."

The definite article is present before "faith" (in brackets, above). Paul uses *diá tas pístis*, "through the faith," in Romans, 2 Corinthians, Galatians, Ephesians, Philippians, Colossians, and 2 Timothy (but the article is not translated). The phrase indicates the subjective means by which one is saved. Wuest gives an expanded translation[1] of Ephesians 2:8–9 that communicates the Greek text as the first readers would have understood them:

> For by the grace have you been saved in time past completely, through faith, with the result that your salvation persists through present time; and this (salvation) is not from you as a source. Of God it is the gift; not from a source of works, in order that no one might boast;

Grace, *cháris*—here it is the dative[2] grammatical form c*hárití*—is the means or cause of salvation, and therefore salvation is "by grace." It is only on the basis of grace that a sinner is saved (and it is only on the basis of grace that one's salvation is maintained). Grace is the objective cause or basis of salvation, and "faith" is the subjective means by which one is saved. The distinction is important both in the Greek grammar of the sentence and in the theology of salvation. The subjective act of faith is to receive salvation. God, through his grace, is the objective cause which initiates and maintains salvation. Since God, by his grace, is the initiator, then salvation cannot rest in the merit of the one being saved, but in the one doing the saving—God. (It is also reasonable that grace, not faith, maintains the believer in a state of salvation, because the salvation initiated by grace is a "past completed action

---

[1] Wuest, *Ephesians*, 71.
[2] Hoehner, *Ephesians*, 340.

Saving Faith

with continuing results"; therefore its maintenance cannot be by the believer's efforts but by God's grace.)

The reason faith cannot be the objective basis of salvation is because the sinner has no merit of his own to overcome the demerit of his or her sin. He or she cannot perform works to earn merit, because all a sinner's works originate in the sin attribute. Therefore any work, no matter how religious, charitable, or meritorious in the world's estimation, only results in additional demerit, because all the sinner's works originate in his sin attribute.

Nor can a sinner do meritorious works on behalf of another. If a sinner could earn merit, then it must be applied to his or her own demerit, leaving none for another person. Also, sin is personal, individually part of each soul, innate to and residing in each person's human essence, so that it cannot be affected by the works of another human being. Nor can merit be earned by a human organization and given to a sinner. An organization is not a sentient being, and the individuals in any organization are sinners who have no merit and therefore cannot earn merit for themselves or another because of their sin. Only the merit of Christ can save a soul. Nor can someone who was saved, died, and is now in heaven apply his or her merit to someone on earth. The person in heaven has no merit but that which belongs to Christ, and Christ requires each person to seek and make an individual application of his merit to their own soul by personal faith.

Because sin is a condition affecting individuals, the application of Christ's infinite merit for salvation must be individual, definite, and personal. This is where faith acts. The merit of Christ's propitiation must be individually applied to each sinner, in order for the total demerit of a person's sin to be completely overcome by the infinite merit of Christ. The means by which the merit of Christ's propitiation is applied to save the soul from sin is by the sinner having personal faith in God's promise of salvation through the merit available in Christ. The infinite merit of Christ's propitiation does for eternity satisfy all the guilt and all the penalty of all the sinner's sins. The grace which caused Christ's infinite merit to be available to the sinner is the objective cause of salvation, and the sinner's personal faith is the subjective cause that applies Christ's infinite merit to the sinner's personal demerit.

This truth of available infinite merit requiring personal individual application was designedly illustrated by the Old Testament sacrifices. The provision for forgiveness was always available, but applied only to those who brought an appropriate sacrifice by faith. In the New Testament the proper sacrifice is Christ, and a sinner is saved only when he or she puts trust in Christ as God's provision for the judicial guilt of their sin. The biblical prescription is not to believe on Christ's death, or his resurrection, or some other aspect of his life. The biblical prescription is always "believe on the Lord Jesus Christ, and you shall be saved." Trust and confidence—faith—in the Person is to receive him as Savior, which incorporates all Jesus has accomplished to secure and maintain the believer's salvation.

Again, the Old Testament provides an illustration. Abraham believed God, and his faith was accounted to him for righteousness (Romans 4:3), meaning, that by means of his personal faith in God Abraham was saved. Although Abraham later did many good works, it was his faith in God, which was prior to his works, which was the means by which he was saved. Paul makes this clear in Romans 4:4–5. The argument of James 2:21–24 is that Abraham's faith was demonstrated by the works that followed. The earlier report made of Abraham's faith, Genesis 15, was shown to be a just and accurate report as demonstrated by his faith, some 30–35 years later, Genesis 22, in his willingness to sacrifice Isaac. Thus Abraham's faith was justified, i.e., shown to be real, by his works. (Paul uses "justified" in its legal sense; Abraham uses justified in the sense of demonstrate or validate.) Salvation is by grace, the objective cause, through personal faith, the subjective means.

What, then, is faith? The word *pístis* means "trust, reliance, confidence, faith."[1] A simple illustration will communicate the biblical meaning. I have a comfortable and sturdy chair at my desk. I may proclaim the chair will support my weight, discuss it endlessly with others, pray about it, study it, test it, get schematics and diagrams and engineering reports to confirm its ability to support me, evaluate the experiences of others, and come to a conclusion that this chair is suitable and trustworthy for sitting. While such actions may be a necessary prelude to faith, none of those actions is faith. Faith occurs when I sit in the chair, putting all the facts to practical use, in confidence trusting the chair will hold my weight without failure. Faith in the chair accepts the merit of the chair, that

---

[1] Zodhiates, *WSDNT*, s. v. "4102."

is, that the chair, and only the chair, can satisfactorily meet my personal need. Faith is the means by which the greater merit is applied to the problem: in this analogy the problem is the need to sit; in life, it is the need to overcome the demerit of sin.

Saving merit, then, is not in one's self or works; it is the chair, not my faith in the chair, which supports my weight. In regard to one's soul, the merit that overcomes the guilt of sin must come from an infinitely meritorious source. Christ is that source of infinite merit which overcomes sin. The sinner can be saved only when he applies by faith Christ's payment for his (the sinner's) sin debt, as paid in full by Christ on his behalf. Faith is the sinner's decision that because of what Christ has done on his behalf God will save his soul.

In its simplest aspect salvation is the resolution of this question: "where will I spend eternity?" Will I spend an eternity of joy with God in heaven; or an eternity of punishment separated from God? The unsaved sinner has faith in himself. Returning to the chair analogy, the sinner believes that it is his faith that supports him in the chair, even if the chair is broken, rickety, decidedly unsafe, and unable to support his weight. In spiritual terms, the sinner believes that his efforts alone will cause him to merit heaven.

But the sinner with faith in Christ believes that the merit of Christ alone can and will deliver him safe and sound to heaven. When one has faith, one puts the eternal destiny of his or her soul into Christ's hands for safe-keeping. From the human point of view, faith is acting on what God says about sin, salvation, and the Savior, just because I am convicted that God is telling me the truth. Faith is believing in the reality of God's promise of salvation; faith is the certainty that salvation will be received when I trust in Christ as my Savior. It is perhaps necessary to add that faith is not blind nor is it ignorant. Faith is not (figuratively speaking) taking a step into the darkness hoping (in the sense of anxiety) there is a floor, not a chasm. Faith is taking that step into darkness because God's word says that, even if I cannot see it, there is solid ground. Faith is believing in the promise of an unseen God that salvation is secured in an unseen Savior, just because I am convicted by God's testimony—the Bible—that Jesus saves. In that perspective, from the God-ward point of view, faith is God giving certainty (conviction) through the gift of grace-faith-salvation concerning his testimony. From the man-ward point of view faith is the positive response of the soul to God-given conviction of truth: one receives God's gift of grace-faith-salvation. Saving faith results in repentance of sin, confidence in Jesus as Savior, salvation of the soul, and public confession of one's faith in Christ.

Saved by the Gift of God

That part of the Greek text of Ephesians 2:8 which refers to the gift of God is translated by the NKJV, "and that not of yourselves; it is the gift of God." The text more literally translates, "and this (*toúto*[1]) not of you. Of God [is] the gift."[2] The meaning is clear: the source of salvation is God not man. There is a grammatical question to be answered, but it does not affect the meaning. The grammatical question is, to what does *toúto*, "this," ("that" in the NKJV translation) refer? The word *toúto* is a neuter demonstrative pronoun. In an earlier discussion I noted that in English the meaning of a sentence is established by word order, but in Greek meaning is decided by word endings. This was an accurate but oversimplified explanation.

Grammatical issues such as the tense, voice, and mood of the verb, the case of the noun, the antecedent to pronouns, the association of adjectives and adverbs to nouns and verbs, gender, and number, are decided by word endings. For example, the root word of *toúto* is *hoútōs*. *Toúto* is the neuter nominative (or accusative) singular form of *hoútōs*; *toútois* is the dative plural masculine (or neuter) form; *toúton* is the accusative singular masculine form; and there are four more grammatical variations which are indicated by their respective word endings. Each form of the word has an effect on translation. Whether "the cat ate the rat" or "the rat ate the cat" is decided in Greek by the word endings on each word. The "gender" of a word is indicated by word endings and is an important factor necessary to understand the relationships of the words in a sentence. Word endings determine whether a word is masculine, feminine, or neuter. (Gender is for grammatical use, that is to say, it does not relate to any innate characteristic. A word might be feminine in one use, but masculine or neuter in other uses.) As a general rule, words that should be associated together have the same gender (as in all languages there are

---

[1] Ibid., s. v. "5124"
[2] Marshall, *Interlinear*, 762.

Saving Faith

exceptions to the general rule). Thus, in "the cat ate the rat," the words "rat," and "ate," would be of the same gender to indicate that the action of the verb "ate" is happening to the noun "rat." The issue is more complicated than this simplified explanation, but will serve for the discussion of vv. 8–9.

The neuter pronoun *toúto* could refer to the feminine noun "grace", or the feminine noun "faith", or the masculine participle "you are saved."[1] However, neither the feminine nor the masculine matches the neuter pronoun in gender. Hoehner, citing a number of sources ancient and modern,[2] believes "it is best to conclude that *toúto* refers back to the preceding section . . . 2:4–8a and more specifically 2:8a, the concept of salvation by grace through faith." He illustrates by noting the *toúto* in 1:15 refers back to 1:3–14; in 3:1 it refers back to 2:11–22; in 3:14 it refers back to 3:1–13.[3] Robertson (one of Hoehner's sources), writes, "the words 'and that' (*kaí toúto*) refer to the act of being saved by grace conditioned on faith on our part. Paul shows that salvation does not have its source in men, but from God. Besides, it is God's gift (*dorón*[4]) and not the result of our work."[5] The best view is that the neuter *toúto* refers to the complete salvation principle: saved by grace through faith. The importance of thus understanding *toúto* cannot be overstated. Some want to make salvation the gift, others want to have faith to be God's gift, and still others want grace to be the gift of God. Let us not divide what the Holy Spirit, Paul, biblical theology, and Greek grammar do not divide, which is that "salvation by grace through faith" is God's gift: grace-faith-salvation is the gift of God. These cannot be separated so that one, but not another, is the gift.

Paul says the gift of grace-faith-salvation "is not of yourselves," indicating the origin or source of the gift is not in man. The gift of God is given in his mercy because of his love, vv. 4–5. The word "gift" is *dorón*, which was used in the LXX to refer to a sacrificial offering, although not necessarily a blood offering as, for example, the grain offering, first–fruits, and wave offering. It is also used in the Old and New Testaments of people giving a gift to one another.

---

[1] The verb "you are" is *esté*, the predicate *sesosménoi* is "saved." Together the noun and verb form the masculine participle "you are saved."
[2] Hoehner, *Ephesians*, 343, n. 1.
[3] Ibid., 343.
[4] Zodhiates, *WSDNT*, s. v. "1435."
[5] Robertson, *Word Pictures*, 4:525.

This is the only use where God gives man a gift. The case of the noun indicates origin: the gift is from God. The text is better translated, "and this [gift of grace-faith-salvation] is not from you as a source. Of God is the gift." Although, as discussed above, the nearest antecedent to *toúto* is "faith," in light of the grammatical gender associations, the better view is to understand the antecedent as the whole concept of salvation. Every aspect of salvation—election, love, mercy, grace, faith—originates in God. In an illustration:

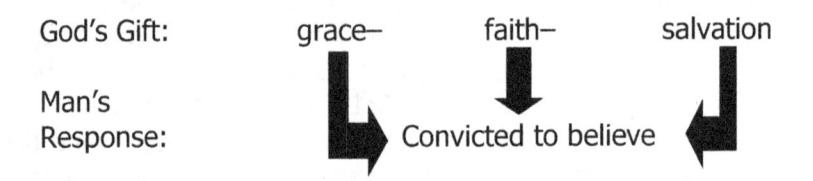

```
God's Gift:      grace–      faith–      salvation
                    ↘          ↓          ↙
Man's
Response:              Convicted to believe
```

Faith comes from God's gift of conviction concerning man as sinner and Christ as Savior, and faith is man's response to God's gift of conviction.

Not Saved by Works

From God's point of view, grace, not works, is the basis of salvation. From man's point of view, faith, not works, is the means to salvation. Paul wants us to know that there is no innate merit in the sinner and no work of merit he or she can do to obtain salvation. The Scripture is very clear that works and grace are opposites: Romans 3:20, 28; 4:1–5; 9:32; Gal 2:16; 3:2–5, 7, 9. If salvation is due a person by reason of works (whether works he performed or works performed on his behalf), then God owes him a debt. A person could say he or she merited or deserved salvation; that he (or she) earned the right to be saved; that God is unjust if the person is not saved by his works. Grace, however, is when something freely given is totally unmerited. Therefore, salvation is not a debt due the sinner; salvation is given for no other reason than that God decided to give, a truth encompassed by the doctrine of election.

The conclusion must be that neither saving faith, nor the exercise of saving faith, is the result of man's works. As to the first, the originating cause of saving faith is not in the sinner. There is

Saving Faith

nothing in the sinner's soul to initiate saving faith. If this were not true, if a person could, independent of God, initiate faith to save him or herself from sin, then saving faith, and thus salvation, would not be God's work. As to the second, saving faith is the means, an instrument, by which man is saved. The physical hand is the instrument of the mind to reach out and take hold of the material thing desired. Even so, faith is the spiritual hand of the soul reaching out to receive the salvation offered by God. To hold out one's hand to receive a gift is no work by the recipient, but is rather volition to put the prior decision of the will into effect. Salvation is the gift of God, conviction-faith is the infallible persuasion of God, and a man's faith is the open hand of his soul (the choice of a human nature spiritually enlightened and convicted by God) extended to receive the gift of God. Therefore, boasting is excluded, blessed be God! who chose us and saved us in Christ.

PART FOUR

Concerning persevering faith and the good works of the saved person.

9. PERSEVERING FAITH

STATEMENT OF THE DOCTRINE

To persevere in the faith is to continue in the faith by faith all the way through life and death. Perseverance is a grace God gives the believer to overcome all spiritual and physical obstacles to faith and thereby continue in the faith, and persevering faith is the believer using the means of grace God has provided for him or her to continue in the faith.

EXPLANATION OF THE DOCTRINE

Why should the believer persevere?

Scripture's main focus, as to perseverance, is on the believer's responsibility to continue in the faith by faith throughout life after salvation. By means of the grace of perseverance every believer must and will persevere in the faith all the way through the end of mortal life and into eternity. Hebrews 10:36–38 describes the kind of persevering faith that must be exercised by the believer.

> For you have need of endurance, so that after you have done the will of God, you may receive the promise: "For yet a little while, and he who is coming will come and will not tarry. Now the just shall live by faith; But if anyone draws back, my soul has no pleasure in him."

In brief, perseverance is required to do the will of God all the way to the time when the promise will be received. What is the promise? The Hebrews Writer is applying Habakkuk 2:3–4 to Christ's promise to return, changing "It will surely come," a reference to judgment, to "he who is coming will come," a reference to Christ. Christ *is* coming in judgment, at the end of the Tribulation period, to judge his enemies and set up his millennial kingdom. For example, the Day of the Lord in Joel's prophecies, the Lord's return in Luke 18:8, and Christ's prophecy of the Tribulation period and the judgment to follow his second advent, Matthew 24, 25. These things apply to those persons who experience the Tribulation.

However, Christ's return for the New Testament believer is based on a different promise, and it is that promise the Hebrews Writer is applying to his readers. The whole of Hebrews 11 is an exhortation of 10:36–38, to wit, the Writer gives examples of perseverance from the Old Testament saints in order to exhort and encourage his readers by their example to persevere in their faith and receive the promises in person at the Lord's return. The New Testament promise the Writer is looking to is John 14:1–4, specifically v. 3 of that passage. Jesus said, "And if I go and prepare a place for you, I will come to receive you to myself, that where I am, there you may be also." This is his promise to return, remove the believer from the world, and take the believer to heaven. Paul explained at 1 Corinthians 15:50–54 and 1 Thessalonians 4:13–18 how that promise would be accomplished. Christ would return to take the church from the world to be "caught up together in the clouds to meet the Lord in the air." This is not the place to defend Christ's return for the church, which is the rapture, versus Christ's return at his second advent to receive the Davidic-Millennial Kingdom. Let me simply note here that the church is "caught up in the clouds to meet the Lord in the air," but at the second advent "in that day his feet will stand on the Mount of Olives" which will be "split in two from east to west . . . thus the Lord my God will come, and all the saints with you," Zechariah 14:4, 5. That last, "and all the saints with you," corresponds with Revelation 19:14, the second advent. To put the rapture and second advent into historical (i.e., prophetic) perspective, the rapture occurs before the Tribulation period (Revelation 6:1–19:10), and the second advent ends the Tribulation (Revelation 1911–21). The rapture of the church is the fulfillment of the promise of Christ's return of John 14: 1–4, and is not the same as Christ's return the second advent.

Therefore, there is a promise of Christ returning to catch the living believer away from the earth and "thus shall we always be with the Lord." This is the promise for which the believer has "need of endurance, so that after you have done the will of God, you may receive the promise." One must persevere in the faith, all the way through life, to receive the promise.

What of those who have died before the rapture? Paul said Jesus would bring the dead saints with him at the rapture, 1 Thessalonians 4:14. Their dead bodies would be resurrected and be reunited with their souls. Compare 1 Corinthians 15:51, "we shall not all sleep [physically die], but we shall all [living and dead believers] be changed. Therefore, those who had persevered in the faith throughout their life into physical death shall also receive the promise. Paul describes the goal of perseverance for those, who like him, would die before the rapture. There is a promise of an immediate entry into heaven should physical death take place before the rapture of the church.

> Philippians 1:21-25, For to me, to live is Christ, and to die is gain. But if I live on in the flesh, this will mean fruit from my labor; yet what I shall choose I cannot tell. For I am hard-pressed between the two, having a desire to depart and be with Christ, which is far better. Nevertheless to remain in the flesh is more needful for you. And being confident of this, I know that I shall remain and continue with you all for your progress and joy of faith.

> 2 Corinthians 5:6-8, So we are always confident, knowing that while we are at home in the body we are absent from the Lord. For we walk by faith, not by sight. We are confident, yes, well pleased rather to be absent from the body and to be present with the Lord.

For Paul there was no doubt. "When I die," he said, "I will go to be with Christ."

To summarize: some believers shall die before the rapture of living believers, but all dead and living believers shall be changed at the rapture, being transformed from mortal to immortal, from corruptible to incorruptible. "The dead in Christ will rise first. Then we who are alive and remain shall be caught up together with them in the clouds to meet the Lord in the air. And thus we [both raptured and resurrected saints] shall always be with the Lord." So there is a goal to perseverance, which is to be with Christ at the end of one's mortal life, whether that ending is physical death, or rapture. Until that day, the believer must persevere in the faith.

What is "the faith?" The faith is more than saving faith; it encompasses the entire testimony of Scripture. Jude, v. 3, exhorted his readers to "contend earnestly for the faith which was once for all delivered to the saints." Jude intended his readers to understand "the faith" as the body of God's revelation delivered to the Old Testament and New Testament believers; in a word, the Bible. When the Hebrews Writer said "the just shall live by faith" he meant two related things. One, the saved person will continue to live his or her life with the same confidence and trust in the Lord that led to salvation. Two, the saved person will continue to live his or her life according to the faith once for all delivered to the saints. We might simply summarize, as does the Hebrews Writer, 10:36, by saying the New Testament believer is to persevere in the will of God until he or she receives the promise.

The Will of God

The believer perseveres in the faith by doing the will of God. What is the will of God? All too often believers think of the will of God as, "What must I do in the future?" Believers want to know their future employment, spouse, etc. The prayer, "Should I take this job or that one . . . should I marry this person or another" is not the same as, "Lord, guide me in making a choice that honors you." The second prayer asks to be guided in making a choice that agrees with God's values and the principles and precepts of Scripture. The choices one makes in order to live in the world must meet this simple test: will this choice help me or hinder me in practicing my faith? Every choice that allows the believer to live according to God's commandments is an acceptable choice. The perfect job, spouse, friend, education, career, church, etc., is the one wherein the believer can live for God and persevere in the faith. In that sense there is no one perfect choice. Choices that allow the believer to practice their faith are of equal value in the will of God.

However, even choices of equal value have different consequences, and it is the consequences that determine the believer's path in life. The small, every day decisions—the one's dealing with life's every-day consequences—have more impact on a life of faith and perseverance than the ones that seem, to us, more important. Shall I read my Bible today, or not; give an offering to support my church's ministries, or not; direct my web browser to something immoral, or not? Perseverance extends upwards to the "big" decisions and downward to the moment-by-moment "small" choices. The will of God in which the believer must persevere covers every aspect of life.

What is the will of God? The will of God is to live according to God's values, principles, and precepts (commandments). God's commandments, or rules for living, are the "do this" and "don't do that" principles and precepts found throughout the Bible (with the understanding that some of the Old Testament rules have been superseded or updated by the New Testament). Practicing God's values is maintaining a righteousness manner of living and performing righteous acts that put one's Christianity into practice for the spiritual and physical well-being of one's self and others. In the demonstrative sense is it doing righteous acts, using sound speech, and practicing sound doctrine, all of which demonstrate one's profession of saving faith in Jesus Christ is genuine. In the daily practice of faith, every act of obedience by faith returns greater spiritual power to the believer. Every surrender to temptation is enslavement; every denial is freedom. "If you love me," said Jesus, "keep my commandments." Obedience is the key that turns on every spiritual power needed to persevere in the faith.

Genuine believers are known (in part) by the fact that they do so endure in the faith by their faith. Their perseverance in the faith by their faith demonstrates they are among the saved, both in the fact they endure, and in the underlying spiritual truth that their endurance is made possible by the grace God gives for their perseverance. Although neither the first New Testament believers, nor their spiritual descendants in the intervening years between Christ's ascension and the present time, have received the promise, yet all those who persevere in the faith will by faith receive the promise of Christ's return. Their faith in the promise, which is (part of) the ground by which they persevere, is itself both the guarantee of receipt and the actuality of receipt: faith—conviction, confidence, doing the will of God—gives substance to the promises.

WHAT IS PERSEVERING FAITH?

Hebrews 11 is an encouragement-by-example of 10:36, "For you have need of endurance, so that after you have done the will of God, you may receive the promise." Hebrews 11:1 states, "Now faith is the substance of things hoped for, the evidence of things not seen." In chapter 11 the writer intends to describe the kind of faith which is required to live a life pleasing to God, through the example of others who lived by faith. Does the Writer mean saving faith or persevering faith? There is one faith (Ephesians 4:5), which may be categorized by its two main uses in Scripture. Those uses are "saving" faith, that brings deliverance from the penalty of sin, and "persevering" faith, that delivers the saved soul intact to heaven through the trials and tribulations of this life. In an illustration, saving faith opens the car door and then by persevering faith we remain in the car as its heavenly driver, the Holy Spirit, takes us to heaven. "Faith" in Hebrews 11 is not saving faith, it is persevering faith. The Writer is not defining faith so much as he is describing the character of faith in which perseverance is accomplished. As with many biblical words, a different context brings out different aspects. For example, in Hebrews 3:7–4:13, faith might be defined as that practical exercise of belief that brings the believer to live settled in God's rest, which is living in the here-and-now of this mortal life by God's power according to God's rules and values. Chapter 11 illustrates through historical example the endurance that receives the promise. Here are men and women of faith who were able to persevere under trial and disappointment because they had unshakeable confidence in the fulfillment of God's promises. Just as the Old Testament saints endured through faith to receive the promises, even so New Testament saints must endure through faith to receive God's promises made to them.

Faith in Hebrews 11 is specifically viewed through the lens of the promise of God's imminent presence. I am using the term "imminent presence" because many generations of saints lived before the Spirit gave the specific prophecies of Christ's first and second advents through David, Isaiah, Paul, etc. Yet, every saint from Adam forward has lived "by faith" in the expectation of the imminent presence ("soon appearing") of God. Seth and contemporaries "called upon the name of the Lord" (Genesis 4:26) as the means to experience God's presence. Enoch walked with God to experience God's presence. Noah looked to forward to God's soon arrival to execute justice against a hopelessly sin-filled world; he worshiped and worked within that context. These believers received prophetic promises that caused them to look to God's imminent presence in worship (Abel), daily life (Enoch), judgment (Noah), inheritance (Abraham), deliverance (Moses), rest (Joshua), or advent (Hebrews 11:39–40). In the New Testament context set by Hebrews 10:19–25, the exercise of persevering faith in these present times is still that same unwavering continuance practiced by the Old Testament saints. The Old Testament saints persevered in the faith by their faith—that unshakable confidence that the promise of the imminent presence of God was certain, Hebrews 10:25, 36–38; 11:13–16, 39; 12:1. Thus, beginning with Abel, the Hebrews Writer presents persevering faith in the "imminent presence" promise in two ways: objectively, as to the spiritual reality of the promise, Hebrews 11:1; subjectively, as to its effect on the heirs to the promises 11:2–40.

Objectively, persevering faith is the substance (*hupóstasis*[1]) of

---

[1] Zodhiates, *WSDNT*, s. v. "5287."

things "hoped" for. The word "hope" in Scripture, *elpízō*,[1] means to expect with desire; the word "expect" is the key to understanding Bible-based hope. This is not the "I hope it does (or doesn't) . . ." of common speech; that brand of hope indicates uncertainty, perhaps anxiety. The hope of Scripture is certain: "I know with absolute assurance that Jesus is returning, because he who promised, John 14:3, is faithful." The "things hoped for" are the promises God has made to believers concerning the future. How then is "faith" the *hupóstasis* (substance) of the promises? The Writer's point is that faith gives certainty to the promises (the things hoped for/not seen). Faith is believing God who cannot lie. Faith is informed by God's word, and therefore acts on the reality described by that word. Faith, then, is the *hupóstasis* of the promises—their substance, their present reality—that gives certainty to the expectation of receiving those promises.

How is faith itself the *hupóstasis*? The word *hupóstasis* always means the real presence. A photograph or a sculpture of a person is representation. When the person is literally, physically standing before you, that is *hupóstasis*, the real presence. This Greek word occurs in Hebrews 1:3. There the Writer says that Jesus is the visible "exact reproduction" (*charaktér*[2]) of the *hupóstasis* (person/essence/substance) of the invisible God. The word *hupóstasis* at 1:3 means the Person of God was literally present: to see Jesus was and is to see God. Jesus was not a sculpture of God, not a photograph, not a hologram, not an appearance or manifestation; he was God in person. As Jesus said to Philip, "he who has seen me has seen the Father," a statement indicative of sensual perception; compare the heard, seen, and touched of 1 John 1:1. The incarnate God-man, Jesus the Christ, revealed the transcendent[3] reality of the Father. Jesus the Christ is the physical, visible, audible presence of the reality of God in our universe, 1 John 1:1; John 14:9. In the second use of this word, Hebrews 3:14, the Writer exhorted the believer to "hold the beginning of our *hupóstasis* (confidence) steadfast to the end." The word in the context of 3:14 could be translated "title deed." A title deed describes real property, such as land, a home, or a car. When one

---

[1] Ibid., s. v. "1679."
[2] Ibid., s. v. "5481."
[3] Transcendent: existing apart from and not subject to the limitations of the material universe. Not subject to normal, physical human perception/experience.

legitimately possesses the title deed, then he holds physical proof of possession of the property. Therefore, in 3:14, *hupóstasis* refers to that certain reality in which one's faith is resting confident and assured. Just as Jesus is the real presence of the reality of God, 1:3, even so, the proclamation of saving faith in Jesus, 3:1, 2, is a description of the reality (*hupóstasis*, 3:14), on which faith rests "steadfast to the end." As the messenger of the confession of faith, 3:1, Jesus is the real presence of the reality of God in which believers share, 3:14.[1]

In Hebrews 11:1 faith is the real presence, the *hupóstasis*, of things hoped for. This is the kind or quality of faith in which the believer perseveres. When a believer has genuine God-given faith in the promises, then the reality of those promises is really present with the believer—his faith is his title deed to the promises. Not promises wished for or wondered about, nor an anxious "I hope so," but the steadfast assurance that the promises are real, genuine, imminent. God knows the doubts sin injects into our confidence, weakening our resolve to believe and persevere. He has given us promises, and faith as the title deed to the promises, to encourage us to persevere. By faith I am absolutely and completely assured of the reality of the things God has promised, and do in fact by the hand of faith hold them in my soul as a present reality.

In Hebrews 11:1, the word "substance," *hupóstasis*, and the word "evidence," *élegchos*,[2] are parallel descriptions. Faith is the presence of the reality, *hupóstasis*, of things hoped for. Faith is the "evidence," *élegchos*, of things not seen. The Greek word *élegchos* is used in one other place in the New Testament, 2 Timothy 3:16, "All Scripture . . . is profitable . . . for *élegchos*, where it is translated "reproof" in the NKJV, a subjective use of the word. *Élegchos* can be used in an objective sense: "proof"; or a subjective sense: "means of proof." In Timothy *élegchos* bears the subjective meaning "means of proof with a view to refuting," thus translated "reproof" or "rebuke." In 11:1, is *élegchos* subjective or objective? The answer affects whether *hupóstasis* is subjective or objective, because *hupóstasis* and *élegchos* are parallel descriptions of faith. In one interpretation of Hebrews 11:1, *hupóstasis* and *élegchos* are interpreted as subjective: faith is the means of proof and persuasion

---

[1] Kittle, *Dictionary*, 8:587.
[2] Zodhiates, *WSDNT*, s. v. "1650."

of the things hoped for, not seen. A subjective interpretation means that the more faith you have (the quantity of faith), the stronger your belief in the promises. A small or weak faith cannot hold onto the promises; a large or strong faith holds fast to the promises. This puts the burden of perseverance solely on the believer, but Scripture teaches that God gives grace to persevere, e.g., Hebrews 13:5; Romans 8:28-39, grace which the believer is to receive and put to use in his or her life. Moreover, the Bible never speaks of the quantity of faith, but its quality, e.g., Matthew 17:20, where a tiny amount of faith is able to resolve big problems. Jesus' point was that one has faith, or does not. Quality, not quantity, is how faith perseveres.

An objective interpretation of *élegchos* is more in keeping with the use Hebrews makes of *hupóstasis*. For example, at 1:3, Jesus is not the means of proof demonstrating there is a God. Jesus is the objective presence of God. Since in Hebrews 11:1 *hupóstasis* and *élegchos* are parallel descriptions of persevering faith, then both must bear an objective meaning: the presence of faith is the objective reality (*hupóstasis*) and demonstration (*élegchos*) of things hoped for, not seen. An objective interpretation means God gives a believer that quality of faith which results in the steadfast assurance that the promises are genuine and imminent. An objective faith places the burden of "proof" on God and emphasizes the believer's moral responsibility to receive and use the grace God gives for perseverance.

Another reason both *hupóstasis* and *élegchos* must bear an objective meaning is that the things promised, hoped for, and not seen are present in the spirit domain, i.e., in heaven. If the faith described in Hebrew 11 is subjective, then man is trying to discern the reality of things in heaven through his sensual and rational faculties. This is not possible. Spiritual things are perceived through the spiritual faculty of the soul, not the sensual and rational faculties by which man subjectively understands the material world. The unsaved sinner cannot understand the things of God, just because they are spiritually discerned (1 Corinthians 2:14), and the unsaved sinner's spiritual perception is dead because of sin. Nor can the saved sinner perceive spiritual things through his material senses, because these were designed and created to perceive the material world. Faith is the means of perceiving the spirit domain because God the Holy Spirit is the source of spiritual perception (1

Corinthians 2:10–11). He reveals spiritual things to material man through the spiritual faculty of perception employed by faith.

A subjective faith originates in the worshiper. If faith is only subjective, then faith is limited by man's sensual and rational faculties. However, the reality of the promises of God cannot in or of themselves be sensually or rationally perceived within the limitations of our material existence. Our physical senses, including the capability for rational thought, were designed to perceive and understand our material universe. But through objective faith the believer perceives spiritual realities through the spiritual senses of his or her born-again soul and the work of the Holy Spirit.

The source of objective faith is God, e.g., God's gift of grace-faith-salvation, Ephesians 2:8. God gives faith, man does not self-generate faith. Man receives the gift of faith from God and puts that faith to practical use: he believes and is saved; he believes and perseveres. An objective faith is itself the reality of the spiritual presence of the things hoped for and not seen, because the origin of objective faith is God. Faith does not *make* these things real to the believer, for that would be persuasion, a subjective reality. Faith itself *is* the reality of the things hoped for and not seen.

Therefore, faith—the soul's positive response to God's testimony—is the *hupóstasis*, the objective substance, the title deed, to the spiritual realities the believer is certain to receive; and they will be received through persevering in life by means of that faith (10:36). Just as Jesus is the real presence of the Spirit-being God, a person's faith is the real presence of spiritual realities hoped for and not seen. When one has faith in the certainty of the promises, one has certainty he will receive the promises, because that kind of faith—the conviction given only by God—is itself the real presence of the promises. Faith itself is the continuing objective presence of the reality of the promises. That quality of faith creates perseverance.

Saving and persevering faith is not being persuaded by means of sensual or rational proof that spiritual things are true. No proof susceptible to man's sensual or rational faculties will be sufficient to cause faith in, for example, the second advent of Christ. The "proof" of this proposition is seen in the lack of faith the Jews had concerning Jesus' claim to be their Christ (Messiah). Although Jesus fulfilled all the several parts of Jewish Scripture relating to the first advent of Messiah, the Jews were not convinced by any proof susceptible to their sensual or rational faculties. Even when they compared the declarations of Scripture against the actions of Jesus, they were not convinced. Some of them did later become convinced, but that conviction was directly caused by the act of God the Holy Spirit, Acts chapters 2, 8, 10. Faith is certainty that God's testimony is absolute truth; only God can cause certainty in man's soul concerning his testimony (1 Corinthians 2:9–14). Faith is not the subjective persuasion that God's promises are genuine. The spiritual reality the Old Testament saints looked toward in faith was the promise of the imminent presence of God in worship, judgment, promise, rest, or advent. For New Testament saints the spiritual reality is the promise of Christ to return, take them to heaven, and return with them to set up his kingdom on earth. Faith itself is the objective presence of the spiritual reality of God's promises. The presence of faith in the believer objectively demonstrates the presence of the spiritual reality we are certain of, but do not yet see. Since, as is the case, faith is the gift of God, then the presence of faith is the objective proof of the reality of the promises made by God, and the certainty the believer has of receiving them.

Allow me to answer the question, "What is faith," from a different point of view. We are too used to thinking of faith as a feeling, a subjective perception or persuasion of spiritual reality. Faith is nothing of the sort. Yes, it is true that since we are sensual and rational creatures we tend to understand and express our personal faith in terms of emotions and reason; and God uses our emotions and reason to help us understand our immediate spiritual state (in sin; in fellowship). Our emotions, in relation to the state of our faith, are like the dashboard lights in a car—they tell us all is alright or something might not be right. They are not the reality of the car but are a "snapshot" of the current state of the car. So our emotions give a subjective moment-to-moment snapshot of the condition of our faith and the state of our fellowship with God.

But faith, whether saving faith or persevering faith, is not based in subjective perception. The efficient cause of genuine, soul-changing faith is God. Faith is the objective, unshakeable, unchanging certainty that what God has said is true. That objective certainty can only be given by God. Through his rational faculties a person can develop an understanding of God's word. However, an objective, soul-changing conviction that God's word is absolute truth speaking to the condition the soul is a conviction given only by God.

When, for example, one believes with undoubting certainty that the God revealed in the Bible is the one and only supreme being, that act of faith is caused by Holy Spirit convicting the soul of the absolute truth of God's objective existence. That certainty is 100 percent spiritual and 100 percent real. Yes, the Spirit does work through our rational faculties to create understanding, but the absolute certainty that God's testimony is genuine absolute truth without error is a conviction that only God can impart. Scripture facts may be rationally known by natural intelligence, and spiritually comprehended when revealed and explained by the Spirit; but the *certainty*, the *conviction*, that these facts are God's absolute genuine truth comes only from God.[1] The certainty of spiritual reality is beyond the finite limitations of material existence. Only God can give an absolute assurance of the certainty of spiritual reality.

When the Holy Spirit informs a person that God exists, this is not a matter of "feeling" God exists, but is a matter of absolute and certain knowledge that God exists, because God has revealed his existence to that person's essential being, i.e., in his soul. The same is true of saving faith, which is a matter of Holy Spirit-revealed absolute and certain knowledge that I am a sinner and Jesus is "my" Savior. Yes, the soul does make a subjective response to the knowledge of the guilt of sin and of redemption in the Savior. That subjective response—repentance of sin and confession of faith in Jesus as Savior—is based in the objective knowledge of the spiritual reality that I am a sinner and only Jesus can save me. The Holy Spirit communicates to the soul the objective spiritual reality of sin and salvation. Perceptually, i.e., through the senses and reason, the sinner understands his personal crime of sin, his personal sentence of condemnation, and his personal need of salvation. Objectively, in his soul, he is persuaded by Holy Spirit-revealed absolute knowledge of the reality of Jesus as the only Savior. One's faith in the knowledge of sin, the Savior, and salvation is certain or sure because the certainty of it comes from God. Thus saving faith is not a matter of feeling saved, but a matter of the presence of the reality (*hupóstasis*) of sin, and the presence of the reality (*hupóstasis*) of the Savior, and then acting in personal faith to apply

---

[1] As noted in an earlier chapter, Satan persuades men to believe in a destructive counterpart, a fanatical zeal.

these truths to the spiritual need of the soul for salvation. We call this spiritual presence of reality "conviction," and because we "feel" convicted (guilt, need), we associate conviction with our senses, i.e., subjectively. The spiritual reality is that conviction of sin, the Savior, and salvation must begin as objective revelation from God the Holy Spirit, if it is to consummate in the subjective reality of choosing salvation in Jesus as "my" Savior (e.g., 2 Thessalonians 2:13). Conviction is first knowing, then feeling; first absolute knowledge, then taking action because our understanding of that knowledge is certain. Conviction, as concerning biblical, scriptural, spiritual matters, is knowing truth after the same manner God knows truth: as absolute, objective, genuine truth. Conviction of spiritual reality is knowing as God knows, because God has effectively communicated both knowledge and certainty.

The same is true of persevering faith. Persevering faith is based on the absolute knowledge—the objective conviction—that spiritual realities hoped for but not seen are real and are certain to be received. Persevering faith is possible because the believer knows by conviction God keeps his promises. This is not a matter of human perception, nor is it a matter of feeling persuaded. I objectively know God keeps his promises, because the spiritual reality of the matter has been revealed to me by God. Yes, a personal rational comprehension of Scripture is essential to perseverance, because God has created us to be rational beings whose choices are supported by reason. There is a difference, however, between being certain because of experience, and having experience validated by the certainty of faith. The certainty of faith validates our experiences as genuine or false. The certainty of faith causes us to make the choice to persevere and informs us when the practice of our faith, perseverance, is based upon spiritual reality. In Hebrews 11:1 the writer is not talking about the choice to persevere, he is addressing the basis for perseverance: faith is the real presence of things hoped for, the objective evidence of things not seen.

Persevering faith begins as, and is always supported by, God-given conviction: I know God is keeping his promises because God has convicted me that he is faithful. That certainty is the basis of persevering faith. Therefore, my choice to persevere in my Christian life must be based upon that Holy Spirit-revealed knowledge of absolute, genuine spiritual reality. Worldly circumstances can discourage, but not destroy. I can endure a great struggle with sufferings because I know, by Spirit-given, Spirit-convicting absolute knowledge, that God who cannot lie will be faithful to his promises to me. The presence of Holy Spirit-given faith is itself the objective reality of God's promises. We can say, then, that faith itself is the substance (*hupóstasis*) of God's promise (the thing hoped for) in the same sense in which Jesus is called (1:3) the exact reproduction (*charaktér*) of the substance (*hupóstasis*) of God. Just as Jesus is the reality of the presence of God, even so faith is the reality of the promises of God.

Faith is also the objective demonstration (*élegchos*) of the spiritual reality of the things not seen. I can't say this more plainly: objective faith is given by God, not created by man. Man's faith is more subjective: I know, therefore I act. I persevere in faith, a subjective act, because I have an objective faith in the reality of the promise. Because one has God-given faith, one has certainty in the things not seen: the presence of faith is the demonstration of the things not seen. Since we are sensual, rational creatures, I will say this in a more familiar way: one's faith gives the perception of immediate presence to spiritual realities. Put another way, perseverance is knowing that God said it, that settles it, I'm going to believe it and do it. In secular Greek *hupóstasis* could be used to describe real property, thus, faith is the "title deed"[1] of things hoped for; a title deed is the objective proof of legal possession. The objective certainty that God gives in the promises is itself the proof the believer possesses the promises, because that (kind or quality of) faith comes only from God. If one has God-given faith, then one has the certainty needed to persevere and receive the promises.

PERSEVERING FAITH BY EXAMPLE

For by faith the elders obtained a good testimony (Hebrews 11:2). This is the announcement of the Writer's theme in chapter 11. We will not discuss these examples of persevering faith, except to say the Writer will concern himself with the fruits and consequences which follow faith. Faith is the basis of perseverance, for without spiritual conviction there is nothing upon which to base one's perseverance. However, the examples of persevering faith

---

[1] Moulton and Milligan, *Vocabulary*, 659–660.

answer the question, Must the believer act in persevering faith? If, as is the case, God is the origin of faith, saving and persevering, then what is the believer's part in perseverance?

Faith in the promises provides the basis for perseverance. I have God-given certainty concerning the goal or end result of perseverance: to receive the promises. Faith is not, however, the efficient cause of perseverance. The act of persevering is a choice: I am persevering in the practice of my faith because I intend to receive the promises. If this were not true, if a decision need not be made to persevere, then the Writer would not have written 10:25–29, or 11:1–39; indeed, he could have ended his epistle at 10:25. The exhortation, "do not cast away your confidence," 10:35, has its counterpart in "you have need of endurance," v. 36. Both express the choice to be made. The exhortations, as illustrated by the example of the elders (patriarchs, ancestors), are intended to encourage the believer to make the right choice: to have endurance, i.e., to persevere in the faith by faith. Manton called this faith "sanctifying faith,"[1] a typically Puritan emphasis on separation from sin and dedication to God. The testimony of the elders illustrates the experiential sanctification required of believers, meaning, that what one believes one must do. Faith must influence all the parts of the spiritual life. Without faith perseverance is noble morality (or ignoble stubbornness). Perseverance by means of faith is the self-motivated personal pursuit of that experiential sanctification which conforms the life to God's commandments; in this case, to maintain unswerving confidence in God's promises.

The choice to persevere includes the choice to use the means of grace to maintain one's faith. Here again I am not speaking of certainty, but the use one makes of that certainty: the inner conviction should result in an appropriate outward action. The text here is *en taúta gár*, "for in this" ("for by this"), that is, "because of this kind of faith," the elders obtained, etc. What is intended is that through the exercise of their faith the elders obtained a good report or testimony concerning their perseverance in and by their faith. Their inner conviction was the basis for an appropriate choice. That this phrase, *en taúta*, is meant to guide the interpretation of subsequent verses in seen in the word translated "by faith", the Greek *pístei*. The use is anarthrous, i.e., without the definite article.

---

[1] Manton, *By Faith*, 51.

Use of the definite article would have indicated "faith" referred to the body of revealed truth, the Word of God. Without the definite article the kind or quality of faith is emphasized, corresponding to the grammar of *en taúta* in v. 2.

The words *pístei*, *pístin*, and *písteos* are grammatical forms of *pístis*, "faith, persuasion, conviction, belief." Ellingworth notes that *pístei* is "essentially synonymous with *en taúta* [by this] in v. 2, *kata pístin* [in faith] in v. 13, *diá písteos* [through faith] in v. 33, and *diá tas písteos* [through the faith] in v. 39"[1] and later states that "*pístei* denotes means."[2] Lane opines that *pístei* "can be read as an instrumental dative ('by means of faith'), or a dative of manner ('accordance with the modality of faith'), or a causal dative ('because of faith')."[3] In keeping with these opinions, the use of *en taúta* and *pístei* indicates that by the *exercise* of their faith ("Abel offered," "Enoch . . . pleased God," "Noah prepared, "Abraham obeyed," etc.) the elders *maintained* their perseverance. Thus, the choice to persevere includes the choice to use the means of grace necessary to maintain one's faith.

We should never forget that in this mortal life, in all things spiritual, there is a God-ward side and a man-ward side. God's responsibility is convicting his people of the certainty of spiritual reality and empowering their soul to achieve the goal of successful perseverance, which is receiving the promises. Man's responsibility is to use the appropriate means of grace God provides to strengthen, mature, and encourage the believer in his or her faith, in order to continue to live according to faith, that he (or she) might endure and receive the promises. What, then, are the means by which we are empowered to persevere? The persevering faith of the elders is demonstrated in that they took action based upon what they held to be true—were convicted was true. The Writer has not only presented the truths of the Christian faith in his epistle, he has exhorted his readers to the practical expression of these truths. The more immediate context is what I have called the privileges and obligations, or duties, of the faith, 10:19–25. Faith is not some ambiguous feeling; faith, if it is genuine, God-given, soul-saving, persevering faith, looks toward the promised future as a solid and

---

[1] Ellingworth, *Hebrews*, 561.
[2] Ibid., 592.
[3] Lane, *Hebrews 9–13*, 326, n. "h."

sure reality that demands appropriate action. The certainty of faith causes the believer to make the choice to persevere and informs the believer when the practice of faith, his or her perseverance, is based on spiritual reality. The choice and the practice are equally essential to the maintenance of faith. Although the conviction of truth is objective and absolute, the recognition and practical application of that conviction is subjective within the soul. One might liken faith to a spiritual "muscle" that requires constant exercise to maintain its tone and strength. Without constant exercise through practical application the subjective recognition of faith weakens. The result is that one comes less often into God's presence, uses prayer and devotion less frequently, becomes apathetic toward his believing brethren, and calloused toward their suffering in the world; ultimately, one abandons gathering together with his Christian brethren (thus the exhortations in Hebrews 10:19–25). As these wrong actions become habitual perseverance is lessened and faith is weakened.

We are, in this physical frame, creatures of subjective sense and rationality, whose faith must be practiced in practical expressions to be maintained all the way through the end of life to the promised reward. The certainty of faith causes us to make the choice to persevere, and informs us when the practice of our faith, perseverance, is based upon spiritual reality. No wonder, then, the Writer of Hebrews energetically exhorted his readers to press forward to spiritual maturity by putting their faith into practice, as did their spiritual predecessors. We too, in this modern day and age, as we wait for the soon-appearing of Christ, must persevere in the faith, both spiritually and practically.

10. GOOD WORKS

Statement of the doctrine. The believer was saved to perform those good works which God foreordained as the necessary and certain result of salvation.

Good works are part of the doctrine of predestination, as Ephesians 2:10 makes clear. Believers are the work of God's hands, saved for a purpose, a purpose foreordained and innate to their election in Christ. The outworking of their predestination is to be like Christ, a purpose fulfilled as they live out their salvation through perseverance and good works. The doctrine of being zealous for and maintaining good works is based on Ephesians 2:10; Hebrews 10:24; Psalm 15:1, 2; Titus 2:14, and other scriptures.

SAVED TO DO GOOD WORKS

Salvation, then Good Works

The key passage is Ephesians 2:10.

> For we are His workmanship, created in Christ Jesus for good works, which God prepared beforehand that we should walk in them.

A more literal translation according to the Greek text (literal word order):

> His for we are workmanship, created in Christ Jesus for works good, which previously prepared God in order that in them we should walk.

Ephesians 2:9 emphasizes salvation is not man's achievement but has God for its origin and source. Ephesians 2:10 indicates God is also the origin and source of the believer's good works. The order is clear: salvation, then good works. Christianity begins at the point, salvation, which other religions attempt to achieve through good works. The Christian's salvation results in good works. Some religions believe their salvation is maintained by good works. But, as we have amply demonstrated in earlier chapters, salvation is obtained by grace through faith not works, and maintained by grace through faith not good works. Good works are the natural and expected result of salvation purchased for the believer and maintained for him by God.

Paul has not created this principle—salvation then works—out of thin air. Jesus had previously stated the relationship between salvation and good works. In John 12:26 Jesus said, "If anyone serves me, let him follow me." The person who would serve must first follow, for one cannot serve Jesus without first possessing that relationship here defined as "following." Those listening would have understood: a follower was a disciple—one committed to learning from their master and reproducing his teachings in their life. Any service not based on following was not service to the master. In the case of Jesus, that "following" relationship was to be found only through saving faith. Any person may imitate Jesus, but only the saved can follow and serve.

One follows then serves: salvation, then works. Unless one has a faith-based salvific relationship with Jesus they cannot serve Jesus. A mundane example may help make the point. To mow someone's lawn without permission from the landowner may be a service, but since there was no pre-existing relationship with the landowner the work will be unrewarded. A relationship, not the work itself, is the basis for serving.

This truth is dramatically exampled at Matthew 25:41–46.[1] Those cursed whom Jesus will send to the lake of fire protest their condemnation by asking, v. 44, "when did we . . . not minister to you?" They were giving food to the hungry, drink to the thirsty, clothing and medicine to the naked and sick, and visiting those in prison. They were certain they would be rewarded with heaven because they were doing works Jesus had recommended as good works. They were, in fact, doing the same things as those whom Jesus had commended for their works, vv. 34–39. However, they were doing these good works indiscriminately, i.e., not for Jesus' sake. They were those who did not have a faith-based relationship with Jesus. They served, but they did not follow. They did not have a relationship with Jesus, else they would have been among the ones Jesus called "my brethren" (cf. Matthew 7:21–23; Luke 6:46). Without a relationship as the basis for serving, one is serving one's

---

[1] Although the judgment of Matthew 25:31–46 concerns faith and good works during the Tribulation period (and the judgment itself takes place after the second advent) the principles of following and serving are relevant to any time and place.

self, whatever good cause or motive may be externally applied as the reason for the service. To do what one thinks is a good work without permission and guidance from the Master of good works is to work at one's own pleasure, not serve the Master. To do the works of God one must believe on the one, Jesus, whom God has sent; faith in Jesus as Savior comes before good works. Therefore, if anyone would do the works of Christ he must be in a salvific relationship with Christ. Any work one might do is Christ's work only when Christ is doing the works through his follower and servant: the faithful believer in Christ as Savior. When one follows Jesus to salvation, then where Jesus is working there the believer will be working.

Created in Christ to do Good Works

Returning to the literal word order of Ephesians 2:10, we read "His for we are workmanship." By placing the word *autón*, "his" as the first word, Paul emphasizes that salvation is God's achievement. The opening *gár*, "for," looks back to the argument and conclusion of vv. 8–9. The words "we are" are the translation of *ésmen*, the present active indicative first person plural of *eimí*. The grammatical form *ésmen* indicates a condition existing during the time the speaker is making the statement. The Ephesians are, by reason of their salvation, God's workmanship. The word workmanship" is *poíēma*,[1] from the noun *poiéō*,[2] "to make." The word *poíēma* describes the result of work. The word is used only here and in Romans 1:20, where it describes the things (of creation) which God made. These Ephesians, who were once sinners, 2:2–3, are now saved, 2:8, whose salvation was solely the work of God, 2:10.

The saved are "created" in Christ Jesus. "Created" is an aorist participle, *ktízō*,[3] indicating the action of being created. This action occurred in the past in relation to the main verb, "you are." Right now, said Paul, as I am writing to you, you are God's workmanship, because previous to my writing this letter God spiritually created and formed you, *ktízō*, in Christ. The word *ktízō* occurs 15 times in the New Testament. This word is used 4 times in Ephesians (2:10, 15; 3:9, 4:24) variously meaning creation from nothing, to fashion

---

[1] Zodhiates, *WSDNT*, s. v. "4161."
[2] Ibid., s. v. "4160."
[3] Ibid., s. v. "2936."

or form out of preexisting materials, or to create and form in a spiritual sense. The last is the meaning here. God took the repentant and believing sinner and created spiritual life in him, by which means God permanently placed him or her in a constant state of "are saved." Thus, *ktízō* corresponds to "born-again," the term that indicates spiritual regeneration. To be *ktízō*, i.e., to be created in Christ Jesus, restates 1:4, chosen in Christ, and 1:7, redeemed in Christ. Salvation is solely the work of God. By reason of election, and by means of redemption by grace through faith in Jesus, sinners are born-again in Christ Jesus out of the sphere of spiritual death into the sphere of spiritual life. The term "Christ Jesus" is used sixty-nine times in the New Testament, eight in Ephesians. The reverse term, "Jesus Christ," is used 188 times in the New Testament, eleven in Ephesians. The two terms are practically synonymous. In Ephesians, "Jesus Christ" tends to refer to the divine Person, whereas "Christ Jesus" tends to refer to the believer's relation with God as incorporated in Christ. Believers are chosen in Jesus Christ (1:3, 4), made alive with Christ (1:5). raised up in Christ Jesus (2:6), and created—saved, made a new creature, born-again—in Christ Jesus (2:10).

Believers are created in Christ Jesus that they should do good works. These are works that God has prepared in advance, or ahead of time. Doing these good works should characterize the believer's manner of life. Before discussing "good works," let us discuss "walk" and "prepared beforehand."

The preposition *ina*, translated "that" ("that" we should walk in them) has the force of "in order that." "We are God's workmanship because we were created in Christ Jesus for the goal of good works 'in order that' (*ina*) we might walk in them."[1] To "walk" is *peripatéō*,[2] a Greek word meaning to walk about. Used in a figurative sense, as it is here, it refers to the manner in which one lives out his or her life. This word was used in 2:2 in reference to the sinner's manner of life; here it refers to the believer's manner of life. The believer once lived according to the world and Satan; he and she have been spiritually regenerated to live according to the ways of God, which ways include good works. To fully understand what Paul is saying in 2:10, we must consider in detail three Greek

---

[1] Hoehner, *Ephesians*, 349.
[2] Zodhiates, *WSDNT*, s. v. "4043."

words and their grammatical form in the sentence.

Good Works Prepared Beforehand

The first of these words is the relative pronoun *oís* (root: *hós*), "which." These are good works "which" were prepared beforehand. There is a small grammatical issue involving the antecedent to *oís*. Either the pronoun refers to believers ("God prepared us beforehand") or it refers to good works ("which [good works] God prepared beforehand"). The antecedent "good works" is the best grammatical choice, and the meaning of the phrase "seems to be, 'in order that we should walk in those works,' they have been prescribed, defined, and adapted to us."[1]

The second word is *proetoímasen*, "prepared beforehand" (a grammatical form of *proetoimázō*). "Prepared beforehand" is an accurate translation. This word is used only here and Romans 9:23. In context, *proetoímasen* communicates the idea of foreordination. In Romans 9:23 believers are vessels of mercy foreordained to display God's glory. In Ephesians the good works a believer is to do in order to glorify God in Christ were foreordained (prepared beforehand) in eternity-past. The good works a believer is to do are part of the decree of foreordination that was the basis for the sinner's election to salvation. Put another way, good works are part of God's plan to manifest his glory: he foreordained that one of the ways in which his glory would be manifested was through the good works performed by his saved people. God's choice to elect to salvation included the works the believer is to perform as a result of salvation. The believer was chosen in Christ for the purpose of demonstrating God's glory; one way in which a believer will do this is by the good works he or she should do.

The third word is the grammatical form *peripatesómen*, "we should walk" (a grammatical form of *peripatéō*). This verb form is the ingressive aorist. The ingressive aorist "is commonly employed with verbs which signify a state or condition, and denote entrance into that state or condition."[3] Paul has set up a contrast. The believer's prior conduct, i.e., their conduct before salvation, was *periepatósate*, 2:2, (a grammatical form of *peripatéō*) indicating

---

[1] Eadie, *Ephesians*, 158–159.
[2] Zodhiates, *WSDNT*, s. v. "4282."
[3] Dana and Mantey, *Grammar*, 196.

their manner of life in their day to day conduct was according to the ways of the world and Satan. Then they became saved, 2:8–9. In 2:10, after their salvation, in contrast to their former manner of life in 2:2, the believer is to enter into, and continue on with, a manner of life which is according to the good works God has prepared beforehand.

In order to understand the full force of *peripatesómen*, "we should walk," we must consider it in connection with *proetoímasen*, "prepared beforehand," which in context indicates two things. One, in consideration of the prefix *pro* (before), it means "God prepared these good works before the believer was created in Christ Jesus."[1] Second, the whole word means "we could not walk in these [good] works unless they had been prepared for us. And therefore, by prearranging the works in their sphere, character, and suitability [*proetoímasen*], and also by preordaining the law which commands, the inducement or appliances which impel, and the creation in Christ which qualifies and empowers us, God has shown it to be his purpose that 'we should walk in them' [*peripatesómen*]."[2] In other words, God foreordained good works for his saved people to do. They are in fact his good works he will do through his saved people, compare John 5:19, 36. He placed his good works in the believer's life path. He gave commandment that they should do his good works. He gave the promise of reward to encourage his people to do his good works. He qualified his people to do his good works by saving them and by giving them spiritual power. In all these things God has shown his saved people that doing his good works should be a vital part of their manner of life. The emphasis of v. 10 is that God's purpose in preparing good works is that believers "should" walk in them.

What Paul intended by "prepared beforehand" and "we should walk [in them]" is the choice to be made by the believer. Good works were prepared beforehand in order that you may come to walk in them. God's purpose is that the Christian's life should incorporate the good works God prepared beforehand. Remember, God's sovereignty works through the believer's responsibility to accomplish his plans and purpose. Good works are one of the many processes by which his plans and purpose are accomplished. The

---

[1] Hoehner, *Ephesians*, 349.
[2] Eadie, *Ephesians*, 159.

individual believer becomes a vital part of the processes by actively cooperating with God to do good works. The believer, therefore, is continuously faced with a choice: to willingly yield to God and do the works, or stubbornly continue in sin and not do the works. God preordained good works for every believer to do; the believer who is in fellowship with God will do them. Note, then, that the believer is to "walk in them" not work in them; thus doing good works is part of a normal Christian life. The plans and purpose of God cannot be frustrated or denied; the good works God has purposed and prepared for his people will be accomplished, if not by one believer, then by another. The believer who willingly becomes part of the processes by which God's good works are accomplished receives blessing and reward.

Good works, by reason of God's purpose and decree, are innate to salvation. The whole by necessity must include the parts. The decree of election must include all the good works the believer should do after salvation, because a perfect choice to save must not only include every means by which it is effected, but also everything which the choice affects. The nature of God as omnipresent, omniscient, and omnipotent means his choices incorporate all means to accomplish them, all consequences resulting from them, and all results—the end or goal—purposed in them.

Therefore, just as the believer was chosen in Christ before the foundation of the world, at the same time the necessary works of his or her Christian life were foreordained as an innate part of his or her salvation. This is not fate, for as discussed earlier God's sovereignty in foreordination causes the free choices a person makes to be part of the processes that work to accomplish his plans to fulfill his purpose. Moreover, viewed in the context of the believer's life, God has given the believer the commandment, the power (a spiritual nature), and the inducement (rewards), to accomplish his plans and thereby his purpose.

The Decision to do Good Works

The believer's point of view is his or her past and present. What the future holds for the individual is unknown, except in a general way that encourages perseverance. For example, every believer knows they will spend an eternity in heaven in God's presence. But, will this occur at death or rapture? Every believer knows he or she is to do good works. But, what are these good works? When will each be accomplished? The experiences of the past inform the actions of the present, but the future is, for the most part, unknown. Put another way, though God has foreordained agents, events, and outcomes, from the human perspective, when the future becomes the present, there are choices to be made—choices which affect one's present and future. In relation to good works, the word "should" in Ephesians 2:10 indicates those choices. Let us look at good works from the point of view of choices and consequences.

The interaction between "God prepared beforehand" and "we should walk in them" indicates that, from the believer's point of view, at every point in life where a decision must be made, many choices are available. Put another way, there are many right choices, and many wrong choices, but there is no one perfect choice, because the sovereignty of God works through man's responsibility to accomplish God's processes, plans, and purpose. God allows people to make free choices, which his sovereignty ensures will accomplish his will. A course of action that is in full agreement with the principles, precepts, and values of God's Word is a right choice. Each choice differs in its mode, method, and progress according to the nature of the person making the choice. Each one of several possible choices at any particular decision point is a means leading to some one end ordained by God. Foreordination is not determinism, it is not fate. Foreordination is God's choices causing man's choices to accomplish his plans and fulfill his purpose. The critical difference in each of several possible choices is not in achieving the end goal, which God's sovereignty will infallibly accomplish, but in the consequences each choice contains for the person making the choice.

In relation to man's point of view, there may be many paths leading from point "A" to point "B." A person decides on a particular path according to his or her nature, his or her faith, his or her state of fellowship with God. God's sovereignty ensures the processes initiated by the believer's choices will accomplish his plans and purpose, through one path or another, if not by one person then by another. The crucial issue for the believer is not so much accomplishing God's will, as it is the consequences of one's choice. Some choices will lead to blessing; others will not. The kind and quality of blessings may differ dependent upon the right choices one makes; just as the consequences for a wrong choice will differ depending upon which wrong choices were made. As an example, prayer is an ordained means to accomplish God's plans. However, if a person impressed by the Spirit to pray does not pray, the plan will be accomplished by another means—another person praying (?)—but the blessing for the person who was supposed to pray, and did not, will be lost. Although this view seems to contradict foreordination, one must realize that God's sovereignty encompasses every consequence of every freely made choice, so that his will is always accomplished, and the believer always receives the appropriate consequence of his or her choice. As discussed in the chapter on foreordination, God knew, through his omniscient wisdom, every possible consequence of his decision to create, and he foreordained which would pass from possible to actual, including the freely made choices of his sentient creatures, and the consequences resulting from those choices. Therefore, God's will is always accomplished, and the freely made choices of his creatures in response to that will of God will determine the just consequences of their choices.

Returning to our subject, the good works each believer is to accomplish through his freely made choices have been foreordained in eternity-past as a vital and necessary part of his or her Christian life. To do or not to do, to serve willingly or by necessity, to choose based upon Scripture principles, precepts, and values or worldly values—these are the crucial choices that lead to success, defeat, or mediocrity. The blessing comes as part of the doing. Moreover, the believer's choices in this life shape the character of his life both now and in eternity.

The Believer Prepared in Advance For Every Good Work

There is another aspect of "prepared beforehand" that I find encouraging. Since good works were decreed in eternity-past, then they wait at a particular moment in the historical-present to meet the believer as he or she progresses through life. Since it is God's will that "we should walk in them," and since they are waiting in the future, then God will prepare the believer to do the good work as he or she journeys through life. When the time arrives for the good work to be performed, the believer has already been prepared to perform it. In an illustration, when Christ places a work of service directly in the path of your life, he will have prepared you through previous experiences to accomplish that work of service. As the believer walks through life, his life-experiences are part of an ongoing process of preparation for future works. Since a believer is saved to do the good works, then he or she must have faith that the God who prepared the works beforehand will also prepare his people beforehand to do the works.

The Place and Manner of Good Works

If, as is the case, the good works one is to do were foreordained in eternity-past, to be accomplished as one meets with them in historical-present, then there is a necessity to understand "good works" as God defines a good work, so each may be recognized and accomplished when met with. Before proceeding to that definition, there are a few other things to discuss. First, as previously noted, salvation is "not of works," but after salvation the believer is to "walk in good works." Therefore, good works are the result, never the cause, of salvation. Good works are the consequence and evidence of salvation.[1]

Second, how does God act in the world to accomplish his good works? God acts both immediately and mediately in the world. To act "immediately" means God takes action by himself. An example is Genesis 1:3, "Then God said, 'Let there be light'; and there was light." Light was created out of nothing by God's sovereign will, omniscient understanding, and omnipotent power.

God, however—based on what Scripture reveals—tends more often to act mediately, i.e., through his creation and creatures. God tends to work through his people to accomplish his will. There is a subtle distinction here that will maintain the proper balance between God's good works through the believer and the good works a person may try to accomplish in his or her own power. When the Holy Spirit empowers a believer to do good works he is acting immediately toward the believer: he gives the believer power to do a good work. When the believer uses that spiritual power then God is acting mediately through the believer, to accomplish his good works. The power and direction to do a good work come from God, and the labor that does the good work comes from the believer. This is the partnership God has with his people. God is the managing partner supplying the plan, power, and resources; the believer is the working partner using God's resources according to

---

[1] Stott, *Ephesians*, 84–85.

his power and plan. One example must suffice. How do sinners hear the word of salvation? God sends his word to sinners through the testimony of his saved people, Romans 10:14–15. In yielding him or herself to God for the work of evangelism, the believer has performed a good work. The believer, then, in being the person through whom God works in the world, is responsible to do God's good works, prepared beforehand for the believer to walk in them.

Third, each believer is to "consider one another in order to stir up love and good works," Hebrews 10:24. In context the call to consider "one another" refers to one's fellow believers. The Writer does not mean the believer is not to express love for the lost (e.g., acts of compassion; a witness of the Gospel), but the believer's focus in the area of "stirring up" is the church not the world. The Greek word translated "consider," *katanoéō*, in this verse means "to have respect to, to regard."[1] That meaning may be applied in several ways. Lane translates "keep on caring,"[2] for one another, and Wuest, "be giving careful attention to"[3] one another. Hughes likes the translation "to pay thoughtful attention to"[4] one another. Westcott seems to capture the meaning: "It is our duty [Hebrews 10:23] to declare what we are and what we look for: it is our duty [10:24] also to consider what others are. The well-being of each believer is bound up with the well-being of the whole body. He is therefore constrained to give careful heed [*katanoéō*] to others in the hope that he may rouse them to nobler action; and again that he may himself draw encouragement and inspiration from nobler examples."[5]

When I think about these various but similar opinions, my interpretation is that each believer is responsible to "observe and encourage" other believers within his circle of association and influence. One is to observe a Christian brother or sister to understand their spiritual state and Christian activity. This is not to catch them doing wrong, but to care for them by gaining a sense of how they are doing in regard to this exhortation, so as to know when they need to receive the loving and good work of encouragement. Christian brethren are to encourage love one

---

[1] Zodhiates, *WSDNT*, s. v. "2657."
[2] Lane, *Hebrews 9–13*, 289.
[3] Wuest, *Translation*, 529.
[4] Hughes, *Hebrews*, 415.
[5] Westcott, *Hebrews*, 324.

toward another, and do good works one toward another. Encouragement is needed at all times and in all circumstances to stimulate love and good works, in order to help one another to practice love and good works and persevere in them.

That this needed encouragement is words and deeds given to the one to be encouraged is found in the words "to stir up." This Greek word, *paroxusmós*,[1] literally means "to provoke" and is usually used negatively, as in to provoke to anger, or irritation. Here it is used in a good sense. Some have suggested the meaning should be "to sharpen" based upon the root meaning and an assumed parallel with Proverbs 27:17. However, root meanings are not the best guides to actual use, and an assumed parallel depends on the root meaning. Who today would interpret "dandelion" by the French root "lion's tooth", or "goodbye" as a contraction of the original, "God be with ye"? The better interpretation retains the basic meaning (thus the KJV "provoke") and "can only have the sense of 'incitement,' 'stimulation,' "[2] and these meanings fit very well with *katanoéō*. Thus, to expand the translation (of Hebrews 10:24) through an interpretation, each believer is to pay attention to, care for, and encourage one another, in order to excite one another to those acts of love and good works that tend to the well-being of one another, and thus promote the well-being of the church.

What are Good Works?

Having now some understanding of the origin of God's good works, and that God tends to work his good works mediately through the believer, and that many good works are intended for the local church body, let us now answer the question, "What are the good works of the believer?"

At their most basic and essential core, good works are God's works, by which I mean their origin, source, intent, use, and result. As explained above, the believer's manner of life is a partnership with God: God supplies all the management, resources, and energy; the believer puts what God supplies to use by expending the energy and resources according to God's plans and purpose. To evangelize the world, God sends Christians to the lost. To supply his church

---

[1] Zodhiates, *WSDNT*, s. v. "3948."
[2] Kittel, *Dictionary*, 5:857.

Good Works

with resources, God gives secular employment to his people. God's works in the world are done by his people in the world. One cannot and should not limit God to working mediately, but mediately is obviously his general and preferred method to accomplish his will. The greatness of God is demonstrated in that he accomplishes his plans and purpose through weak vessels. Thus, good works are God at work in and through the believer. Having discussed the concept in general terms, what are the details?

In fine, good works are righteousness in action. Right–ness is according to God's definition of what is and is not right. The biblical view of a "good work" is seen through the context in which this term is found. In the KJV that use is Matthew 5:16, John 10:32, Acts 9:36, Romans 13:3, Ephesians 2:10, 1 Timothy 2:10; 5:10, 25; 6:18; 2 Timothy 3:17; Titus 2:7, 14; 3:8, 14; Hebrews 10:24; 1 Peter 2:12.

At Matthew 5:16 the term is used in the context of Christ's discourse on the "beatitudes." A beatitude is moral precept used to express the broader moral principles underlying God's commandments. In the immediate context in which Christ stated them, the "Beatitudes" were intended to reveal the perfection required by the Mosaic Law, and therefore the hopelessness of attaining righteousness and justification through the Law: who is able to be perfect as God is perfect? (Matthew 5:48). For the Christian, who has received righteousness and justification in Christ, the beatitudes embody moral principles that guide the practice of faith.

When one practices the beatitudes, then one will be the salt of the earth and the light of the world. These are moral concepts expressed symbolically using physical actions. In the ancient world, without refrigeration or other modern means to preserve food, salt was the preservative (bacteria cannot live in salt). To be "the salt of the earth" is to preserve morality, virtue, and truth through moral convictions and actions. The "light" of the ancient world was a shallow vessel filled with oil, in which a wick was floated. This was the only means of lighting a dark place. To be the "light of the world" is to expose the world's sins and bring knowledge and understanding of God's way of salvation. Moreover, if we go but a little further into Matthew 5, we discover that the beatitudes are a practical summation of God's commandments. When one's manner of life is lived according to the moral principles and values embodied in the beatitudes, then he or she is doing good works. Good works are righteous actions; right actions are defined exclusively by Scripture. The moral principles, precepts, and values embodied in the Beatitudes help define right acts. I am not saying the Beatitudes are the moral code of life. Rather, the principles and values on which they are based are that moral code. The precepts known as the Beatitudes are an expression of those principles and values, but not the only expression found in Scripture. Wherever Scripture says "do this," or "don't do that" we find the principles of righteousness embodied in precepts, the doing of which is good works.

Another insight into good works is John 10:32. Some Jews were about to try and kill Jesus (he had declared himself to be God) and he said to them, "Many good works have I shown you from my Father; for which of those works do you stone me?" In context, Jesus was trying to help them understand he was fulfilling Old Testament messianic prophecy every time he healed someone, but his reference to good works also included his teachings and the compassion that motivated his healing acts. The modern Christian is not divinely empowered to heal people physically, but is spiritually empowered to preach the Gospel to heal sin-sick souls, and exercise compassion and kind acts toward others. These things are good works.

In the epistles, Paul comments that governments are "not a terror" to good works, but to evil. Doing that which is morally right is a good work. Paul wrote to his friend Timothy, pastor of a local church, that, 2 Timothy 3:16–17, "All scripture is given by inspiration of God, and is profitable for doctrine, for reproof, for correction, for instruction in righteousness: that the man of God may be complete, thoroughly equipped for every *good work*" (emphasis mine). For the Christian's work to be a "good" work, the Christian must be informed by Scripture so that the work he or she does conforms to the Scripture's standard of what is, in God's sight, right and good.

In 1 Peter 2:11–12 the apostle speaks of the believer's witness to the unsaved, "Beloved, I beg you as sojourners and pilgrims, abstain from fleshly lusts which war against the soul, having your conduct honorable among the Gentiles, that when they speak against you as evildoers, they may, by your *good works* which they observe, glorify God" (emphasis mine). Here good works are spoken of as "honorable conduct" and contrasted with "fleshly lusts," and "doing evil."

To sum up all the uses of the term, good works means:

Living according to God's rules and practicing God's values.

Righteous actions that put one's Christianity into practice for the spiritual and physical well-being of others.

Righteous actions, sound speech, and sound doctrine that demonstrates one's profession of saving faith in Jesus Christ is genuine.

Scripture is the only means by which the Christian can be informed of God's rules and God's values in this New Testament age. One must be careful to take into account the whole counsel of Scripture. For example, the Old Testament Law of Moses is fulfilled in Christ. Therefore, although Old Testament Scripture defined a good work as bringing a sacrifice, or as stoning an adulterer/adulteress, those laws have been superseded in Christ. In this New Testament age, the Law provides moral principles to inform and guide personal behavior. The Christian way is one of peace, compassion, love, and testifying of salvation by faith in Christ. The Christian life is one of rejection, trials, persecutions, suffering for the testimony of Christ (cf. Acts 5:41), and often little success in worldly attainments and riches. The Christian way is to show the gift of life through his life—good works—and willingly suffer when the offer of eternal life is rejected.

Good works are what one does inwardly and outwardly to conform his (or her) manner of living to all that God says is right and good. To pray for myself is a good work, because in it I confess God as my God; and to pray for others is a good work. To study and meditate on the Scripture is a good work; as is practicing what I have learned; as is proclaiming to others what I have learned. Living out my faith without fear, without wavering in the truth, is a good work, as is helping others striving to do the same. Public and private worship is a good work. Paying attention to and caring for the physical and spiritual well-being of others (both within and without the church, both saved and unsaved) is a good work. Persevering in the faith is a good work. If a believer would know what good works he or she is to do, he need look no further than Scripture. When the believer conforms his life to God's rules and values for living, both inwardly toward himself and outwardly toward others, then he is living in the sphere of good works. One absolutely must take care that the inward and the outward aspects are practiced with equal vigor. God has prepared beforehand good works that his people should live their life in them.

A final thought to tie good works to the doctrine of predestination. We have discussed that the purpose of the believer's predestination was to conform him or her to be like Christ. Jesus said, many times, that he came do the works his Father had sent him to do. Just as he did for the believer, Ephesians 2:10, God had foreordained—prepared beforehand—good works for Jesus to accomplish. Every time Jesus met a good work on his life-path he did that good work. Jesus knew God's will and had God's resources to do the works that came from his Father, John 14:10, "the Father who dwells in Me does the works." Believers also know God's will—the principles and precepts of Scripture for holy and righteous living—and have the same power and guidance—the indwelling Holy Spirit—to do God's good works. The predestination of the believer—part of the reason he was predestined to be conformed to the image of Christ, Romans 8:29—is to do the works of his heavenly Father; the works God has prepared beforehand that we should live in them.

APPENDIX: MOLINISM, FOREORDINATION, AND ELECTION

After the initial publication of this work, some began to compare my doctrines of foreordination and election with the doctrinal view known as Molinism. Molinism is not easy to understand, and this discussion concerns only two aspects of the doctrine. I am indebted to an article by Dr. Kirk R. MacGregor for my understanding of Molinism.[1]

There are two places where I disagree with original (as described by Molina) Molinism. As we discuss Molina's view of foreordination and election, and what I believe is the scriptural view, keep in mind we are talking about the eternity before God created anything.

Molina was concerned to maintain both God's sovereignty and libertarian human freedom (free will) in regard to God's sovereign election of some to salvation. That human beings have free will is certain. God gave Adam the moral authority to make choices. All human choice is limited by human nature, whether physical nature, moral nature, or spiritual nature. In Adam, his spiritual nature was not limited by sin, until he sinned. In his descendants, the spiritual nature is limited by sin in its choices. No unsaved human being is capable of initiating saving faith. God must give grace in order for the sinner to choose to exercise saving faith. The grace that God gives to effectuate salvation is known as "prevenient grace." How and when that prevenient grace is given is at the heart of my disagreement with Molinism. (Prevenient Grace is the biblical teaching that God gives grace to enable the sinner's faith. The issues surrounding prevenient are not the fact God gives this grace, Ephesians 2:8, but when God gives this grace.)

Molina taught that God gives every human being coming into the world prevenient grace, as the special supernatural empowerment to place saving faith in God, an empowerment which, in Molina's view, a human being may or may not freely decide to use, or not.

---

[1] *Evangelical Dispensationalism Quarterly Journal*, vol. 3, num. 2. Published online by Scofield Biblical Institute and Theological Seminary.

Appendix

Molina also taught that in the world God determined to create, out of all possible worlds he might have created, any individual whom God knew, in that world, who would freely embrace and use the prevenient grace he would give to all, that person God elected to salvation.

One must understand that, in Molina's view, God could have created a world in which none would use his prevenient grace, or he could have created a world in which all would use his prevenient grace, but God chose to create a world in which some would use his prevenient grace. In that world where some would use the prevenient God gives to all, those whom God knew would use that prevenient grace are the ones whom God decided to elect to salvation.

By saying God choose which kind of world to create, Molina maintained both God's sovereignty and human free will. In Molina's view, God sovereignly choose who would be saved, by choosing to create a world in which some would freely choose to use the gift of prevenient grace God would give to all. Those individuals whom God knew, in this particular world, would use his prevenient grace, those were the ones God elected to salvation.

My problem with Molinism, is though God sovereignly chose what to create, his election in that creation is based on foreknowledge of who would believe, not on his sovereign choice to unconditionally elect.

In response to, "God gave prevenient grace to all," in my understanding of Scripture, God gives prevenient grace *only* through his choice of specific individuals to whom he will give his gift of grace-faith-salvation, Ephesians 2:8. This is counter to Molina's view and the Arminian view. Arminian soteriology views prevenient grace as God giving every sinner, at some time after birth, the grace needed to freely decide for him or herself whether or not to believe the gospel and be saved.

In the biblical view of prevenient grace, before God created anything or anyone, God unconditionally choose which individuals, out of the entire mass of individuals, to whom he would give his prevenient grace—his gift of grace-faith-salvation—thereby electing those certain individuals to salvation, without any consideration of merit or lack of merit, faith or lack of faith, in the individual. Only those to whom God chose to give the gift of prevenient grace would receive the gift of prevenient grace.

Appendix

In response to, "creating a world in which only some individuals would choose to use the prevenient grace God would give to all," I view foreordination differently. God, before he created anything, before he made any choices concerning election to salvation, God first chose to allow all human beings to become sinners through Adam's sin, and therefore God saw all human beings as sinners, before choosing whom to elect to salvation.

God therefore, before his decision to elect certain individuals to salvation, knew every human being's freely made choices would always be to rebel against God and reject salvation, because all were sinners. Election, then, is God's choice to give his gift of grace-faith-salvation to certain individuals, without decreeing the reprobation of any others, because by their sinful nature all human beings were and would remain reprobate, without God's gift of prevenient grace. In other words, God sovereignly chose whom he would save from a just reprobation by specifically giving his gift of grace-faith-salvation to those individuals whom he specifically elected to salvation.

Election, then, is the choice of a sovereign God, 1) to give the gift of grace-faith-salvation to effect the salvation of some sinners, and 2) to take no action, positive or negative, to either effect or deny salvation to other sinners. The decree of election includes all means necessary to effectuate salvation in those elected.

Foreordination is, the decree of God occurring between his decision to create and his act of creation as to which agents, events, and outcomes, out of all possible agents, events, and outcomes potential in the decision to create, would pass from possible to actual, in which the liberty or contingency of secondary causes is established, in which God is not the author of sin, and in which no violence is done to the free will of his creatures. (Perhaps more simply, God effectuated from possible to actual certain freely made choices, thereby maintaining both his sovereignty and the moral authority he would give his creatures.)

God effectuated salvation in some, not because he saw who would believe—because none would—but because he chose in whom he would initiate saving faith through giving his gift of grace-faith-salvation to those whom he chose to salvation.

Reprobation means to be disqualified from heaven and subject to judgment and eternal punishment. All unsaved sinners are by nature, not by decree, reprobate. The Calvinistic doctrine of

Appendix

Reprobation is the election of some to eternal damnation. That is not the biblical doctrine, but is intuited from the doctrine of election, which is to say, there is no Scripture concerning a decree of reprobation.

The reprobation of every human being occurred prior to the decree of election. God chose to effectuate Adam's freely made choice to sin. Because God chose that Adam would represent all humanity seminally (all are born of Adam) and federally (legally), Genesis 4:1–2; 5:3; 1 Corinthians 15:22; Romans 5:12–14, then Adam's freely made choice to sin would make all his descendants sinners, and thus God viewed all human beings as reprobate before he elected some to salvation. After decreeing to effectuate Adam's choice to sin, God then chose (elected) to save some of those reprobate sinners, by giving those specific individuals prevenient grace through God's gift of grace-faith-salvation. In choosing to elect some sinners to salvation God justly passed by the rest, taking no action to effect or deny their salvation.

Because God does not take any action to deny the salvation of the non-elect, the proclamation of salvation to all is just. Any person not elected could, if they would, come to God through faith in God and God's testimony of the way to salvation. That the non-elect cannot make that choice is because they are sinners in rebellion against God. Their sin is not God's fault, because God did not 1) make Adam sin, it was his freely made choice; and 2) God does not prevent any from coming and believing and being saved, it is their desire to remain sinners that prevents their salvation.

One final effect of Molina's doctrine of, "prevenient grace to all," is how that affects the doctrine of perseverance. The biblical doctrine of perseverance is a grace God gives the believer to overcome all spiritual and physical obstacles to faith, and perseverance in the faith is the believer using the means of grace God has provided for him or her to continue in the faith by faith. Molina's doctrine is, in the world God selected to create, God knows that no individual who responds to his prevenient grace would fall away. That is not the same as God giving grace to persevere.

To sum up. In my understanding of Molinism, as explained by Molina, God elects because he foreknows, not because he foreordained. To say God elects by sovereignly deciding to create a world in which he knows who will believe and be saved ,is to say God makes his electing choice as a response to human free will. To me, a sovereign God initiates salvation, through the sovereign and unconditional bestowal of prevenient grace to a specific individual, thereby changing the spiritual boundary of that individual's human nature, to efficaciously and irresistibly initiate saving faith in the elect sinner.

BIBLIOGRAPHY AND SOURCES

Ames, William. *The Marrow of Theology*. 1648. Reprinted, Durham, PA: The Labyrinth Press, 1983.

Baker, Warren, ed. *The Complete Word Study Dictionary Old Testament*. Chattanooga, TN: AMG Publishers, 1994.

Bancroft, Emery. *Elemental Theology*. 1932. Reprinted, Grand Rapids, MI: Zondervan, 1986.

Berkhoff, Louis. *Systematic Theology*. 1941, Reprinted, London: The Banner of Truth Trust, 1959.

Berry, George Ricker. *The Interlinear Literal Translation of the Greek New Testament, with the Authorized Version*. 1958. Reprinted, Grand Rapids, MI: Zondervan, 1977.

Boettner, Loraine. *The Reformed Doctrine of Predestination*. 1932. Reprinted, Philadelphia, PA: The Presbyterian and Reformed Publishing Company, 1973.

Brown, John. *An Analytical Exposition of the Epistle of Paul to the Romans*. 1857. Reprinted, Grand Rapids, MI: Baker Book House, 1981.

Buswell, J. Oliver. *A Systematic Theology of the Christian Religion*. Grand Rapids, MI: Zondervan, 1962.

Calvin, John. *Calvin's Calvinism*. Translated by Henry Cole. 1552. Reprinted, Grand Rapids, MI: Reformed Free Publishing Association, n. d.

———. *Calvin's Commentaries*. Vol. 21. *Ephesians*. Grand Rapids, MI: Baker Book House, 1996.

———. *Institutes of the Christian Religion*. Henry Beveridge, Translator. 2 vols. 1559. Reprinted, Grand Rapids, MI: Eerdmans Publishing, 1971.

———. *Sermons on the Epistle to the Ephesians*. 1562. Reprinted, Carlisle, PA: The Banner of Truth Trust, 1973.

Chafer, Lewis Sperry. *The Ephesians Letter*. New York, NY: Loizeaux Brothers, 1935.

———. *Systematic Theology*. 1947. Reprinted, Grand Rapids, MI: Kregel Publications, 1993.

Craigie, Peter C. *Psalms 1–50*. Word Biblical Commentary. Waco, TX: Word Books, 1983.

Dana, H. E., and Julius R. Mantey. *A Manual Grammar of the Greek New Testament*. New York, NY: The Macmillan Company, 1927.

Dictionary.com. Culpable. *Merriam-Webster's Dictionary of Law*. Merriam-Webster, Inc. Online: http://dictionary.reference.com/browse/culpable.

Eadie, John. *Ephesians*. The John Eadie Greek Text Commentaries. Vol. 2. 1869. Reprinted, Grand Rapids, MI: Baker Book House, 1979.

Ellingworth, Paul. *The Epistle to the Hebrews*. The New International Greek Testament Commentary. Grand Rapids, MI: Eerdman's Publishing, 1993.

Elwell, Walter A., ed. *Evangelical Dictionary of Theology*. Grand Rapids, MI: Baker Book House, 1984.

Fisk, Samuel. *Divine Sovereignty and Human Freedom*. Neptune, NJ: Loizeaux Brothers, 1973.

Grudem, Wayne. *Systematic Theology*. Grand Rapids, MI: Zondervan, 1994.

Haldane, Robert. *An Exposition of the Epistle to the Romans*. 1858. Reprinted, McLean, VA: MacDonald Publishing, n. d.

Harris, R. Laird; Gleason L. Archer, Jr.; and Bruce K. Waltke. *Theological Wordbook of the Old Testament*. 2 vols. Chicago, IL: Moody Press, 1980.

Harrison, Everett, F., ed. *Baker's Dictionary of Theology*. Grand Rapids, MI: Baker Book House, 1960.

Hodge, Archibald A., and Benjamin B. Warfield, *Inspiration*. 1881. Reprinted, Grand Rapids, MI: Baker Book House, 1979.

Hodge, Charles. *A Commentary on the Epistle to the Ephesians*. 1856. Reprinted, Grand Rapids, MI: Baker Book House, 1980.

———. *A Commentary on Romans*. 1835. Rev. 1864. Reprinted, Carlisle, PA: The Banner of Truth Trust, 1972.

———. *Systematic Theology*. 3 vols. 1871–73. Reprinted, Grand Rapids, MI: William B. Eerdmans Publishing Company, 1981.

Hoehner, Harold W. *Ephesians, an Exegetical Commentary*. Grand Rapids, MI: Baker Academic, 2002.

Hughes, Philip Edgcumbe. *A Commentary on the Epistle to the Hebrews*. Grand Rapids, MI: Eerdman's Publishing, 1977.

Kittle, Gerhard, and Gerhard Friedrich. *Theological Dictionary of the New Testament*. 10 vols. Translated by Geoffrey W.

Bibliography and Sources

Bromiley. Grand Rapids, MI: Eerdmans Publishing, 1967.

Lane, William L. *Hebrews 9–13*. Word Biblical Commentary. Waco, TX: Word, Inc., 1991.

Lincoln, Andrew T. *Ephesians*. Word Biblical Commentary. Vol. 42. Dallas, TX: Word Books, 1990.

Manton, Thomas. *By Faith, Sermons on Hebrews 11*. 1873 ed. Reprinted, Carlisle, PA: The Banner of Truth Trust, 2000.

Marshall, Alfred. *The Interlinear Greek-English New Testament, the Nestle Greek Text with a Literal English Translation*. 2nd ed. 1959. Reprinted, Grand Rapids, MI: Zondervan, 1971.

Melton, J. Gordon. ed. *American Religious Creeds*. New York, NY: Triumph Books, 1991.

Moulton, J. H., and G. Milligan. *Vocabulary of the Greek Testament*. 1930. Reprinted, Peabody, MA: Hendrickson Publishers, 1997.

O'Brien, Peter T. *The Letter to the Ephesians*. The Pillar New Testament Commentary. Grand Rapids, MI: Eerdmans Publishing, 1999.

Owen, John. *Biblical Theology, the History of Theology from Adam to Christ*. 1661. Reprinted in an English translation by Stephen P. Westcott. Grand Rapids, MI: Soli Deo Gloria Publications, 1994.

———. *The Works of John Owen*. 16 vols. 1850–53 edition. Reprinted, Carlisle, PA: The Banner of Truth Trust, 1965–68.

Packer, J. I. *A Quest for Godliness, the Puritan Vision of the Christian Life*. Wheaton, IL: Crossway Books, 1990.

Perowne, J. J. Stewart. *The Book of Psalms*. 1878. Reprinted, 1 vol. ed. Grand Rapids, MI: Zondervan, 1976.

Pink, Arthur W. *The Sovereignty of God*. 1918. Reprinted, Grand Rapids, MI: Baker Book House, 1977.

Quiggle, James D. *Adam and Eve, A Biography and Theology*, Published in e-book for Nook and Kindle, and in print by Createspace, 2011.

———. *Antichrist, His Genealogy, Kingdom, and Religion*. Published in e-book for Nook and Kindle, and in print by Createspace, 2011.

———. *A Private Commentary on the Bible: Ephesians*. Published in e-book for Nook and Kindle, and in print by Createspace, 2012.

———. *A Private Commentary on the Bible: Hebrews*. Published in e-book format for Nook and Kindle, and in print by Createspace, 2012.

Roberts, Alexander, and James Donaldson. *Ante-Nicene Fathers*. Vol. 1. 1885. Reprinted, Peabody, MA: Hendrickson Publishers, 1995.

———. *Ante-Nicene Fathers*. Vol. 2. 1885. Reprinted, Peabody, MA: Hendrickson Publishers, 1995.

———. *Ante-Nicene Fathers*. Vol. 4. 1885. Reprinted, Peabody, MA: Hendrickson Publishers, 1995.

———. *Ante-Nicene Fathers*. Vol. 7. 1886. Reprinted, Peabody, MA: Hendrickson Publishers, 1995.

Robertson, A. T. *Word Pictures in the New Testament*. Vol. 4. *Epistles of Paul*. Nashville, TN: Broadman Press, 1932.

Ryrie, Charles, C. *Dispensationalism*. Chicago, IL: Moody Press, 1995

Schaff, Philip. *The Evangelical Protestant Creeds*. The Creeds of Christendom. Vol. 3. 1931. Reprinted, Grand Rapids, MI: Baker Book House, 1983.

———. *Nicene and Post-Nicene Fathers*, First Series. Vol. 1. 1886. Reprinted, Peabody, MA: Hendrickson Publishers, 1999.

———. Nicene and Post-Nicene Fathers, First Series. Vol. 2. 1887. Reprinted, Peabody, MA: Hendrickson Publishers, 1999.

———. *Nicene and Post-Nicene Fathers*, First Series. Vol. 3. 1887. Reprinted, Peabody, MA: Hendrickson Publishers, 1999.

———. *Nicene and Post-Nicene Fathers*, First Series. Vol. 5. 1887. Reprinted, Peabody, MA: Hendrickson Publishers, 1999.

———. *Nicene and Post-Nicene Fathers*, First Series. Vol. 11. 1889. Reprinted, Peabody, MA: Hendrickson Publishers, 1999

———. *Nicene and Post-Nicene Fathers*, First Series. Vol. 13. 1889. Reprinted, Peabody, MA: Hendrickson Publishers, 1999.

Schaff, Philip, and Henry Wace. *Nicene and Post-Nicene Fathers*, Second Series. Vol. 4. 1892. Reprinted, Peabody, MA: Hendrickson Publishers, 1999.

———. *Nicene and Post-Nicene Fathers*, Second Series. Vol. 7. 1894. Reprinted, Peabody, MA: Hendrickson Publishers, 1999.

Shedd, W. G. T. *Dogmatic Theology*. 1863. 3 vols. Reprinted, Nashville, TN: Thomas Nelson Publishers, 1980.

———. *Theological Essays*. 1877. Reprinted, Minneapolis, MN: Klock

Bibliography and Sources

& Klock Christian Publishers, 1981.

Snodgrass, Klyne. *Ephesians*. The NIV Application Commentary. Grand Rapids, MI: Zondervan, 1996.

Sproul, R. C. *Grace Unknown, the Heart of Reformed Theology*. Grand Rapids, MI: Baker Books, 1997.

Spurgeon, C. H. *The C. H. Spurgeon Collection*, AGES Digital Library. CD-ROM, AGES Software, RIO, WI: 2001.

Strauss, Lehman. *Devotional Studies in Galatians and Ephesians*. Neptune, NJ: Loizeaux Brothers, 1957.

Stott, John R.W. *The Message of Ephesians*. The Bible Speaks Today. Downers Grove, IL: Inter- Varsity Press, 1979.

Thomas, W. H. Griffith. *The Principles of Theology*. 4th ed. London: Church Room Book Press Ltd., 1951.

Venning, Ralph. *The Sinfulness of Sin*. 1669. Reprinted, Carlisle, PA: The Banner of Truth Trust, 1997

Warfield, Benjamin B. *The Works of Benjamin B. Warfield*. Ten volumes. 1927. Reprinted, Grand Rapids, MI: Baker Book House, 1991.

Westcott, B. F. *The Epistle to the Hebrews*. Grand Rapids, MI: Eerdman's Publishing, 1955.

Wuest, Kenneth S. *Ephesians*. Word Studies in the Greek New Testament. Vol. 1. Grand Rapids, MI: Eerdman's Publishing, 1973.

———. *The New Testament, an Expanded Translation*. Grand Rapids, MI: Eerdmans Publishing, 1961.

Zodhiates, Spiros, ed. *The Complete Word Study Dictionary New Testament*. Revised. Chattanooga, TN: AMG Publishers, 1993.

Made in the USA
Las Vegas, NV
17 May 2024